Presented To:

_____

By:

_____

Date:

_____

God's Little Devotional Journal

Honor Books
Tulsa, Oklahoma

God's Little Devotional Journal
ISBN 1-56292-758-2
Copyright © 2000 by Honor Books
P.O. Box 55388
Tulsa, Oklahoma 74155

God's Little Devotional Journal

Introduction

As teenagers, many of us wrote in diaries with tiny locks or scrawled our thoughts in spiral notebooks that have long been thrown away. Occasionally, we may have splurged on journals with beautiful covers that were never opened. But when we actually recorded our hopes and dreams on paper, how much more real they became!

Keeping a journal is a valuable and time-honored tradition—one that has been practiced by kings and queens and philosophers for centuries—but has gained popularity recently. Psychologists support the therapeutic benefit of writing down our thoughts. Teachers encourage journalizing as a proven method of improving communication skills. Business leaders suggest using a journal for setting and keeping goals. But one of the greatest benefits of writing regularly in a journal is spiritual growth.

In the opening words of his first journal entry on September 3, 1822, Eugène Delacroix—a nineteenth-century French artist—writes: "I am carrying out my plan, so long formulated, of keeping a journal. What I most keenly wish is not to forget that I am writing for myself alone. Thus I shall always tell the truth, I hope, and thus I shall improve myself."

God's Little Devotional Journal brings you an inspirational story each day to uplift and motivate you to share your thoughts in this beautifully crafted 365-day journal. Commit to reading it daily and sharing your thoughts with God. At the end of the year, you will be amazed at how much you've grown spiritually. Read and write with an open heart, and let God speak to you today!

Acorns, Pumpkins, and God

Humble yourselves therefore under
the mighty hand of God, that he
may exalt you in due time.

1 PETER 5:6

An old poem tells the story of a woman who was walking through a meadow one day. As she strolled along, meditating on nature, she came upon a field of golden pumpkins. In the corner of the field stood a majestic oak tree.

The woman sat under the oak tree and began musing about the strange twists in nature. Tiny acorns hung on huge branches and huge pumpkins sat on tiny vines. She thought, *God blundered with creation! He should have put the small acorns on the tiny vines and the large pumpkins on the huge branches.*

Before long, the warmth of the late autumn sunshine lulled the woman to sleep. A tiny acorn bouncing off her nose awakened her. Chuckling to herself, she amended her previous thinking, *Maybe God was right after all!*

In every situation, God knows far more about the people and circumstances involved than we can ever know. He alone sees the beginning from the ending. He alone knows how to create a master plan that provides for the good of all those who serve Him.

Only God knows what lies ahead for your life. Today, trust in Him and His plan—it may seem backwards, but He always does what is best for you.

Most people wish to serve God—
but only in an advisory capacity.

What "MISTAKES" DO I UNJUSTLY ATTRIBUTE TO GOD?

A Mirror of Truth

And herein do I exercise myself, to have always a conscience void of offence toward God, and toward men.

ACTS 24:16

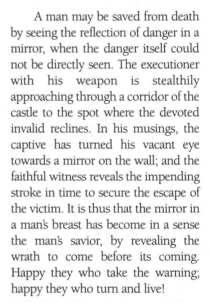

Today, MY CONSCIENCE IS PROMPTING ME TO...

_____

_____

_____

_____

_____

_____

_____

_____

_____

_____

_____

_____

_____

_____

A man may be saved from death by seeing the reflection of danger in a mirror, when the danger itself could not be directly seen. The executioner with his weapon is stealthily approaching through a corridor of the castle to the spot where the devoted invalid reclines. In his musings, the captive has turned his vacant eye towards a mirror on the wall; and the faithful witness reveals the impending stroke in time to secure the escape of the victim. It is thus that the mirror in a man's breast has become in a sense the man's savior, by revealing the wrath to come before its coming. Happy they who take the warning; happy they who turn and live!

These lines from Dr. Arnot give an interesting description of a person's conscience.

It has been said that man's conscience was given to him after the Fall in the Garden of Eden. Man's desire to know good and evil had been granted. But in His mercy, God gave man a way of discerning good from evil. That mechanism, which He placed in man's heart, was the conscience. Don't ignore the prompting of your conscience. When you do, it becomes callused. Your conscience is more than a sixth sense. It's a beacon whose homing signal is Heaven.

Conscience is God's built-in warning system.
Be very happy when it hurts you.
Be very worried when it doesn't.

The Big Picture

A man shall not be established
by wickedness: but the root of the
righteous shall not be moved.

PROVERBS 12:3

In the 1960s, the Federal Drug Administration received nearly seven hundred applications for new medicines each year. The beleaguered New Drug Section had only sixty days to review each drug before granting approval or requesting more data.

A few months after Dr. Frances Kelsey joined the FDA, an established pharmaceutical firm in Ohio applied for a license to market a new drug, Kevadon. In liquid form, the drug seemed to relieve nausea in early pregnancy. It was given to millions of expectant women, mostly in Europe, Asia, and Africa. Although scientific studies revealed harmful side effects, the pharmaceutical firm printed 66,957 leaflets declaring its safety. In anticipation of the drug's approval, the company exerted great pressure on Dr. Kelsey to give permission for labels to be printed.

Dr. Kelsey reviewed the data and said no. Through several rounds of applications, she continued to find the data "unsatisfactory." After a fourteen-month struggle, the company humbly withdrew its application. Kevadon was thalidomide, and by that time, the horror of thalidomide deformities overseas was becoming well publicized in the United States. One firm no by Dr. Kelsey spared many American parents untold agony.

Sometimes standing your ground may be hard and not seem that important, but take courage. In time you will see the "big picture."

I WANT TO BE
COURAGEOUS;
I NEED TO
STAND MY
GROUND
REGARDING . . .

The mighty oak was once a little
nut that stood its ground.

Resting on the Promises

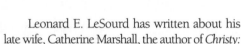

It is written, "Man shall not live by bread alone, but by every word that proceeds from the mouth of God."
MATTHEW 4:4 RSV

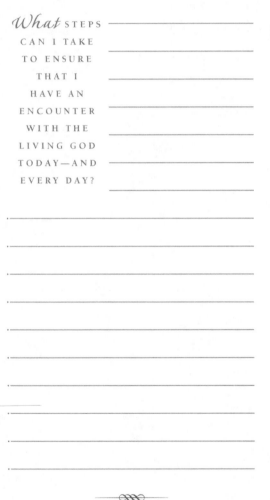

What STEPS
CAN I TAKE
TO ENSURE
THAT I
HAVE AN
ENCOUNTER
WITH THE
LIVING GOD
TODAY—AND
EVERY DAY?

What is a home without a Bible?
'Tis a home where daily bread for the
body is provided, but the soul is never fed.

Leonard E. LeSourd has written about his late wife, Catherine Marshall, the author of *Christy:*

> Bibles were scattered throughout our house. We often went to bed, turned out the light, and listened to a chapter of Scripture on tape. If she could have found a way to spread Bible passages on a slice of bread, Catherine would have devoured it.
>
> When upset or under spiritual assault or in physical pain, Catherine would go to her office, kneel by her chair, and open her Bible. . . . She would read, then pray, then read, then pray some more. She liked to pray with the Bible clutched in her hands. . . . She would rest her case on its promises. Catherine didn't read the Bible for solace or inspiration, but to have an encounter with the Lord. . . . I think these were the most intense moments of her life. . . . Catherine's passion for the Word permeated her whole life. It undergirded her writing. It provided substance to her counseling of people through the mail. I'm convinced it was also the basis for her inner vitality, her charisma, and the mantle of authority she wore with some reluctance.

The Bible is a living, breathing book. Let God speak to you through its pages. Let it transform your thinking and your way of life. Like Catherine Marshall, don't just read your Bible, have an encounter with the living God.

Forgiveness and Freedom

Blessed are the merciful,
For they shall obtain mercy.
MATTHEW 5:7 NKJV

When God forgives, something decisive happens. Likewise, when we forgive, something decisive happens. In *Healing Life's Hurts,* Matthew and Dennis Linn tell of an inner-healing workshop they observed. All of the men and women present were once divorced and had remarried. They had come to the retreat hoping for healing of the anger and hostility they felt toward their former spouses. During the weekend sessions, the couples were slowly and prayerfully shown ways in which they could grow from their past relationships and use what they had learned to build new patterns of behavior in their current marriages.

After a year, the group gathered to discuss the outcome of the retreat. The Linns reported: "Out of the seven who forgave a former spouse after years of resentment, five found that their former spouses had suddenly made an effort to forgive and build a bridge toward them. One unexpectedly called a week after the workshop, another traveled two thousand miles to see his family, and another wrote his first letter in ten silent years."

Forgiveness frees a person to receive love, and in experiencing love, they are much more likely to express it! Make every effort to walk in forgiveness daily, so that you and those around you can experience and express God's love.

Whom DO I NEED TO FORGIVE TODAY?

Forgiveness is giving love
when there is no reason to.

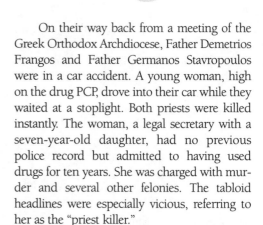

Divine Justice

I say unto you, Love your enemies, bless them that curse you, do good to them that hate you, and pray for them which despitefully use you, and persecute you.

MATTHEW 5:44

How CAN I TRANS-FORM MY RESENTMENT INTO LOVE, BLESSING, AND KINDNESS?

On their way back from a meeting of the Greek Orthodox Archdiocese, Father Demetrios Frangos and Father Germanos Stavropoulos were in a car accident. A young woman, high on the drug PCP, drove into their car while they waited at a stoplight. Both priests were killed instantly. The woman, a legal secretary with a seven-year-old daughter, had no previous police record but admitted to having used drugs for ten years. She was charged with murder and several other felonies. The tabloid headlines were especially vicious, referring to her as the "priest killer."

Father Demetrios' son, George, responded with forgiveness, not anger. He offered to help provide the woman with a lawyer and expressed the hope that if she was convicted, the sentence would be short. He said, "The last thing my father would have wanted was to make an example [of her]. This woman is anguished and troubled to begin with . . . we have to look after the innocent one, the child. It is extremely important that her child be told that we forgive her mother."

George Frangos loved his father and grieved for him, but more important to him than "legal justice" was "divine justice"—that this woman and her little girl know the love of Jesus Christ.

When faced with a devastating situation, remember that God's love is greater than any circumstance you might encounter. When you express His love in forgiveness, you receive that love back in greater measure.

Those who deserve love the least need it the most.

Hands that Touch Eternity

Store up for yourselves treasures in heaven,
where moth and rust do not destroy, and
where thieves do not break in and steal.

MATTHEW 6:20 NIV

Although we do not have the original manuscripts of the New Testament, we do have more than 99.9 percent of the original text because of the faithful work of manuscript copyists over the centuries.

Copying was a long, arduous process. In ancient days, copyists did not sit at desks to write, but stood or sat on benches or stools with a scroll on their knees. Notes at the end of some scrolls tell of the drudgery of the work:

- "He who does not know how to write supposes it to be no labor; but though only three fingers write, the whole body labors."

- "Writing bows one's back, thrusts the ribs into one's stomach, and fosters a general debility."

- "As travelers rejoice to see their home country, so also is the end of a book to those who toil."

Even so, without the work of the faithful copyists, we would not have the Christian Scriptures today. As one scribe aptly noted: "There is no scribe who will not pass away, but what his hands have written will remain forever."

If you truly want your work to last, do work that touches the eternal truth and nature of God and do it with excellence.

The greatest use of life is to spend it
for something that will outlast it.

What ARE SOME PRACTICAL WAYS I CAN CREATE ETERNAL VALUE IN THE WORK I DO?

Four Percent Prayer

*Seek first the kingdom of God and
His righteousness, and all these things
shall be added to you.*

MATTHEW 6:33 NKJV

What IS
GOD'S PLAN
FOR MY DAILY
ROUTINE?

A pastor's wife was amazed when she heard a person say, "One hour is only 4 percent of a day." She had never thought about time that way. Sensing the need for more prayer time in her life, she thought surely she could give God at least 4 percent of her time. She resolved to try it.

Rather than try to fit prayer into her schedule, she decided to fix a prayer time and then fit the rest of the day around it. At the time, her children were old enough to travel to school alone. By 8:30 each morning, the clamor of morning preparations was over and a hush fell over her home. She knew her best hour for prayer would be between 8:30 and 9:30 A.M. To guarantee she was not interrupted, she made it known in the parish that except for emergencies, she would be grateful if people didn't call her until after 9:30 in the morning.

To her surprise, no one in the church was offended. Instead, they responded very positively. Several other women began to follow her example by setting aside the same hour for their own daily prayer time!

When you seek God's plan first, all of your other plans will have a way of falling into place.

---

*Be more concerned with what
God thinks about you than what
people think about you.*

Just Cause?

Do not judge so that you will not be judged.
For in the way you judge, you will
be judged; and by your standard of
measure, it will be measured to you.

MATTHEW 7:1-2 NASB

Willie had good cause to judge his father. His dad and mom had been teenage sweethearts and had married at age eighteen. But when his mother became pregnant, his father abandoned her. Willie didn't meet his father until nineteen years later.

He said,

> I was eager but nervous to meet my father. I didn't know what to expect. What I discovered was a kind, loving, sincere person, who actually cared for me. He and I talked for a long time. I began to understand his reasons for running away. I learned a lot about life and about myself from that conversation. I never held a grudge against my father. . . .
>
> My father had his reasons for leaving. It wouldn't be fair to compare his life with mine. It would be like comparing baseball and football. I simply accepted my father as he was. I didn't offer judgment on what he had done, and I eventually grew to love him for who he was.

Willie Stargell, an all-star outfielder who played twenty years for the Pittsburgh Pirates, had good reason to criticize the father he never knew as a child, but he chose not to.

You may think you have good cause to criticize another—but is it ever a good enough reason? Criticism is a result of judgment. Jesus told us that if we judged others, we ourselves would be judged. He encouraged us to look at others the same way He looks at us, through the eyes of His grace.

I KNOW THAT I NEED TO STOP JUDGING PEOPLE WHO . . .

———— ✐ ————

Attention Men: Before you criticize another,
look closely at your sister's brother.

Raised in Love

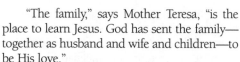

*Let love and faithfulness never leave
you; bind them around your neck,
write them on the tablet of your heart.*

PROVERBS 3:3 NIV

I CAN SHOW
MY FAMILY
HOW MUCH
I LOVE
THEM BY . . .

*When Mother Teresa received her
Nobel prize, she was asked, "What can
we do to promote world peace?" She replied,
"Go home and love your family."*

"The family," says Mother Teresa, "is the place to learn Jesus. God has sent the family—together as husband and wife and children—to be His love."

In *Words to Love By*, Mother Teresa writes,

Once a lady came to me in great sorrow and told me that her daughter had lost her husband and a child. All the daughter's hatred had turned on the mother. She wouldn't even see the mother.

So I said, "Now you think a bit about the little things that your daughter liked when she was a child. Maybe flowers or a special food. Try to give her some of these things without looking for a return."

And she started doing some of these things, like putting the daughter's favorite flower on the table, or leaving a beautiful piece of cloth for her. And she did not look for a return from the daughter.

Several days later the daughter said, "Mommy, come. I love you. I want you."

It was very beautiful.

By being reminded of the joy of childhood, the daughter reconnected with her family. She must have had a happy childhood to go back to the joy and happiness of her mother's love.

Today, think of some special ways to remind your family of your love for them, then put them into action!

Poised for Prayer

Humble yourselves in the sight of the Lord, and he shall lift you up.

JAMES 4:10

One stormy day, a woman, along with two experienced guides, climbed the Weisshorn in the Swiss Alps. As they neared the peak, exhilarated by the view before her, the woman sprang forward and was almost blown away by a gust of wind. One of the guides caught her and pulled her down, saying, "On your knees, madam! You are safe here only on your knees."

We typically regard kneeling as the standard position for prayer, but talking to God isn't limited to a certain posture. He can hear us, regardless.

Three Christian women were talking once about the best position for prayer. One argued the importance of holding one's hands together and pointing them upward. The second advocated stretching out on the floor. The third thought standing was better than kneeling. As they talked, a telephone repairman listened as he worked on a nearby phone system. Finally, he could contain himself no longer and interjected, "I have found that the most powerful prayer I ever made was while I was dangling upside down from a power pole, suspended forty feet above the ground."

Pray while driving in your car (with your eyes open, of course). Pray while cleaning your house. Pray while working in your office. And pray while kneeling in your quiet place. The important thing is not your position of prayer, but the fact that you do pray! Because when you do, God hears you.

What MAN-MADE RULES HAVE BEEN LIMITING MY PRAYER LIFE LATELY?

You are never so high as when you are on your knees.

From Victim to Victor

Love ye your enemies, and do good, and lend, hoping for nothing again; and your reward shall be great, and ye shall be the children of the Highest: for he is kind unto the unthankful and to the evil.

LUKE 6:35

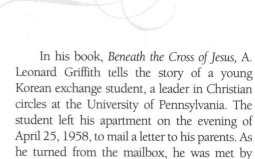

What RADICAL MEASURE CAN I TAKE TO EXPRESS THE LOVE OF GOD TO THOSE WHO HAVE ·HURT ME DEEPLY?

In his book, *Beneath the Cross of Jesus,* A. Leonard Griffith tells the story of a young Korean exchange student, a leader in Christian circles at the University of Pennsylvania. The student left his apartment on the evening of April 25, 1958, to mail a letter to his parents. As he turned from the mailbox, he was met by eleven leather-jacketed teenage boys. Without a word, they beat him with a blackjack, a lead pipe, and their shoes and fists—and left him lying dead in the gutter.

All of Philadelphia cried out for vengeance. The district attorney planned to seek the death penalty for the arrested youth. And then the following letter arrived, signed by the boy's parents and twenty other relatives in Korea:

> Our family has met together and we have decided to petition that the most generous treatment possible within the laws of your government be given to those who have committed this criminal action. . . . In order to give evidence of our sincere hope contained in this petition, we have decided to save money to start a fund to be used for the religious, educational, vocational, and social guidance of the boys when they are released. . . . We have dared to express our hope with a spirit received from the Gospel of our Savior Jesus Christ who died for our sins.

When you forgive, you are no longer a victim, but a victor.

The best way to get even is to forget.

Blessed, Faithful

He will not allow your foot to slip;
He who keeps you will not slumber.

PSALM 121:3 NASB

When Penny saw her daughter's scarlet cheeks, she became alarmed. Candi had undergone a liver transplant as an infant, and when Penny rushed Candi to the hospital, her fears were confirmed: The fever signaled a serious infection. Six-year-old Candi would need another liver transplant.

The same day, Candi's best friend Jason also became ill. He, too, had undergone a liver transplant. Penny and Jason's mom, Nancy, spotted each other in a hospital corridor in the heat of the crises, each unaware of the other's latest problem. Then the children's surgeon presented Penny with the toughest choice of her life. A liver had been found, and it was suitable for either child. The medical team had assigned the liver to Candi, but now the team felt Jason's need was more urgent. Was Penny willing to give up the liver intended for Candi so Jason might have it? Yes.

Jason's transplant went smoothly, but after two weeks, no liver had been found for Candi. Her condition was becoming desperate. At what seemed like the last moment, a liver was found. Candi went home three weeks after the operation. Penny recalls, "I gave Candi's liver to Jason, knowing that somehow God would provide for Candi. I thank Him every day!"

Trust God today, even in your greatest need. He will always provide an answer at just the right time.

What IS ONE NEED THAT I HAVE BEEN UNABLE TO COMPLETELY ENTRUST TO GOD?

Give your troubles to God;
He will be up all night anyway.

Kingdom Residents

By this shall all men know that ye are my disciples, if ye have love one to another.

JOHN 13:35

How DOES
MY DAILY
BEHAVIOR
REFLECT THE
KINGDOM I
BELONG TO?

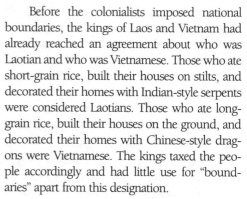

Before the colonialists imposed national boundaries, the kings of Laos and Vietnam had already reached an agreement about who was Laotian and who was Vietnamese. Those who ate short-grain rice, built their houses on stilts, and decorated their homes with Indian-style serpents were considered Laotians. Those who ate long-grain rice, built their houses on the ground, and decorated their homes with Chinese-style dragons were Vietnamese. The kings taxed the people accordingly and had little use for "boundaries" apart from this designation.

These kings knew it was not the exact location of a person's home that determined their culture or loyalty. Instead, each person belonged to the kingdom whose values they shared.

So it is with a Christian. Regardless of our culture or nationality, we belong to God's kingdom. We live according to the values, standards, and commandments He has established. When we pray, "Thy kingdom come, Thy will be done," we are asking that the heavenly law of love be established in our lives here on earth. We are His people, regardless of our address.

As you go through your day, remember who you are and to whom you belong. The greatest witness you can give your neighbors lies not in what you say, but in what you do. Let your behavior reflect that of the kingdom you belong to.

It's good to be a Christian and know it, but it's better to be a Christian and show it!

He Can Put the Letters Together

What is man, that thou art mindful of him? and the son of man, that thou visitest him? For thou hast made him a little lower than the angels, and hast crowned him with glory and honour.

PSALM 8:4-5

A little shepherd boy was watching his sheep one Sunday morning. As he heard the bells ringing the faithful to church, he watched the people walking along the lane next to the pasture. He began to think that he, too, would like to communicate with God. *But what can I say?* he thought. He had never learned a prayer. So on bended knee, he began to recite the alphabet—a, b, c, d, and so on to z, repeating his "prayer" several times.

A man, who was passing by, heard the boy's voice and stopping to look through the bushes, saw the child kneeling with folded hands and closed eyes, saying, "j k, l, m. . . . " He interrupted the boy, asking, "What are you doing, my little friend?" The boy replied, "I was praying, sir." Surprised, the man said, "But why are you reciting the alphabet?"

The boy explained, "I don't know any prayers, sir. But I want God to take care of me and help me to care for the sheep. So I thought if I said all I knew, He could put the letters together and spell all that I want to say and should say." The man smiled and said, "Bless your heart. You're right, God will!" then went on to church, knowing he had already heard the finest sermon he could possibly hear that day.

Jesus told us to have faith like a child. When you go to God in prayer, don't worry if you don't know what to say. He can put your thoughts and feelings together and send you the answer you need, even when you don't know exactly what that is.

How CAN I PRAY FROM THE HEART, EVEN WHEN I DON'T HAVE THE WORDS TO EXPRESS MY NEED?

⤜⤛

Every child comes with the message that God is not yet discouraged of man.

Sure Covenant

With God all things are possible.
MATTHEW 19:26

I NEED TO
WAIT FOR
GOD'S
APPROVAL
AND TRUST
HIS TIMING
REGARDING...

When Ferdinand de Lesseps heard that his childhood friend, Mohammed Said, had been named viceroy of Egypt, de Lesseps wasted no time in getting to Cairo. Both men were in high spirits when they met outside Alexandria on November 13, 1854.

The primary reason de Lesseps had come to Egypt was to discuss with Said an idea he had for a canal, but he did not bring it up immediately. Instead, he waited for a sign from God. One day, when he rose before dawn, he knew the moment had come. He later wrote: "The sun's rays were already lighting up the eastern horizon; in the west it was still dark and cloudy. Suddenly I saw a vivid-colored rainbow stretching across the sky from east to west. I must admit that I felt my heart beat violently, for . . . this token of a covenant . . . seemed to presage that the moment had come for the consummation of the union between East and West."

De Lesseps immediately rode to Said's tent, and before the day was out, his proposal for the Suez Canal had been approved.

God may not send you a rainbow as a sign, but His covenant with you is sure. Why not look to Him today for His answers—both for the innovative ideas you need and for the precise timing in which to implement them?

❊❊❊

Impossibilities vanish when a man and his God confront a mountain.

The Light of the World

Let your light so shine before men, that
they may see your good works, and
glorify your Father which is in heaven.

MATTHEW 5:16

One day while backpacking, fifteen-year-old Heidi doubled over with stomach pain. After being rushed to the hospital and undergoing surgery to stop her internal bleeding, Heidi seemed to recover quickly. Then tests revealed an adrenal tumor. Heidi underwent more surgery, followed by extensive radiation. She asked her father, Paul, "Why me, Dad?" Her father answered, "Honey, I don't know. But the book of Matthew says, 'Ye are the light of the world. . . . Let your light so shine before men, that they may see your good works, and glorify your Father which is in heaven.' I know you have accepted Jesus as your personal Savior and have become one of His lights, sweetheart. Just keep shining."

Two years later, Paul watched his "light" receive her high-school diploma, and then the cancer struck again, this time in her lungs. As Paul embraced his daughter, he could only say, "Honey, all we can do is call on the Lord for His strength." Another surgery followed, and the following Christmas, Paul was again filled with joy when Heidi married. The following April, she died as a result of brain cancer.

How hard it is for a father to be a Christian when his daughter is suffering and dying! Paul saw Heidi as one of God's "lights," but surely he was also a light to her in her greatest hours of need.

Our light often shines the brightest in the midst of difficulties. Today, no matter what you may face, let your light shine on. It will spark embers of hope in the hearts of all those around you.

How CAN I BE SURE THAT MY LIGHT IS SHINING TODAY DESPITE THE DIFFICULTIES THAT MAY ARISE?

If a man cannot be a Christian in
the place where he is, he cannot
be a Christian anywhere.

Raising by Praising

*I tell you that men will have to give
account on the day of judgment for every
careless word they have spoken.*

MATTHEW 12:36 NIV

I CAN
HELP RAISE
MY CHILD'S
SELF-
ESTEEM BY
PRAISING...

A banker was appalled when his awkward teenage son began wearing ragged clothing and an earring in his ear. His first impulse was to demand that his son "shape up and clean up." But before he said anything, he thought, *My son must feel that he isn't a part of the school crowd. He's dressing this way to feel accepted. Rather than work on his dress, I need to work on his self-esteem.*

So a few weeks later, the father invited his son to go with him to his annual bankers' club banquet. The two had a great time. Even though the son sported an orange streak in his hair, he wore a suit to the event and behaved superbly, recalling the names of his father's friends and confidently conversing with them. He had responded to the unspoken message of his father's affirming words: *Son, I'm proud of you.*

Criticism wounds and tears down. Praise heals and builds up. Your child will encounter plenty of criticism in his or her life, without any of it coming from you. An important part of raising a child is to raise their self-esteem, their sights, and their faith. That kind of raising is the product of praising.

───❧───

*A torn jacket is soon mended; but hard
words bruise the heart of a child.*

Even the Morsels Shine

Whatsoever ye do, do it heartily,
as to the Lord, and not unto men.

COLOSSIANS 3:23

Former *Good Morning America* cohost Joan Lunden recalled,

> When I first came on [the] program in 1978, hosting with David Hartman, he got to interview all the celebrities and politicians and kings. I got the information spots. . . . I received piles of letters from women who were unhappy that I was allowing myself to be used in this way. Well, the fact was, I enjoyed those spots and I was good at them. I had to accept that it was either that way or no way at all. I got very good advice from Barbara Walters, who said: "Joan, don't buck city hall or you're gonna end up where all your female predecessors ended up—out there somewhere. Do the absolute best with what they give you and make those little morsels shine. And then go out and make the bigger interviews happen on your own."
>
> I can't see any reason to spend your time frustrated, angry, or upset about things you don't have or you can't have or you can't yet do. I drill this into my children when I hear them say, "I don't have this." I'll say, "Don't focus on what you don't have. Focus on what you do have and be grateful for it."

God created each of us with certain gifts and talents. When we focus on the gifts and talents we don't have, and envy others who do have them, we get nowhere. God never asks us to become something that we aren't; all He asks is that we use our gifts to the best of our ability. As we work to develop our gifts, our best gets better.

How CAN I BE MORE FAITHFUL WITH THE "LITTLE MORSELS" I'VE BEEN GIVEN?

_____
_____
_____
_____
_____
_____
_____
_____
_____
_____
_____
_____
_____
_____

The price of success is hard work, dedication to the job at hand, and determination that whether we win or lose, we have applied the best of ourselves to the task at hand.

Programming Your Mind

Keep watching and praying that you may not come into temptation.

MARK 14:38 NASB

I COULD BE ON THE ROAD TO A PURER THOUGHT LIFE IF I WOULD STOP WATCHING SHOWS THAT...

As a teen, Megan arrived home from school just in time to watch an hour of soap operas before doing her homework. She enjoyed the escape into the TV world and wasn't really aware that the programs were creating in her an inordinate amount of sexual curiosity. Over months and even years of watching her "soaps," Megan's perspective on life shifted. She began to think, *Relationships don't need to be pure—in fact, the impure ones seem more exciting. Fidelity doesn't matter, as long as a person is "happy."*

As a college student, Megan found it easy to participate in "one-night stands." Then after a short marriage ended in catastrophe as a result of her infidelity, she sought help from a counselor. At the outset, it was difficult for the counselor to understand why Megan had engaged in extramarital affairs. As far as her public behavior was concerned, she had been a model teenager at home, at church, and at school. Finally, the counselor discovered the source of the temptation that drove Megan to participate in her hidden life.

What we see on television inevitably becomes a part of our memory bank, becoming background information for justifying our behavior. If what you see isn't what you want to do, then change the channel!

Watch out for temptation—the more you see of it the better it looks.

Perfect People

The beginning of wisdom is this:
Get wisdom, and whatever
you get, get insight.

PROVERBS 4:7 RSV

In *One Woman's Liberation*, Shirley Boone writes:

> Talk about blind adoration! When Pat and I married, I was so much in love I didn't have any sense at all. Pat has said in interviews that we married fully aware of the serious adjustments we'd have to make and the financial crises we'd face, but he was speaking strictly for himself. As far as I was concerned, I wasn't aware of anything except that he was wonderful and that life without him would be miserable.
>
> I understood exactly how Mary, Queen of Scots, must have felt when she said of James Bothwell, her third husband, "I'd follow him to the ends of the earth in my petticoat," because that's how I felt about Pat. . . . If Pat had suggested it, I would have gone with him to Timbuktu without batting an eye. He was my life. To me, he was perfect, and that was the beginning of our troubles, because anyone placed on a pinnacle can go in only one direction: down.

Recognizing the fact that nobody's perfect frees us to forgive our spouses when their behavior is imperfect. It means recognizing the good and forgiving them when the less-than-perfect behavior surfaces.

Shirley and Pat Boone worked through their differences to create a strong and lasting marriage, but the beginning of their true success as a couple came when they each recognized this cardinal truth: Nobody's perfect . . . except God.

How CAN I
TREAT MY
SPOUSE
BETTER
DURING
THOSE TIMES
WHEN I FEEL
I'VE BEEN
WRONGED?

Nothing beats love at first sight
except love with insight.

29

Calculated Risk

*Peter got out of the boat, and walked
on the water and came toward Jesus.*
MATTHEW 14:29 NASB

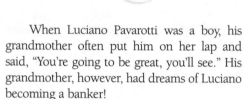

What SAFE
PATH AM I ON
THAT GOD IS
PROMPTING
ME TO LEAVE?

When Luciano Pavarotti was a boy, his
grandmother often put him on her lap and
said, "You're going to be great, you'll see." His
grandmother, however, had dreams of Luciano
becoming a banker!

Instead, he became a teacher. He taught
elementary school for a while, singing infre-
quently at special events. His father was the one
who goaded him into developing his voice,
chiding him for singing below his potential.

Finally, at age twenty-two, Pavarotti
stopped teaching to sell insurance. He continued to look for something financially stable to
rely on just in case he couldn't make it in the
music world. However, the insurance business
allowed him time to take voice lessons, and the
rest is history. The opera star now says,
"Studying voice was the turning point of my
life. It's a mistake to take the safe path in life."

He adds with a twinkle in his eye, "My
teacher groomed me. But no teacher ever told me
I would become famous. Just my grandmother."

It takes courage to leave a position you
consider safe and launch out into a new direction. But without taking a risk, you can never
realize your potential or find out all God created you to be.

*Man cannot discover new oceans unless he
has the courage to lose sight of the shore.*

Drops of Character

The integrity of the upright
shall guide them.

PROVERBS 11:3

Have you ever watched an icicle form? Did you notice how the dripping water froze, one drop at a time, until the icicle was a foot long or more?

If the water was clean, the icicle remained clear and sparkled brightly in the sun; but if the water was slightly muddy, the icicle looked cloudy, its beauty spoiled.

Our character is formed just like an icicle. Each thought or feeling adds its influence. Each decision we make—both great and small—contributes its part. Everything we take into our minds and souls—impressions, experiences, images, or words—helps create our character.

At all times, we must be aware of the "droplets" we allow to drip into our lives. Acts that develop habits of hate, falsehood, and evil intent mar and eventually destroy us, but habits born of love, truth, and goodness silently mold and fashion us into the image of God.

———

Character is what you are in the dark.

What IS FORMING A MUDDY ICICLE IN MY LIFE?

Recognizing God

The fool hath said in his heart,
There is no God.

PSALM 53:1

How CAN I
"SEE" GOD IN
MY EVERYDAY
WALK WITH
HIM?

One Sunday in the Netherlands, a plainly dressed, scholarly-looking man went into a church and took a seat near the pulpit. A few minutes later, a woman approached the pew. Seeing the stranger, she curtly advised him that he was in "her seat" and asked him to leave. The man graciously apologized and moved to one of the pews reserved for the poor. There, he devoutly joined in the service and left afterward without further incident.

When the service was over, one of the woman's friends asked her if she knew who it was whom she had ordered out of her pew. "No," the woman replied casually, "only some stranger, I suppose."

To the woman's great dismay, her friend informed her, "It was King Oscar of Sweden. He is here visiting the queen."

People who refuse to acknowledge the existence of God simply aren't aware of who is walking beside them day by day. We can refuse to recognize God, but that doesn't mean He ceases to exist or that He stops reaching out to us with His great love. Although the Lord may be invisible to us now, He is more real than anything we can see with our natural eyes. Rest in the knowledge that God is with you today, tomorrow, and forever.

An atheist is a man who has no
invisible means of support.

Too Late for Truth

What will it profit a man
if he gains the whole world
and forfeits his life?
MATTHEW 16:26 AMP

As former campaign manager for President George Bush and chairman of the Republican National Committee, Lee Atwater had accomplished the two things he had set out to do by the time he was forty. Then he was diagnosed with a malignant brain tumor. Shortly before he died, he wrote,

> I acquired more than most. But you can acquire all you want and still feel empty. What power wouldn't I trade for a little more time with my family? What price wouldn't I pay for an evening with friends? It took a deadly illness to put me eye to eye with that truth, but it is a truth the country can learn on my dime.

> I lie here in my bedroom, my face swollen from steroids, my body useless. The doctors still won't answer that nagging question: How long do I have? Some nights I can't go to sleep, so fearful am I that I will never wake up again.

> I've come a long way since the day I told George Bush that his "kinder, gentler" theme was a nice thought, but it wouldn't win us any votes. I used to say that the president might be kinder and gentler, but I wasn't going to be. How wrong I was. There is nothing more important in life than human beings, nothing sweeter than the human touch.

It's not too late for you. Evaluate your priorities. Most likely, they are in the proper order on paper, but are they in practice? Resolve today to realign your life according to your priorities.

I CAN
REALIGN MY
LIFE TODAY
BY . . .

Men will spend their health getting wealth; then gladly pay all they have earned to get health back.

Calm at the Core

The peace of God, which transcends all understanding, will guard your hearts and your minds in Christ Jesus.

PHILIPPIANS 4:7 NIV

What AM I AFRAID OF THAT HAS LEFT ME "CRIPPLED"?

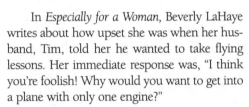

In *Especially for a Woman,* Beverly LaHaye writes about how upset she was when her husband, Tim, told her he wanted to take flying lessons. Her immediate response was, "I think you're foolish! Why would you want to get into a plane with only one engine?"

Tim asked her to pray about the matter, but she writes, "I started right off giving God my opinions and drawing my own conclusions. My fear . . . was controlling me." Tim suggested, "Be open with the Lord. . . . Let Him know you're afraid of flying but that you're willing to be changed if that's what He would have."

Beverly did just that. Tim took flying lessons, and she repeatedly committed her fears—and their lives—to the Lord.

Years later, she was a passenger in a commuter plane that was caught in a storm. As the plane bounced in the sky, the LaHaye's attorney—normally a very calm man—was sure they were going to crash. He looked over and saw that Beverly was asleep! He asked her later, "How could you sleep so peacefully?"

Beverly responded, "It had to be God. Only He could have brought me from that crippling fearfulness . . . to a place where I could fly through such a storm and be at peace."

The only way to truly overcome our fears is to commit them to the Lord. When we let go of our fears and let God deal with them, He can replace them with His peace and we can sleep right through the storms.

Sometimes the Lord calms the storm; sometimes He lets the storm rage and calms His child.

Which Morality?

Marriage should be honored by all, and the marriage bed kept pure, for God will judge the adulterer and all the sexually immoral.

HEBREWS 13:4 NIV

The 1960s were known for many rebellions, among them the sexual revolution. "Free love" spilled over from the hippie movement into mainstream American culture. Premarital sex, sanctioned by the "new morality," was openly flaunted.

One of the unexpected results of this trend, however, received little publicity. As reported by Dr. Francis Braceland, past president of the American Psychiatric Association and editor of the *American Journal of Psychiatry,* an increasing number of young people were admitted to mental hospitals. In discussing this finding at a National Methodist Convocation on Medicine and Theology, Braceland concluded, "A more lenient attitude on campus about premarital sex experience has imposed stresses on some college women severe enough to cause emotional breakdown."

Looking back over the years since this "new morality" was introduced into our American culture, we find a rising number of rapes, abortions, and divorces. Premarital pregnancies; single-family homes; and cases of sexually transmitted diseases, including herpes and HIV; rare occurrences in previous decades—have multiplied many times over. The evidence is compelling: The old morality produced safer, healthier, and happier people.

———❧———

The Bible has a word to describe "safe" sex: It's called marriage.

How CAN I KEEP THE OLD MORALITY ALIVE IN MY OWN LIFE?

Refusing the "Inevitable"

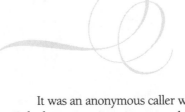

I have set the LORD always before me:
because he is at my right hand,
I shall not be moved.

PSALM 16:8

I've
NOTICED
MY OWN
CHARACTER
BEGINNING
TO BEND;
I NEED
TO STAND
STRAIGHT
AND TALL
REGARDING...

It was an anonymous caller who informed Erik that a certain priest named Bernard was delivering sermons aimed at subverting Germany's racial policies. Erik knew little about the priest's background and could not imagine what had compelled him to take this rash course. After all, the majority of churches, both Catholic and Protestant, had either supported the policies or remained discreetly neutral. Erik attended an evening service and found the church less than a third full. During his sermon, Father Bernard proclaimed Christ's love and asked those gathered to pray for the Jews. Several parishioners left as he preached.

As Father Bernard was removing his vestments, Erik said to him, "You are gravely misinformed." The priest looked at him with tired, sensitive eyes and said simply, "I know what is happening to the Jews. And so do you, Captain." When the priest died in Dachau, Erik concluded, "I feel a bit sorry for him. He simply did not understand the need to run with the tide, to accept the inevitable."

Although Erik and Bernard are fictional characters in Gerald Green's book, *Holocaust,* they make a strong point: Character does not bend to politics.

Character is not made in crisis,
it is only exhibited.

Bridging Heaven and Earth

With God all things are possible.

MATTHEW 19:26

Walking on the moon was once considered to be impossible, yet Neil Armstrong and Buzz Aldrin did just that on July 20, 1969. Michael Collins, the astronaut who remained aloft in the *Columbia,* writes of another seeming impossibility overcome that day:

> They hadn't been out on the surface very long when the three of us got a big surprise. The President of the United States began talking on the radio! Mr. Nixon said, "Neil and Buzz, I am talking to you by telephone from the Oval Office at the White House, and this certainly has to be the most historic telephone call ever made. . . . Because of what you have done, the heavens have become a part of man's world. As you talk to us from the Sea of Tranquillity, it inspires us to redouble our efforts to bring peace and tranquillity to earth."

Our prayers are like an unseen communication link, spanning Heaven and earth. Things once regarded as impossible become possible when that link is firmly established.

❈

The world is moving so fast these days that the man who says it can't be done is generally interrupted by someone doing it.

If I TRULY BELIEVE GOD CAN DO THE IMPOSSIBLE, THEN I BELIEVE THAT ON MY BEHALF HE WILL . . .

The Right Equipment

*I am the light of the world: he that
followeth me shall not walk in darkness,
but shall have the light of life.*

JOHN 8:12

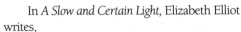

What
"STUFF" AM I
RELYING ON
INSTEAD OF
GOD ALONE?

In *A Slow and Certain Light*, Elizabeth Elliot writes,

> Two young Americans with high adventure in their hearts arrived in the city of Quito, Ecuador, on their way to the "Great Amazon Rain Forest" east of the Andes. They were going on a six-week trek and planned to write a book about their experiences. . . . They had been to an army surplus store before they left home and bought everything the salesman told them they would need. . . . What more could they want? There was, it occurred to them when they reached Quito, one thing—the language—and when they learned that a jungle missionary was in town, they came to see me. . . . "Just give us a few phrases," they said. . . . They described their equipment to me with great pride, and I could see that it was not going to be of much use. I wanted to tell them that what they ought to have was a guide. . . .
>
> Sometimes we come to God as the two adventurers came to me—confident and, we think, well-informed and well-equipped. But it has occurred to us that with all our accumulation of stuff something is missing. . . . What we really ought to have is the Guide Himself.

*The strength of a man consists in finding out
the way God is going and going that way.*

Who Are You?

It shall not be so among you: but whosoever will be great among you, let him be your minister; and whosoever will be chief among you, let him be your servant.

MATTHEW 20:26-27

The following set of contrasting remarks has been offered as a character sketch of a good leader. For a personal challenge, as you read through the list, circle the words you believe most closely describe you!

- Self-reliant but not self-sufficient
- Energetic but not self-seeking
- Steadfast but not stubborn
- Tactful but not timid
- Serious but not sullen
- Loyal but not sectarian
- Unmovable but not stationary
- Gentle but not hypersensitive
- Tenderhearted but not touchy
- Conscientious but not a perfectionist
- Disciplined but not demanding
- Generous but not gullible
- Meek but not weak
- Humorous but not hilarious
- Friendly but not familiar
- Holy but not holier-than-thou
- Discerning but not critical
- Progressive but not pretentious
- Authoritative but not autocratic

Ask God to help you develop the positive attributes you can't circle yet.

Put others before yourself, and you can become a leader among men.

I COULD CIRCLE THE POSITIVE ATTRIBUTES IF ONLY I WOULD LEARN TO . . .

Innovative Success

How long will you lie down,
O sluggard? When will you
arise from your sleep?
PROVERBS 6:9 NASB

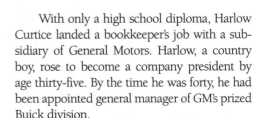

How CAN I
APPLY THESE
THREE
PRINCIPLES
TO THE
PROBLEM
AREAS OF
MY LIFE?

With only a high school diploma, Harlow Curtice landed a bookkeeper's job with a subsidiary of General Motors. Harlow, a country boy, rose to become a company president by age thirty-five. By the time he was forty, he had been appointed general manager of GM's prized Buick division.

Curtice made his way to the top of his profession with a flair for taking new ideas and putting them into action. He dared to design new styles and develop new models. Furthermore, he personally traveled throughout the United States to inspire dealers and instill in them a renewed enthusiasm for their Buick products.

The result? Even though his career was forged in the middle of the Depression, sales of Buick cars quadrupled! His division became the second biggest moneymaker in General Motors' history.

To what did Harlow Curtice attribute his success? He cited these three things: 1) he set goals for himself and required the same of the people around him, 2) he took pride in confronting and overcoming obstacles that blinded his vision, and 3) he was willing to do things losers refused to do. Therefore, winning became a habit!

By putting these principles into practice, you, too, can develop the habit of winning.

The way to get to the top is
to get off your bottom.

Our Refuge and Strength

*They that wait upon the LORD shall renew
their strength; they shall mount up with wings
as eagles; they shall run, and not be weary;
and they shall walk, and not faint.*

ISAIAH 40:31

Norma Zimmer, a well-known singer for Lawrence Welk, had a difficult childhood as a result of her parents' drinking. Singing was her way to escape. As a high school senior, Norma was invited to be a featured soloist at the University Christian Church in Seattle. When her parents heard she was going to sing a particular song, they both insisted on attending the service. She says about that morning: "I stole glances at the congregation, trying to find my parents . . . then in horror I saw them—weaving down the aisle in a state of disheveled intoxication. They were late. Few empty seats were left. . . . The congregation stared. I don't know how I ever got through that morning."

After she sang and took her seat, her heart pounding and her cheeks burning from embarrassment, the pastor preached, "God is our refuge and strength, a tested help in time of trouble." She says, "My own trouble seemed to bear down on me with tremendous weight. . . . I realized how desperate life in our family was without God, and that day I recommitted my life to Him. . . . Jesus came into my life not only as Savior but for daily strength and direction."

The salvation God offers us is not only for our future benefit, but also for our day-to-day needs in the present. He is an ever-present help in times of trouble. Rely on Him daily for peace and direction. Let Him be your refuge and your strength.

My MOST
PRESSING
DAY-TO-DAY
NEED IS . . .

*True faith and courage are like a kite—
an opposing wind raises it higher.*

Tough Enough to Be Tender

*You have also given me the shield of Your
salvation, and Your right hand upholds me;
and Your gentleness makes me great.*

PSALM 18:35 NASB

How CAN
I SHOW
COMPASSION
TO A LOVED
ONE IN
NEED TODAY?

In *God Works the Night Shift,* Ron Mehl writes of Joe Knapp, who was as "fearless and aggressive as a bulldozer." He drove a beer truck down the Oregon highways and had a mean streak that went clear to the bone. But Joe found the extended hand of God on a cold, snowy night in Portland, Oregon. Trying to navigate the slick streets, his beer truck stalled (of all places) in front of a church. Hearing singing from within the building, he went in and was converted to Christ. Joe eventually went to the mission field and became the pastor of a large Protestant church in Colombia. Joe fearlessly preached Christ. He was bombastic and tough, though his wife, Virginia, was a quiet, gracious woman.

What lingered the most in Ron's mind, however, was not Joe's toughness, it was "his extraordinary tenderness and care shown his wife as she lay in a rest home. Joe knew she was afraid to be alone, so every day this dear man who, years earlier could have single-handedly tossed everyone out of a bar, would visit with his little wife long into the night. Every day as Joe sat at her side, he would tell her how much he loved her. . . . But most of all, he would hold her hand." Joe was strong enough to be tender.

Toughness does not preclude tenderness—it enhances it. God gives us His strength so we can show His compassion to a world in need of His courage.

*Nothing is so strong as gentleness.
Nothing is so gentle as real strength.*

Honor the Positive

Honour thy father.
EXODUS 20:12

During war games, Private Glenn Sollie and Private Andrew Bearshield of the Fifteenth Infantry were ordered to make their way to a bridge and stand guard there until they were relieved.

The two were faithful soldiers. They went to the bridge and guarded it . . . and guarded it. They remained at their post for three days and nights, with neither food nor blankets. Eventually, they were not "relieved," but found. The privates had been guarding the wrong bridge. They had lost their way and taken their battle stations at a bridge seven miles away from the one they were supposed to guard. One might think they were reprimanded for making such a mistake. On the contrary, they were given military honors for guarding their position with such faithfulness!

Parents often make mistakes in life. They can take "wrong turns" or follow foolish pursuits. But rather than criticize or blame them for their errors, we can choose to focus on what our parents did right. In turning our attention to their positive qualities and deeds—however meager they may be—we usually find we have no difficulty giving them honor.

❦

My dad and I hunted and fished together.
How could I get angry at this man
who took the time to be with me?

In WHAT AREAS HAVE MY PARENTS BEEN FAITHFUL?

The Humility of a Servant

*He that is greatest among you
shall be your servant.*
MATTHEW 23:11

In MY DAILY
ROUTINE, I
CAN SERVE
OTHERS BY...

People often think of heart surgeons as the prima donnas of the medical world. But those who know Dr. William DeVries, the surgeon who pioneered the artificial heart, couldn't disagree more. Coworkers at Humana Hospital Audubon in Louisville, Kentucky, describe DeVries as the kind of doctor who shows up on Sundays just to cheer discouraged patients. He occasionally even changes dressings, traditionally considered a nurse's job, if a patient wants him to stick around and talk.

Friends say DeVries is an "old shoe" who fits in wherever he goes. He likes to wear cowboy boots with his surgical scrubs, and he often repairs hearts to the beat of Vivaldi or jazz. "He has always got a smile lurking," says Louisville cardiologist Dr. Robert Goodin. "And he's always looking for a way to let it out."

No matter how high you rise, never forget that you started out at ground zero. Even if you were born to great wealth or privilege, you were born as a helpless babe, nonetheless. Real success comes not in thinking you have arrived at a place where others should serve you, but in recognizing that in whatever place you are, you have arrived at a position where you can serve others.

---

*It needs more skill than I can tell
to play the second fiddle well.*

An Argument for Honesty

Be ye doers of the word,
and not hearers only,
deceiving your own selves.

JAMES 1:22

A reporter once asked Sam Rayburn, Speaker of the House of Representatives at the time:

"Mr. Speaker, you see at least a hundred people a day. You tell each one yes or no. You never seem to make notes on what you have told them, but I have never heard of your forgetting anything you have promised them. What is your secret?"

Rayburn's eyes flashed as he answered, "If you tell the truth the first time, you don't have anything to remember."

Truth extends to honesty. If you are honest in all of your dealings, you never have to remember whom you may have cheated.

Truth extends to encouragement. If you speak a positive truth about all people, you never have to avoid anyone.

Truth extends to implications. If you refuse to give false impressions, you never feel the need to cover anything up.

If you refrain from twisting the truth, you will never need to unravel a relationship gone awry.

Live truth instead of professing it.

Sometimes I TWIST THE TRUTH WHEN I . . .

Don't Forget the Captain

Take fast hold of instruction; let her
not go: keep her; for she is thy life.
PROVERBS 4:13

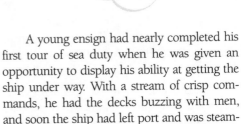

How HAVE I
TRIED TO
GET MY LIFE
UNDER WAY—
WITHOUT THE
CAPTAIN?

A young ensign had nearly completed his first tour of sea duty when he was given an opportunity to display his ability at getting the ship under way. With a stream of crisp commands, he had the decks buzzing with men, and soon the ship had left port and was steaming out of the channel.

The ensign's efficiency was remarkable. In fact, the deck was abuzz with talk that he had set a new record for getting a destroyer under way. The ensign glowed at his accomplishment and was not all that surprised when another seaman approached him with a message from the captain. He was, however, a bit surprised to find that it was a radio message, and he was even more surprised when he read, "My personal congratulations upon completing your underway preparation exercise according to the book and with amazing speed. In your haste, however, you have overlooked one of the unwritten rules—make sure the captain is aboard before getting under way."

The Bible is God's manual for getting our life under way. However, we should never become so bound to the Book that we forget the author of it and the relationship He desires to have with us on the voyage.

If a first you don't succeed,
try reading the instructions.

A Soldier's Obedience

The wise in heart accept commands,
but a chattering fool comes to ruin.

PROVERBS 10:8 NIV

The story is told of a great military captain who, after a full day of battle, sat by a warm fire with several of his officers and began talking over the events of the day.

"Who did the best today on the field of battle?" the captain asked them.

One officer told of a man who had fought bravely all day, and then just before dusk, he had been severely wounded. Another told of a man who had taken a hit for a fellow soldier, sparing his friend's life but possibly losing his own. Yet another officer told of the man who had led the charge into battle. And still another told of a soldier who had risked his life to pull a fellow soldier from danger.

The captain heard them out and then said, "No, I fear you are all mistaken. The best man in the field today was the soldier who was just lifting up his arm to strike the enemy, but upon hearing the trumpet sound the retreat, checked himself, dropped his arm without striking the blow, and retreated. That perfect and ready obedience to the will of his general is the noblest thing that was done today on the battlefield."

God's Word tells us that obedience is better than sacrifice (1 Samuel 15:22). God desires that we learn to obey Him and walk in His will for our lives. He will never lead us astray.

He that has learned to obey
will know how to command.

I NEED TO
BE MORE
OBEDIENT TO
GOD BY . . .

Putting the Pieces Together

This Daniel was preferred above the presidents and princes, because an excellent spirit was in him; and the king thought to set him over the whole realm.

DANIEL 6:3

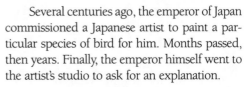

What
SINGULAR DETAIL OF MY LIFE NEEDS THE MOST ATTENTION RIGHT NOW AS I WORK TOWARD EXCELLENCE?

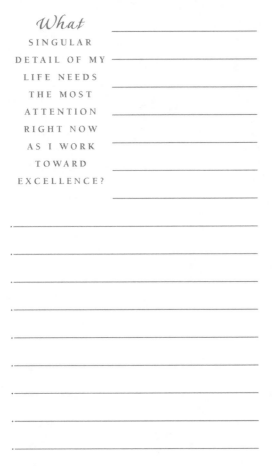

Several centuries ago, the emperor of Japan commissioned a Japanese artist to paint a particular species of bird for him. Months passed, then years. Finally, the emperor himself went to the artist's studio to ask for an explanation.

The artist set a blank canvas on the easel and within fifteen minutes had completed a painting of the bird. It was a masterpiece! Admiring both the painting and the artist's great skill, the emperor asked why there had been such a long delay.

The artist then went from cabinet to cabinet in his studio. He pulled out armloads of drawings of feathers, tendons, wings, feet, claws, eyes, and beaks—virtually every aspect of a bird from every conceivable angle. He placed them before the emperor, who nodded in understanding. The magnificence of any finished product can never be greater than the magnificence of any singular detail.

To have an excellent life, strive for an excellent year. Within that year, strive for an excellent month, and within that month, strive for an excellent day. Within a day, strive for an excellent hour. An excellent life is the sum of many excellent moments!

It's the little things in life that determine the big things.

Glorious Moments

Thou hast been faithful over a few things,
I will make thee ruler over many things:
enter thou into the joy of thy lord.

MATTHEW 25:21

Once when speaking to a group of ministers, Fred Craddock noted the importance of being faithful in the little things of life.

To give my life for Christ appears glorious. To pour myself out for others . . . to pay the ultimate price of martyrdom—I'll do it. I'm ready, Lord, to go out in a blaze of glory.

We think giving our all to the Lord is like taking a $1,000 bill and laying it on the table—"Here's my life, Lord. I'm giving it all."

But the reality for most of us is that He sends us to the bank and has us cash in the $1,000 for quarters. We go through life putting out 25 cents here and 50 cents there. Listen to the neighbor kid's troubles instead of saying, "Get lost." Go to a committee meeting. Give a cup of water to a shaky old man in a nursing home.

Usually, giving our life to Christ isn't glorious. It's done in all those little acts of love, 25 cents at a time. It would be easy to go out in a flash of glory; it's harder to live the Christian life little by little over the long haul.

Ask the Lord to show you how you can spend your life well—25 cents at a time.

These ARE THE LITTLE ACTS OF LOVE I CAN PERFORM FAITHFULLY:

Happiness is a dividend
on a well-invested life.

Equal and Opposite

*Till I die I will not remove mine integrity
from me. My righteousness I hold fast,
and will not let it go: my heart shall not
reproach me so long as I live.*

JOB 27:5-6

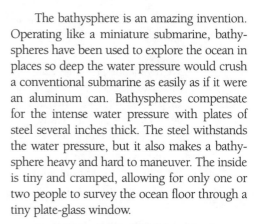

What
NEGATIVE
CIRCUM-
STANCES DO I
NEED TO SEE
IN TERMS OF
BUILDING UP
MY SPIRITUAL
FORTITUDE?

The bathysphere is an amazing invention. Operating like a miniature submarine, bathyspheres have been used to explore the ocean in places so deep the water pressure would crush a conventional submarine as easily as if it were an aluminum can. Bathyspheres compensate for the intense water pressure with plates of steel several inches thick. The steel withstands the water pressure, but it also makes a bathysphere heavy and hard to maneuver. The inside is tiny and cramped, allowing for only one or two people to survey the ocean floor through a tiny plate-glass window.

Amazingly, divers find fish and other sea creatures at every depth of the ocean. Some of these creatures are quite small and have normal-looking skin—no heavy metal for them! They swim freely, remaining flexible and supple in the inky waters.

How is it that fish can live at these depths without being crushed? They compensate for the outside pressure with equal and opposite pressure from inside.

Spiritual fortitude works in the same way. The more negative the circumstances, the greater the need to allow God's power to work within us to exert an equal and opposite pressure.

———❦———

*Let us not say, "Every man is the architect
of his own fortune"; but let us say, "Every
man is the architect of his own character."*

Forgiven and Forgotten

Be ye kind one to another, tenderhearted,
forgiving one another, even as God
for Christ's sake hath forgiven you.

EPHESIANS 4:32

A much-loved minister of God once carried a secret burden of a long-past sin buried deep in his heart. He had committed the sin many years before, during his seminary training. No one knew what he had done, but they did know he had repented. Even so, he had suffered years of remorse over the incident without any sense of God's forgiveness.

A woman in his church deeply loved God and claimed to have visions in which Jesus Christ spoke to her. The minister, skeptical of her claims, asked her, "The next time you speak to the Lord, would you please ask Him what sin your minister committed while he was in seminary?" The woman agreed.

When she came to the church a few days later, the minister asked, "Did He visit you?" She said, "Yes."

"And did you ask Him what sin I committed in seminary?"

"Yes, I asked Him," she replied.

"Well, what did He say?"

"He said, 'I don't remember.'"

The forgiveness we receive in Christ is complete. As far as God is concerned, our sin is finished and forgotten. We need to rest in His forgiveness and release the guilt and shame of our sin, so that we may walk in God's rest and peace.

Right NOW,
I RELEASE
TO GOD THE
GUILT AND
SHAME I FEEL
ABOUT . . .

Every person should have a special
cemetery plot in which to bury the
faults of friends and loved ones.

The Reality of Life

*I can do all things through Christ
which strengtheneth me.*
PHILIPPIANS 4:13

In WHAT
AREA OF MY
LIFE DO I
NEED TO SEE
THE POWER
OF GOD
MANIFESTED
TODAY?

Dr. Walter Eerdman wrote a bestseller some years ago entitled *Source of Power in Famous Lives*. In it, he gave biographical sketches of fifty great men and women of history, among them David Livingstone, Jenny Lind, Clara Barton, Frances Willard, Christopher Columbus, and Oliver Cromwell.

Eerdman drew this conclusion about the people he had profiled: "In their lives, God was a reality."

Truly great people share a common source of power—they simply apply that power in different ways. Some have greater public success and thus attain a greater degree of fame and prominence than others. Many less famous people, however, have also encouraged others with their stories of personal triumphs and victories. This shows that the power which comes from having a real relationship with God isn't limited to the rich and famous. It can be attained by anyone, regardless of wealth or position in society.

Genuine power from God is manifested as hope in times of disaster, calm in times of crises, direction in times of confusion, and an enduring faith in times of fear. Anyone can know this power if they will allow God to become a reality in their lives.

*If God be your partner,
make your plans large.*

Receiving Is Believing

The LORD seeth not as man seeth; for man looketh on the outward appearance, but the LORD looketh on the heart.

1 SAMUEL 16:7

A minister once preached an entire series of sermons on some challenging Scriptures in hopes of winning one particular man of great intellect to Christ. Shortly after the series ended, to the preacher's delight, the man came forward to announce that he had become a convinced Christian and wanted to join the church.

Pleased with himself, the preacher said, "And which of my sermons was it that removed your doubts?" The man replied, "Your sermons? It wasn't any of your sermons."

"What was it then?" the preacher asked, greatly surprised and disappointed.

"The thing that set me thinking was when a poor woman came out of the church and stumbled down the steps right beside me," the man said. "When I put out my hand to help her, she smiled and said, 'Thank you' and then added, 'Do you love Jesus Christ my blessed Savior? He means everything to me.' I did not then, but I thought about what she had said. I found I was on the wrong road. I still have many questions, but now Jesus means everything to me, too."

Faith is not based on convincing God of our goodness. Faith is receiving God's goodness, which He has given us through Jesus Christ.

If I HAD AN OPPORTUNITY TO TELL OTHERS ABOUT GOD'S GOODNESS TO ME, I WOULD TELL THEM HOW HE . . .

When God measures a man, He puts the tape around the heart instead of the head.

Shining Floodlights on Your Soul

May your love and your truth
always protect me.
PSALM 40:11 NIV

God
FLOODED MY
SOUL WITH
LIGHT WHEN
HE . . .

_____

_____

_____

_____

_____

_____

_____

_____

_____

_____

_____

_____

_____

_____

_____

_____

_____

_____

_____

_____

In his November 11, 1942, war report to the British House of Commons, Winston Churchill referred to "the soft underbelly of the Axis." On the surface, Hitler's regime seemed anything but soft. The powerful blitzkrieg of Nazi troops, the bravado and pageantry of the Third Reich, seemed unstoppable. What the British prime minister perceived, however, was the hidden side of the German dictator: his lack of character, his insecurity, and his racially biased fears. Churchill saw the moral darkness of Hitler's soul and predicted that when that darkness was exposed, it would create a black hole into which all of the Nazi ideals would be sucked into oblivion.

Mark Twain used a similar word picture when he said, "Everyone is a moon and has a dark side which he never shows to anybody."

When you face up to your own sinful darkness, you can either embrace it and pursue it—which leads to condemnation—or you can repent and turn from it. Trust God to forgive you and flood your soul with light. In doing so, you will discover that you have no risk of exposure, because there's nothing to expose!

———— ⟡ ————

The man who fears no truths has
nothing to fear from lies.

Holy Comfort

Even though I walk through the valley of the shadow of death, I fear no evil, for You are with me; Your rod and Your staff, they comfort me.

PSALM 23:4 NASB

In *Women Who Do Too Much*, Patricia Sprinkle writes,

> Three months before I spoke with Nancy, her husband lost a four-year battle to a degenerative brain disease. She said, "This was a brilliant man, a gentle man, a man with a terrific sense of humor. I grieved as he lost his ability to walk, pick up things from the floor, write, speak clearly. We had been married for thirty years and expected to grow old together. Suddenly, in one day, our life changed. He flew to Mayo Clinic one morning and called me that night with the doctor's diagnosis. They could do nothing for him.
>
> "I remember thinking after I hung up the phone, life is never going to be the same again. Nobody gets a rehearsal for this. You don't get to practice.
>
> "I was furious with God—banged my fist on many tables. But I learned to thank God that God is God. God didn't get bowled over by my fury. Instead, He told me, 'I won't leave you. I'm as sad about this as you are. I grieve with you.' The shared grief of God gets me through my own."

Jesus called the Holy Spirit the "Comforter." He alone is with us every moment of our lives.

I THANK GOD THAT HE SHARED MY GRIEF WHEN...

The best comforter isn't a down-filled quilt.

Having a Say

He that reproveth a scorner getteth to himself shame: and he that rebuketh a wicked man getteth himself a blot.

PROVERBS 9:7

I CAN SPEND
MY TIME
BLESSING
OTHERS
BY . . .

When Charles Spurgeon was still a boy preacher, he was warned about a certain woman with a reputation for being extremely quarrelsome. He was told that she intended to give him a tongue-lashing the moment she saw him next.

Spurgeon said, "All right, but that's a game two can play."

Shortly thereafter, the woman met him and began to assault him with a barrage of verbal abuse. He simply smiled back at her and said, "Oh yes, thank you. I am quite well. Thank you for asking. I hope you are the same."

His remarks were followed by another tirade of know-it-all complaints, this time voiced at a slightly higher volume. He responded again, smiling quietly, "Yes, it does look rather as if it might rain. I think I had better be getting on."

"Bless the man!" the woman exclaimed and then concluded, "He's as deaf as a post. What's the use of storming at him!"

Never again did she assault Spurgeon with her arguments. Nor did he ever tell her what he had done. There's no point in arguing with know-it-all people. It's better to let them have their say and walk on. Instead, spend your valuable time blessing the lives of others!

The only fool bigger than the person who knows it all is the person who argues with him.

Right Is Right, Regardless

Humble yourselves therefore under
the mighty hand of God, that he
may exalt you in due time.

1 PETER 5:6

In 1953, a *Chicago News* columnist named Harris had a large and faithful readership. One of his most famous statements was one he called, "A Prayer for the President." It said, in part, "O Lord . . . give him the courage, not of convictions, but of Your commandments."

Harris seemed to be echoing the sentiments of an earlier patriot, William Penn, who said, "Right is right, even if everyone is against it, and wrong is wrong, even if everyone is for it." Clearly the commandments of God are right for every generation, regardless of public opinion. God's law—His ideal plan for mankind—is never subject to popular vote.

When we compare our lives to God's ideal, we invariably come up short. In fact, the Word of God predicts this will be the case! The guilt we feel, however, is not intended to overwhelm or plunge us into despair. Rather, we are to draw closer to God—to seek His forgiveness, to ask for His help—that we might become more like His Son, Jesus Christ. As we seek and receive God's help, we are transformed into people who no longer seek easy tasks or simple lives. Instead we become willing to take on hard tasks and difficult challenges.

Only when we have knelt before
God can we stand before men.

What HARD TASK OR DIFFICULT CHALLENGE DO I NEED TO TAKE ON—WITH GOD'S HELP?

Finding the Path

I will lift up my eyes to the mountains; from where shall my help come? My help comes from the LORD, who made heaven and earth.

PSALM 121:1-2 NASB

What

PATHLESS "JUNGLE" IS GOD LEADING ME OUT OF TODAY?

E. Stanley Jones tells the story of a missionary who became lost in an African jungle. Looking around, he saw nothing but bush and a few clearings. He stumbled about until he finally came across a native hut. He asked one of the natives if he could lead him out of the jungle and back to the mission station. The man agreed to help him.

"Thank you!" exclaimed the missionary. "Which way do I go?" The native replied, "Walk." And so they did, hacking their way through the unmarked jungle for more than an hour.

Pausing to rest, the missionary looked around and had the same overwhelming sense that he was lost. All he saw was bush and a few clearings. "Are you quite sure this is the way?" he asked. "I don't see any path."

The native looked at him and replied, "Bwana, in this place, there is no path. I am the path."

When you have no clues, remember that God is omniscient—all-wise. When you run out of time, remember that God is omnipresent—all time is in His hand. When you are weak, remember that God is omnipotent—all power belongs to Him.

⸺⊶⊷⸺

It is impossible for that man to despair who remembers that his Helper is omnipotent.

Doctor's Orders

Pride only breeds quarrels, but wisdom
is found in those who take advice.

PROVERBS 13:10 NIV

Next to the patient who doesn't pay his bill, the physician's most difficult patient is the one who refuses to follow "doctor's orders." One study revealed that up to 90 percent of all patients fail to take a complete round of antibiotics, enabling bacteria to mutate into more resistant strains. A similar percentage of patients were found to cheat on diets, continue to smoke, and fail to return for required follow-up visits to their physicians—even if their lives were considered to be in jeopardy.

One researcher noted that teachers seemed to be among the least obedient patient groups, thinking that they could modify anything doctors told them. Young executives also presented a problem in attitude. "Just give me enough to get by," was their philosophy. According to one study, engineers made the best patients, since they seemed to be compulsive about following explicit orders.

The net result of failing to follow a physician's prescription is nearly always less health in the long run, even though a condition might temporarily clear up or a disease be overcome.

That's true for the advice given by most professionals and especially so for the wisdom of God's Word. Wise up! Take God's advice today.

Many receive advice—
only the wise profit by it.

How HAVE I FAILED TO FOLLOW "DOCTOR'S ORDERS" RECENTLY?

What's the Rush?

*He that gathereth in summer is a wise
son: but he that sleepeth in harvest
is a son that causeth shame.*

PROVERBS 10:5

If I REALLY
BELIEVED
THE LORD
WAS GETTING
READY TO
RETURN, I
WOULD . . .

An old legend recounts how Satan once called three of his top aides so that they might make a plan for stopping the effective outreach of a particular group of Christians.

One of the aides, Rancor, proposed, "We should convince them there is no God." Satan sneered at Rancor and replied, "That would never work. They know there's a God."

Bitterness then spoke up and said, "We'll convince them that God does not really care about right or wrong." Satan thought about the idea for a few moments, but then rejected it. "Too many know that God cares," he finally said.

Malice then proposed his idea. "We'll let them go on thinking there is a God and that He cares about right and wrong. But . . . we will keep whispering that there is no hurry, there is no hurry, there is no hurry."

Satan howled with delight! The plan was adopted, and Malice was promoted to an even higher position in Satan's malevolent hierarchy.

Who can tell how many souls have been lost or lives sorely wounded because someone succumbed to procrastination? Is it time for you to gather in the harvest?

---

*The wise does at once
what the fool does at last.*

Whittled to Your Essence

*The memory of the righteous
will be a blessing, but the
name of the wicked will rot.*

PROVERBS 10:7 NIV

In *Grand Essentials,* Ben Patterson writes,

> I have a theory about old age. . . .
> I believe that when life has whittled
> us down, when joints have failed and
> skin has wrinkled . . . what is left of
> us will be what we were all along, in
> our essence.
>
> Exhibit A is a distant uncle. . . .
> All his life he did nothing but find
> new ways to get rich. . . . He spent his
> senescence very comfortably, drooling
> and babbling constantly about the
> money he had made. . . . When life
> whittled him down to his essence, all
> there was left was raw greed.
>
> Exhibit B is my wife's grand-
> mother. . . . The best example I can
> think of was when we asked her to
> pray before dinner. She would reach
> out and hold the hands of those sit-
> ting beside her, a broad, beatific smile
> would spread across her face, her dim
> eyes would fill with tears as she
> looked up to Heaven, and her chin
> would quaver as she poured out her
> love to Jesus. That was Edna in a nut-
> shell. She loved Jesus and she loved
> people. She couldn't remember our
> names, but she couldn't keep her
> hands from patting us lovingly when-
> ever we got near her. When life whit-
> tled her down to her essence, all there
> was left was love: love for God and
> love for people.

Who you are deep on the inside will always
surface at some point in your life. Let God and
His Word transform your essence into love.

Deep INSIDE, I NEED GOD'S WORD TO TRANSFORM MY ABILITY TO LOVE OTHERS, ESPECIALLY . . .

*Beware lest your footprints on the sand
of time leave only the marks of a heel.*

Obedient Choices

The wise in heart accept commands,
but a chattering fool comes to ruin.
PROVERBS 10:8 NIV

What
AUTHORITY
IN MY LIFE
HAVE I BEEN
UNWILLING
TO SUBMIT
TO?

In the eleventh century, King Henry III of Bavaria grew tired of his responsibilities as king, the pressures of international politics, and the mundane worldliness of court life. He made an application to Prior Richard at a local monastery to be accepted as a contemplative so that he could spend the rest of his life in prayer and meditation.

Prior Richard responded, "Your Majesty, do you understand that the pledge here is one of obedience? That will be hard for you since you have been a king."

"I understand," Henry said. "For the rest of my life, I will be obedient to you, as Christ leads you."

Prior Richard responded, "Then I will tell you what to do. Go back to your throne and serve faithfully in the place where God has put you."

After King Henry died, this statement was written in his honor: "The king learned to rule by being obedient."

Each of us ultimately obeys either the righteous commandments of our Heavenly Father or the "rule of lawlessness." We must willingly choose to put ourselves under authority, including the authority of God. To fail to do so is to have no law other than our own whim, an unreliable source at its best.

Obedience is the "virtue-making virtue."

Seven Days of Integrity

*That you may live a life worthy of
the Lord and may please him in every
way: bearing fruit in every good work.*

COLOSSIANS 1:10 NIV

The story is told of two men who met on the street. One man said to the other, "Have you heard about Harry? He embezzled half a million dollars from his company." The other man said, "That's terrible! I never did trust Harry."

The first man continued, "Not only that, he left town and took Tom's wife with him." The other man said, "That's awful! Harry has always been a ne'er-do-well."

The first man said, "Not only that, he stole a car to make his getaway." The other man said, "That's scandalous; I always did think Harry had a bad streak in him."

The first man concluded, "Not only that, they think he was drunk when he pulled out of town." The other man said, "Harry's no good!" After a few moments of reflection, he then asked, "But what really bothers me is this—who's going to teach his Sunday school class?"

Maintaining your integrity is a seven-day-a-week job. It requires an ongoing supply of character and a steady flow of trustworthiness.

The measure of a man is not what he does on Sunday, but rather who he is on Monday through Saturday.

I CAN MAINTAIN MY INTEGRITY BY . . .

Solving the Impossible

He who heeds discipline shows the way to life, but whoever ignores correction leads others astray.

PROVERBS 10:17 NIV

What

MISTAKE
HAVE I MADE
RECENTLY
THAT I KNOW
I HAVE TO
CORRECT?

A janitor at the First Security Bank in Boise, Idaho, once accidentally put a box of 8,000 checks totaling $840,000 on a trash table, which the operator of the paper shredder dutifully dumped into his machine that night, cutting the checks into quarter-inch shreds. He then dumped the paper scraps into a garbage can outside the bank. The next morning when the bank supervisor realized what had happened, he moaned, "I wanted to cry."

Most of the checks had been cashed at the bank and were awaiting shipment to a clearinghouse. Their loss represented a bookkeeping nightmare, since most of the checks were still unrecorded. As a result, the bankers could not know who paid what to whom.

What did the supervisor do? He ordered that the shredded pieces be reconstructed. So fifty employees worked in two shifts for six hours a day inside six rooms, shifting, matching, and pasting the pieces together as if they were jigsaw puzzles, until all 8,000 of the checks were pieced together.

Humpty Dumpty may have fallen from the wall. But did the king's men even try to put him together again? If you make a mistake, make a solution!

An error doesn't become a mistake until you refuse to correct it.

Living Words

My son, attend to my words; incline thine ear unto my sayings. Let them not depart from thine eyes; keep them in the midst of thine heart. For they are life unto those that find them, and health to all their flesh.

PROVERBS 4:20-22

A young woman was packing a suitcase for a long trip. She said to a woman who was watching her, "I'm just about finished. I only have to put in a guidebook, a lamp, a mirror, my favorite love letters, a microscope, a telescope, a volume of fine poetry, a songbook, a few biographies, a package of old letters, a sword, and a set of books I have been studying." The onlooker gasped, "How do you intend to get all that in your suitcase? It's almost full now!"

The young woman replied, "Oh, all that won't take much room." She then walked over to a table, picked up her Bible, placed it in the corner of her suitcase, and closed the lid. Winking at her friend, she said, "And I even got in a loaf of living bread."

The Bible says of itself that it is "fresh" with every reading—it never grows stale. The Bible is always applicable to life, no matter where one lives. The truths of the Bible are unshakable—they will last forever and never go out of style. Voltaire once said that in a hundred years, the Bible would be a forgotten book, found only in museums. When the hundred years were up, however, Voltaire's home was occupied by the Geneva Bible Society! Feed your children a healthy portion of the Bible today. Consider it "heavenly food."

Today MY PORTION OF "HEAVENLY FOOD" NOURISHED ME BY . . .

The Bible is alive, it speaks to me; it has feet, it runs after me; it has hands, it lays hold of me.

True Justice

*A merry heart doeth good
like a medicine.*
PROVERBS 17:22

God IS
PROMPTING
ME TO GIVE
GENEROUSLY
TO . . .

One of New York City's most popular mayors was Fiorello LaGuardia. Nearly every older New Yorker has a favorite memory of him. Some recall the day he read the funny papers over the radio, with all the appropriate inflections, because a strike had kept the Sunday newspapers off the stands. Others remember his outbursts against the "bums," who exploited the poor.

One time, the mayor chose to preside in night court. An old woman was brought before him on that bitterly cold night. The charge was stealing a loaf of bread. She explained that her family was starving. LaGuardia replied, "I've got to punish you. The law makes no exception. I must fine you ten dollars." At that, he reached into his own pocket and pulled out a ten-dollar bill. "Well," he said, "here's the ten dollars to pay your fine, which I now remit." He then tossed the ten-dollar bill into his own hat and declared, "I'm going to fine everybody in this courtroom fifty cents for living in a town where a person has to steal bread in order to eat. Mr. Bailiff, collect the fines and give them to this defendant."

After the hat was passed, the incredulous old woman left the courtroom with a new light in her eyes and $47.50 in her pocket to buy groceries! God is ever merciful.

---

*The young man knows the rules,
but the old man knows the exceptions.*

The Untamed Tongue

*Don't talk so much. You keep
putting your foot in your mouth.
Be sensible and turn off the flow!*

PROVERBS 10:19 TLB

Many analogies have been given for the "untamed tongue." Quarles likened it to a drawn sword that takes a person prisoner: "A word unspoken is like the sword in the scabbard, thine; if vented, thy sword is in another's hand."

Others have described evil speaking as:

- A freezing wind—one that seals up the sparkling waters and kills the tender flowers and shoots of growth. In similar fashion, bitter and hate-filled words bind up the hearts of men and cause love to cease to flourish.

- A fox with a firebrand tied to its tail and sent out among the standing corn just as in the days of Samson and the Philistines. So gossip spreads without control or reason.

- A pistol fired in the mountains, the echo of which is intensified until it sounds like thunder.

- A snowball that gathers size as it rolls down a mountain.

Perhaps the greatest analogy, however, is one given by a little child who came running to her mother in tears. "Did your friend hurt you?" the mother asked.

"Yes," said the girl.

"Where?" asked her mother.

"Right here," said the child, pointing to her heart.

Ask God to place a watch over your tongue. Your words have the power to hurt and tear down, but they also have the power to heal and build up.

The BIGGEST CHALLENGE I HAVE WITH MY "UNTAMED TONGUE" IS . . .

_____

*The best time for you to hold your
tongue is the time you feel you
must say something or bust.*

On the Rebound

Consider it all joy…when you encounter various trials, knowing that the testing of your faith produces endurance. And let endurance have its perfect result, so that you may be perfect and complete, lacking in nothing.

JAMES 1:2-4 NASB

How CAN I
REBOUND
FROM A PAST
FAILURE TO
ACHIEVE
SUCCESS?

Bernie Marcus was a poor Russian cabinet-maker's son from Newark, New Jersey. Arthur Blank was raised in a lower-middle-class neighborhood in Queens, New York. Blank once ran with a juvenile gang, and his father died when he was only fifteen. He has said, "I grew up with the notion that life is going to be filled with some storms."

In 1978, Marcus and Blank worked together at a hardware store in Los Angeles. The store was taken over by a new owner, who fired them both. The day after they lost their jobs, an investor friend suggested they go into business for themselves.

"'Once I stopped stewing in my misery,'" Marcus recalls, "I saw that the idea wasn't so crazy." Marcus and Blank opened the kind of store they had always dreaded competing against; a no-frills, hanger-size outlet with a huge selection and high-grade service. Today, their Home Depot stores are at the top of the fast-growing home-improvement industry.

Marcus enjoys talking to other entrepreneurs. He often asks them, "Was there a point in your life when you despaired?" He was once quoted as saying, "I've discussed this with fifty successful entrepreneurs. Forty had that character-building experience."

Consider your "low time" to be a position from which to rebound, not the place where you plan to stay!

A diamond is a chunk of coal that made good under pressure.

Image Counts

My son, despise not thou the chastening of the Lord, nor faint when thou art rebuked of him: For whom the Lord loveth he chasteneth, and scourgeth every son whom he receiveth.

HEBREWS 12:5-6

As a professional stock-car racer, Darrell Waltrip was once proud of his image as "the guy folks loved to hate." When crowds booed, he'd just kick the dirt and smile. Then things began to change. He miraculously survived a crash and started attending church with his wife, Stevie. They tried to have a family, but his wife suffered four miscarriages.

One day their pastor came to visit. He asked, "Your car is sponsored by a beer company. Is that the image you want?" Darrell had never considered this. He had always loved watching kids admire his car, but the more he thought about it, he discovered he did care about his image. He thought, *If our prayers for a child were answered, what kind of dad would I be?* He remembered his pastor's admonition to "walk the walk, not just talk the talk."

He didn't know how to convince the car's owner to change sponsors, but amazingly, an opportunity opened up for him to sign on with a new racing team sponsored by a laundry detergent company! After much thought and more prayer, he switched teams. Two years later, his daughter Jessica was born, and a few years after that, Sarah. In 1989, he won the Daytona 500.

God honors our obedience and rewards our faithfulness to follow Him.

How CAN I BE MORE CAREFUL ABOUT "WALKING THE WALK" IN MY OWN LIFE?

In order to receive the direction from God, you must be able to receive the correction from God.

Honest Expressions

*Provide things honest in
the sight of all men.*
ROMANS 12:17

How CAN I
BE HONEST IN
EXPRESSING
MY HOPE FOR
THE SUCCESS
OF SOMEONE
THAT I MAY
NOT EVEN
LIKE MUCH?

The editor of the weddings-and-engagements section of a small-town newspaper grew tired of hearing complaints from the town's citizens that she always embellished her reports of parties and celebrations. She decided that in the next issue, she was going to tell the truth and see if she had greater favor with the citizenry. She wrote the following item:

"Married—Miss Sylvan Rhodes and James Collins, last Saturday at the Baptist parsonage, by the Rev. J. Gordon. The bride is a very ordinary town girl, who doesn't know any more about cooking than a jackrabbit and never helped her mother three days in her life. She is not a beauty by any means and has a gait like a duck. The groom is an up-to-date loafer. He has been living off the old folks at home all his life and is now worth shucks. It will be a hard life."

We don't always need to be so brutally honest in telling the truth! Only God, after all, ultimately knows the truth. He alone has the ability to see into the hearts of men and women and know everything involved in any situation or relationship. Instead, we should be honest in expressing our hopes for another person's welfare and success. That is a truth everybody loves to hear.

*Honesty is the first chapter
of the book of wisdom.*

Feeding the Hungry

The righteous shall never be removed.

PROVERBS 10:30

When Brother Denys Cormier says "food," there's a good chance he will pass you a fork. He is part of the Wandering Monks of Emmaus, an ecumenical community established in the fourth century that seeks to feed the poor. In order to do that, Cormier and others founded the Wandering Monks' Guild and Bakery. The proceeds from the restaurant fund the Children's Soup Kitchen, where some 1,130 needy children receive food each day.

At the restaurant, a hearty all-you-can-eat buffet is offered, without a set price. A basket is placed at the end of the food line for donations. Most days, the basket is stuffed with ten and twenty-dollar bills. People seem willing to pay far more than the average cost of a lunch buffet, because they know the money goes toward a worthy cause.

Cormier's main concern today is the one-thousand children that the soup kitchen doesn't reach. He says, "I'm not going to feel right until we can feed them all." Although the monks in his order traditionally wander and minister to communities along the way, Cormier has found a position from which he will not be moved, and at least two doors—one to a restaurant and one to a soup kitchen—that he refuses to allow to be closed.

God presents us with open doors, but we must choose to walk through them and do what He has purposed for us to do.

Has GOD OPENED A DOOR FOR ME THAT I'VE CHOSEN TO IGNORE?

*Personality has the power to open doors,
but character keeps them open.*

A Greater Weapon

Whosoever will save his life shall lose it;
but whosoever shall lose his life for my sake
and the gospel's, the same shall save it.

MARK 8:35

Have I
LOST MY
MISSION
IN LIFE
BY CARING
MORE ABOUT
MYSELF THAN
OTHERS?

Joseph Ton ran away from his native Romania to study theology at Oxford. As he was preparing to return to his homeland after graduation, he shared his plans with several students. They candidly pointed out to him that he would probably be arrested at the border. One asked, "If you're arrested, what hope do you have of being a preacher?"

Ton asked God about this and was reminded of Matthew 10:16: "I send you forth as sheep in the midst of wolves." He thought, *What chance does a sheep have of surviving, let alone converting, the wolves? Yet Jesus sent them out and expected them not only to survive, but to fulfill His mission.*

The young man returned to his country and preached until the day he was arrested. As he was being interrogated by officials, Joseph said, "Your supreme weapon is killing; mine is dying. My sermons are all over the country on tapes now. If you kill me, then whoever listens to them will say, 'This must be true. This man sealed his words with his blood.' The tapes will speak ten times louder than before, so go on and kill me. I win the supreme victory." The officer sent him home!

When Joseph thought to save his life, he was in danger of losing his mission. When he didn't care about losing his life, he won not only life, but freedom.

The world wants your best,
but God wants your all.

A Wealth of Affection

*Wealth is worthless in the day of
wrath, but righteousness
delivers from death.*

PROVERBS 11:4 NIV

The children of a wealthy family were put into the care of a well-qualified nanny, as well as a host of other servants the family employed. When adverse circumstances impacted the family's finances, they moved into a slightly smaller home but kept the children's nanny. Eventually, however, the family's financial situation became severe enough that they had to let the beloved nanny go.

One evening after the father returned home from a day of great financial anxiety and business worry, his little girl climbed up on his knee and threw her arms around his neck. "I love you, Papa," she said, trying to soothe the weariness she intuitively perceived in him.

"I love you, too, darling," the father replied, glad to have such a warm welcome home. The little girl then said, "Papa, will you make me a promise?" The father said, "What is it?"

She said, "Papa, please promise me you won't get rich again. You never came to see us when you were rich, but now we can see you every night and hug you and kiss you and climb on your knee. Please don't get rich again!"

Money cannot buy the affection of our children. They need our presence, our time, and our attention. Their love is more valuable than all the money in the world.

❦

Superfluous wealth can buy superfluities only. Money is not required to buy one necessity of the soul.

I CAN GIVE
MY CHILDREN
MORE TIME
AND
ATTENTION BY
ELIMINATING
THINGS FROM
MY LIFE,
LIKE...

Tempting Choices—Right Decisions

Abstain from all appearance of evil.

1 THESSALONIANS 5:22

What

TEMPTATION
HAVE I BEEN
FLIRTING
WITH
LATELY?

As college roommates, Meg and Ann also became best friends. Then one day, Meg told Ann that John had asked her for a date. Ann was disappointed; she'd had a crush on John for two years. Still, she managed to say, "Have a good time," and later, to put on a happy face at John and Meg's wedding.

Through the years, Meg maintained a close relationship with Ann. Ann enjoyed teasing and laughing with John. When Meg asked Ann to join them at a beachside bungalow for a week, Ann jumped at the chance. One afternoon when Meg went out to visit a friend, Ann and John betrayed Meg's trust. Afterward, Ann felt sick inside. Deep shame welled up within her.

A few minutes of flirtation and passion resulted in more than a decade of misery for Ann. She might never have known happiness again if Meg hadn't confronted her about her refusal to accept a marriage proposal. Ann sobbed, "I'm horrible. You don't know how I've wronged you." Meg said, "I do know, Ann," and one look into her eyes confirmed that Meg had known, loved, and forgiven. With that forgiveness, years of shameful pain melted away—pain that could have been avoided by a few right choices easily made at the beginning of temptation.

Temptation itself is not a sin, but allowing it to continue is. When you find yourself being tempted, God always provides a way of escape. You must simply take it.

If you don't want the fruits of sin,
stay out of the devil's orchard.

Putting a Stop to Gossip

*A talebearer revealeth secrets:
but he that is of a faithful
spirit concealeth the matter.*

PROVERBS 11:13

In 1752, a group of Methodist men, including John Wesley, signed a covenant that every man agreed to hang on his study wall. The six articles of this solemn agreement were as follows:

1. That we will not listen or willingly inquire after ill concerning one another.

2. That, if we do hear any ill of each other, we will not be forward to believe it.

3. That as soon as possible, we will communicate what we hear by speaking or writing to the person concerned.

4. That until we have done this, we will not write or speak a syllable of it to any other person.

5. That neither will we mention it, after we have done this, to any other person.

6. That we will not make any exception to any of these rules unless we think ourselves absolutely obliged in conference.

Talk about an anti-gossip pact! Always remember: The person who tells you "don't tell this to a soul" has probably told all the souls you know.

———— ⨋ ————

*Whoever gossips to you
will be a gossip of you.*

I NEED TO
MAKE AN
ANTI-GOSSIP
PACT
WITH...

75

Beating Adversity

We walk by faith, not by sight.
2 CORINTHIANS 5:7

How CAN
MY FAITH
BE MORE
DARING?

During his two years in the army, David Brenner made the most of his posting to Europe by traveling at every opportunity. To heighten his sense of excitement, he often showed up at a train station and bought a ticket to wherever the next train was going.

One day he bought a ticket for Rome. Since the train was scheduled to leave immediately, he raced across the station but arrived at the track just as the train was pulling away. He chased after it as fast as he could run. Standing on the platform of the last car was a well-dressed man who motioned for him to hand him his bags. He quickly tossed him his smaller bag and then his larger suitcase. By this time, he was growing weary from running, but then he looked into the man's face. The smirk he saw quickly told him that the man had offered his help not altruistically, but criminally. If Brenner didn't make it on board, this man had brand-new clothes and gear!

Brenner kicked up his heels, and running as never before, managed to grab the railing by the entrance to the last car. With all the strength he could muster, he swung himself aboard.

Adversity sometimes comes to rob you. Instead, let the challenges of life motivate your faith to be even more daring.

*Faith is daring the soul to go
beyond what the eyes can see.*

The Value of Manners

A kind man benefits himself.

PROVERBS 11:17 NIV

In 1865, after General Ulysses Grant had moved his occupying army into Shiloh, he ordered a seven-o'clock curfew for the city. One distinguished southern lady, a Mrs. Johnson, was seen walking near the army's downtown headquarters near the curfew time.

General Grant approached her and said, "Mrs. Johnson, it's a little dangerous out there. I am going to ask two of my officers to escort you home."

She replied determinedly, "I won't go."

Grant smiled, went back into his headquarters, and returned in a few minutes wearing an overcoat that covered his insignia and rank.

"May I walk with you, Mrs. Johnson?" he asked.

"Why, yes," Mrs. Johnson replied, nearly blushing. "I'm always glad to have a gentleman as an escort."

Mrs. Johnson would walk with a man she saw as a gentleman, even though she would not walk with a Union soldier. Good manners and genuine politeness go a long way toward covering our perceived faults and mistakes.

Politeness goes far, yet costs nothing.

I COULD BE MORE POLITE TO...

Forgiving an Enemy

When you stand praying, if you hold anything
against anyone, forgive him, so that your
Father in heaven may forgive you your sins.

MARK 11:25 NIV

How CAN
I BETTER
DISPLAY
FORGIVENESS
AND
TOLERANCE
ON A DAILY
BASIS?

In 1946, Czeslaw Godlewski was a member of a gang of youths that roamed and sacked the German countryside. On one isolated farm, they gunned down ten members of the Hamelmann family. Nine of them died, but the father, Wilhelm, miraculously survived four bullet wounds.

As the time approached for Godlewski to complete his twenty-year prison term, the state would not release him, simply because he had nowhere to go. None of his family members offered shelter, and each place the state sought to place him refused to take him. Then the warden received a letter. It contained a simple request, "I ask you to release Godlewski to my custody and care. Christ died for my sins and forgave me. Should I not then forgive this man?" The letter was signed, Wilhelm Hamelmann.

Lord Balfour once advised, "The best thing to give to your enemy is forgiveness; to an opponent, tolerance." If these are the best we can give to our enemies and opponents, how much more should we grant forgiveness and tolerance to those we love!

Forgiveness means giving up
your right to punish another.

Get Your Kernel's Worth

The liberal soul shall be made fat:
and he that watereth shall be
watered also himself.

PROVERBS 11:25

Three young men were once given three kernels of corn apiece by a wise old sage, who admonished them to go out into the world and use the corn to bring themselves good fortune.

The first young man put his three kernels of corn into a bowl of hot broth and ate them. The second thought, *I can do better than that,* and he planted his three kernels of corn. Within a few months, he had three stalks of corn. He took the ears of corn from the stalks, boiled them, and had enough corn for three meals.

The third man said to himself, *I can do better than that!* He also planted his three kernels of corn, but when his three stalks of corn produced, he stripped one of the ears and replanted all of the seeds in it, gave the second ear of corn to a sweet maiden, and ate the third. His one full ear's worth of replanted corn kernels gave him two hundred stalks of corn! And he continued to replant the kernels of these, setting aside only a minimum for eating. He eventually planted a hundred acres of corn. With his fortune, he not only won the hand of the sweet maiden, but he purchased the land owned by the sweet maiden's father. He never hungered again.

God's law of sowing and reaping has never changed: What you sow, you will reap!

—————

One of life's great rules is this:
The more you give, the more you get.

What AM I
SOWING
TODAY THAT
I EXPECT
TO REAP
TOMORROW?

Choosing to Love

Love endures long and is patient and kind . . .
it takes no account of the evil done to it—
pays no attention to a suffered wrong.
1 CORINTHIANS 13:4-5 AMP

Because
NO ONE ELSE
WILL, I
CHOOSE TO
LOVE...

One Christmas morning, little Amy was delighted to find a beautiful golden-haired doll among the presents she unwrapped. "She's so pretty!" Amy squealed in excitement as she hugged her new doll. Then rushing to hug her grandmother, the giver of the doll, she cried, "Thank you, thank you, thank you!"

Amy played with her new doll most of the day, but toward evening, she put it down and sought out one of her old dolls. Amy cradled the tattered and dilapidated old doll in her arms. Its hair had nearly worn away, its nose was broken, one eye was askew, and an arm was missing.

"Well, well," Grandma noted, "it seems as though you like that old dolly better."

"I like the beautiful doll you gave me, Grandma," little Amy explained, "but I love this old doll more, because if I didn't love her, no one else would."

We all know the saying, "Beauty is in the eye of the beholder." A similar saying might be, "Love is the choice of the beholder." When we see faults in others, we can choose to look beyond them. We can choose to love them regardless of their negative attributes, faults, or quirks.

Love sees through a telescope,
not a microscope.

A Last-Place Winner

Whatever your hand finds to do,
do it with your might.

ECCLESIASTES 9:10 NKJV

During the 1984 summer Olympics, a young American long-distance runner, Derrick Redmond, was running in front of the pack, well on his way to winning his race. Suddenly, with only a lap to go, Derrick's hamstring muscle snapped. He fell to the ground in agony, and fellow runners dodged past him. His parents and friends let out a collective groan, as did millions of Americans who were watching by satellite.

Then obviously in great pain, Derrick rose from the track and began hopping on one leg toward the finish line. Late stragglers passed him. People on the sidelines who feared for his health yelled for him to lie down. Yet Derrick hopped on. Long after the race was over, Derrick Redmond kept hopping.

Derrick had about a hundred yards to go when a figure in the stands began jumping over people, chairs, and then the retaining wall. It was his father, Jim. Rushing to his son's side, he placed his arm around Derrick's waist. Derrick slung his arm over his dad's shoulder, and together, they half-bounced, half-ran the rest of the way. Derrick didn't wear a gold medal that day, but all who saw him and his father knew . . . Derrick and Jim Redmond had hearts of gold.

Honor awaits those who finish the race.

⊶⊷

If a task is once begun, never leave it till
it's done. Be the labor great or small,
do it well or not at all.

I MAY BE HURTING AND LIMPING, BUT I PLAN TO FINISH THE RACE BY . . .

Absorbed in Prayer

Evening, and morning, and at noon,
will I pray, and cry aloud: and he
shall hear my voice.

PSALM 55:17

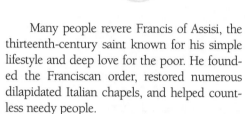

I FIND
MYSELF
BELIEVING
THAT I'M TOO
BUSY TO PRAY
WHEN...

Many people revere Francis of Assisi, the thirteenth-century saint known for his simple lifestyle and deep love for the poor. He founded the Franciscan order, restored numerous dilapidated Italian chapels, and helped countless needy people.

What most people don't know, however, is that Francis spent most of his life in prayer, not in doing good works. Saint Bonaventure wrote about him, "Whether walking or sitting, within doors or without, at toil or at leisure, he was so absorbed in prayer that he seemed to have devoted not only his whole heart and body, but also his whole heart and time." Francis regularly set aside hours throughout the day that he called "appointments with God," and he never missed one, even though he had serious eye, stomach, spleen, and liver problems. On one occasion, as Francis traveled through the large town of Borgo on a donkey, people pressed in upon him from all sides to touch his garments. Francis was so absorbed in prayer that when he arrived at his destination sometime later, he asked when they were going to get to Borgo!

No matter how busy we are, we should never become too busy to pray. It is our prayer life that gives lasting meaning to everything else we undertake.

Most men forget God all day and ask
Him to remember them at night.

Leave the Outcome to God

Know ye that the LORD he is God: it is he
that hath made us, and not we ourselves; we
are his people, and the sheep of his pasture.

PSALM 100:3

A story is told about actor Charlton Heston that illustrates our need to do all we can and then trust God to do what we cannot.

During the making of the great epic, *Ben Hur,* Heston worked long hours with the stunt trainers to learn to drive a chariot for the movie's crucial chariot-race scene. He improved greatly in his mastery over the horses and rig but finally became convinced the task was more of a challenge than he had initially anticipated. He approached the legendary director of the movie, Cecil B. De Mille, about the scene.

"Mr. De Mille," he said, "I've worked very hard at mastering this rig, and I think I can drive it convincingly in the scene. But I don't think I can win the race."

The director replied, "You just drive. I'll do the rest."

Let God coach you through this race called life. He will teach you how to "master" the equipment and resources He's put into your hands. Trust Him to help you cross the finish line. As one engineer has said, "God provides the initial input. We provide the output. And God provides the outcome."

❧

The greatest act of faith is when man
decides he is not God.

I NEED TO
ALLOW GOD
TO COACH
ME AS I TRY
TO . . .

Temptation Defeated

Keep watching and praying that you may not come into temptation.

MARK 14:38 NASB

When MY EARS AND EYES START TO WANDER, I KNOW THAT I MUST...

As the ancient myth goes, when Ulysses sailed out to meet the Sirens, he stopped his ears with wax and had himself bound to the mast of his ship. Apparently, he was unaware that every traveler before him had done the same thing and that wax and chains were no match for the Sirens. Their alluring song could pierce through everything, causing sailors to break all manner of bonds.

The Sirens, however, had a more fatal weapon than their song. It was silence. As Ulysses approached them, the Sirens chose to employ that weapon. Rather than be seduced into straining to hear their song, however, Ulysses concluded that he alone must be the only person who could not hear their song and that he must be immune to their powers. Strengthened in that confidence, he set his gaze on the distant horizon and escaped the Sirens as no man before him.

Temptation starts first in what we see and hear. Choose carefully where your eyes and ears wander.

When you flee temptations,
don't leave a forwarding address.

Seeing Ahead

*Humble yourselves therefore under
the mighty hand of God, that he
may exalt you in due time.*

1 PETER 5:6

For weeks, eight-year-old Susie had been looking forward to a particular Saturday fishing trip with her dad. But when the day finally arrived, it was raining.

Susie wandered around the house all morning, grumbling as she peered out the windows, "Seems like the Lord would know it would have been better to have the rain yesterday than today." Her father tried to explain how important the rain was to the farmers and gardeners. But Susie only replied, "It just isn't fair."

Around three o'clock, the rain stopped. There was still time for fishing, so father and daughter quickly loaded their gear and headed for the lake. Because of the rainstorm, the fish were really biting. Within a couple of hours, they returned with a full stringer of fish.

At the family's fish dinner that night, Susie was asked to say grace. She concluded her prayer by saying, "And, Lord, if I sounded grumpy earlier today, it was because I couldn't see far enough ahead."

When we seek His advice, it's important to remember that God alone can see what lies ahead for us.

I NEED TO
TRUST GOD TO
SEE WHAT
LIES AHEAD
FOR ME
REGARDING...

*If one door shall be shut, God will open
another . . . there's a bright side to all
things, and a good God everywhere.*

The Gifts of God

These things I have spoken unto you, that in me ye might have peace. In the world ye shall have tribulation: but be of good cheer; I have overcome the world.

JOHN 16:33

How HAS GOD GIVEN A HUNDREDFOLD TO ME?

While serving in India, a devout English judge befriended a young Indian man. Having been raised in a prominent family, the young man had been cast out after he converted to Christianity. The judge took the boy into his household, where he happily worked as a houseboy.

It was the custom of the household to have a devotional time every evening. One night the judge read aloud the words of Jesus: "Every one that hath forsaken houses, or brethren, or sisters, or father, or mother, or wife, or children, or lands, for my name's sake, shall receive an hundredfold" (Matthew 19:29).

The judge turned to the lad and said, "Nobody here has done this except you, Norbudur. Will you tell us, is it true what Jesus has said?"

The young Indian man read the verse aloud for himself and then turned to the family and said, "No, there is an error."

Startled, the judge responded, "There is?"

The youth replied, "It says He gives a hundredfold. I know He gives a thousandfold."

Who can truly measure the value of what it means when Jesus Christ comes into a person's life? The things He provides are worth far more than silver or gold.

Jesus is a friend who walks in when the world has walked out.

A Time to Forgive

*If you have been trapped by what you said,
ensnared by the words of your mouth, then do
this, my son, to free yourself, since you have
fallen into your neighbor's hands: Go and humble
yourself; press your plea with your neighbor!*

PROVERBS 6:2-3 NIV

In 1755, a twenty-three-year-old colonel was in the midst of running for a seat in the Virginia assembly when he made an insulting remark as part of a campaign speech. The remark was addressed to a hot-tempered man named Payne, who responded by knocking the colonel down with a hickory stick. Soldiers rushed to the colonel's assistance, and it appeared that a full-blown fight would ensue. But the would-be politician got up, dusted himself off, called off the soldiers, and left the scene.

The next morning the colonel wrote Payne, requesting his presence at a local tavern. Payne obliged but wondered what demands the colonel might make—perhaps an apology or even a duel. To Payne's surprise, the colonel met him with an apology, asking forgiveness for his derogatory remarks and offering a handshake.

Others may have viewed the move as politically expedient, but Colonel George Washington considered it personally imperative if he was to enjoy inner peace as he continued with his campaign.

The moment we feel like demanding forgiveness from others may be the moment when we need to forgive. Is there someone you need to forgive?

*I NEED TO BE
MORE
FORGIVING
TOWARD . . .*

*The best way to get the
last word is to apologize.*

God's Elegant Plan

Go ye into all the world, and preach
the gospel to every creature.
MARK 16:15

Whom
DOES GOD
WANT ME TO
PASS MY
FAITH ON TO?

John Hull, author of *Touching the Rock,* is blind. In telling his life story, he recounts that his mother spent two years attending Melbourne High School, lodging there with Mildred Treloar. While living with Mildred, John's mother began attending weekly Bible classes with her. Over the months, his mother's personal dedication to the Lord was renewed and deepened as the pages of the Bible came alive for her. It was this vibrant faith that she passed on to her son, John.

Where did Mildred Treloar acquire her faith? From her father. Mr. Treloar had desired to become a minister as a young man but was rejected by his denomination. Rather than become bitter, he poured his faith into Mildred. While she lived with Mildred, John's mother spent many hours reading the Bible to Mr. Treloar and vividly recalled for John his great hope of Heaven. Why was Mr. Treloar considered to be unacceptable as a minister? He was blind!

John Hull credits Mr. Treloar with much of his own spiritual formation—a blind man passing on his faith to another blind man over a sixty-year time span!

There is elegance in God's plan when we are faithful to reinvest our faith in others. Today, pass on your faith to another.

———⌘———

A Christian must keep the faith,
but not to himself.

Blind Faith

They that know thy name will put
their trust in thee: for thou, LORD,
hast not forsaken them that seek thee.

PSALM 9:10

Dr. Amanda Whitworth was frustrated as she crept up a hill with eight cars in front of her. They were stuck behind a slow-moving truck, and she was in a hurry. Amanda's last patient had needed more attention than was allotted for regular examinations, and she was late leaving to pick up her daughter from day school. Now she breathed a prayer that she would not be late again. It would be her third time, and because the day school did not tolerate parental tardiness, she would have to make new arrangements for Allie's afternoon care.

Amanda silently fumed at the truck's progress. No one dared pass the truck on the long hill, as it was impossible to see oncoming cars around it. Suddenly, the trucker waved his hand indicating that all was clear ahead. As Amanda zipped past him, it occurred to her that this man was probably a stranger to all who passed him—yet nine people trusted their lives and the lives of their families to this man.

What a tremendous picture of how we do all that we can do and then trust the smallest details of our lives to the care of God, our loving Heavenly Father! It's comforting to know that He can always see exactly what's ahead. Wait for God to give you the go-ahead signal.

God WANTS ME TO WAIT UNTIL HE GIVES THE GO-AHEAD SIGNAL TO . . .

My job is to take care of the possible
and trust God with the impossible.

Amazing Strength

With God nothing shall be impossible.
LUKE 1:37

I NEED GOD TO STRENGTHEN ME SO I MAY BE ABLE TO...

A young man was running a race, and he found himself falling further and further behind his competitors. His friends cheered him on from the sidelines, but to no avail. Then suddenly, his lips began to move, his legs picked up speed, and to the amazement of the entire crowd watching the race, he passed his competitors one by one—and won the race!

After he had been awarded a blue ribbon and received the congratulations of his coach and teammates, he turned to his friends. One of them asked, "We could see your lips moving, but we couldn't make out what you were saying. What were you mumbling out there?"

The young man replied, "Oh, I was talking to God. I told Him, 'Lord, you pick 'em up, and I'll put 'em down. You pick 'em up, and I'll put 'em down!'"

When we live our lives the way we know God's Word commands us and we are believing to the best of our ability that the Lord will help us, we are then in a position to know with certainty what the apostle Paul knew when he said, "I can do all things through Christ which strengtheneth me" (Philippians 4:13).

———⦿———

When we do what we can,
God will do what we can't.

A Secret to Success

*A fool uttereth all his mind: but a wise
man keepeth it in till afterwards.*

PROVERBS 29:11

A small-town newspaper developed a column for interviews with couples in that town who had reached their golden wedding anniversary. A brief history of the couple celebrating fifty years of marriage was outlined. Then the newspaper posed the same question to each spouse: "To what do you attribute the success of your marriage?" Many of the couples approaching this milestone knew they were going to be interviewed, so they gave long thought to the wisest and most practical advice they could give. Some advocated total honesty, others a shared faith, and others abundant communication.

One man lovingly glanced at his wife and then replied, "The secret of our fifty years of marital harmony is quite simple. My wife and I made an agreement the day we were married. If she was bothered or upset about something, she was to get it off her chest and out into the open. We felt it was important for her to get it out of her system. And if I was mad at her about something, we agreed I would take a walk. So I guess you can attribute our marital success to the fact that I have led largely an outdoor life."

In finding a way to release anger and frustration, make sure your loved ones aren't part of your method!

I CAN IMPROVE THE WAY I HANDLE ANGER AND FRUSTRATION BY . . .

❦

*Swallowing angry words is much better
than having to eat them.*

Personal Property

He that keepeth his mouth keepeth his life: but he that openeth wide his lips shall have destruction.

PROVERBS 13:3

What CAN
I DO TO
SQUELCH
GOSSIP
AMONG MY
CIRCLE OF
FRIENDS?

Constance Cameron tells the story of a lesson her mother taught her. One day when she was about eight, she was playing beside an open window. Inside, Mrs. Brown was confiding a personal problem to Constance's mother. After Mrs. Brown had gone, the mother realized that Constance had heard everything that had been said. She called her in and said, "If Mrs. Brown had left her purse here today, would we give it to anyone else?"

"Of course not," the girl said. Her mother went on to say, "Mrs. Brown left something more precious than her pocketbook today. She left a story that could make many people unhappy. That story is not ours to give to anyone. It is still hers, even though she left it here. So we shall not give it to anyone. Do you understand?"

She did. And from that day on, whenever a friend would share a confidence or even engage in careless gossip, she considered what they said to be the personal property of the other person and not hers to give to anyone else.

What a great way to squelch gossip! Look at the confidences of others as their personal property not to be given away to someone else. This old saying bears great truth: If you don't have something positive to say, don't say anything at all.

———

A shut mouth gathers no foot.

Building Friendship Foundations

The light in the eyes [of him whose heart is joyful] rejoices the hearts of others.

PROVERBS 15:30 AMP

It has been estimated that more than 95 percent of all Americans receive at least one Christmas card each year. The average is actually more than seventy cards per family! Millions of cards are mailed each holiday season worldwide. Have you ever wondered where this custom began?

A museum director in the mid-nineteenth century had a personal habit of sending notes to his friends at Christmastime each year just to wish them a joyful holiday season. One year he found he had little time to write, yet he still wanted to send a message of good cheer. He asked his friend, John Horsely, to design a card that he might sign and send to his friends. Those who received the cards loved them, so they created cards of their own. And thus, the Christmas card was invented!

It's often the simple heartfelt gestures in life that best exemplify friendship. Ask yourself today what you can do to bring a smile to the face of a friend. What can you do to bring good cheer into the life of someone who is in need, trouble, sickness, or sorrow? Follow through on your answer. It's not a gift you are giving as much as a friendship you are building!

Good nature begets smiles, smiles beget friends, and friends are better than a fortune.

I CAN BRING GOOD CHEER INTO THE LIFE OF SOMEONE IN NEED BY...

A Slip-up

Though he fall, he shall not be
utterly cast down: for the LORD
upholdeth him with his hand.

PSALM 37:24

How AM I
GUILTY OF
STOMPING
ON OTHERS
WHEN THEY
STUMBLE?

When Colin Powell was a young infantry officer, he served in Frankfurt, Germany. One day, his platoon was assigned to guard a 280-millimeter atomic cannon. Powell alerted his men, loaded his .45-caliber pistol, and jumped into his jeep. Before he had gone far, he realized that his .45 was missing. Knowing well that losing a weapon is serious business, he reluctantly radioed his captain, Tom Miller.

When Powell returned, Captain Miller said, "I've got something for you" and handed Powell his pistol. He said, "Some kids in the village found it where it fell out of your holster." Powell felt a cold chill. Kids had found it? "Yeah," Miller continued. "Luckily, they only got off one round before we heard the shot and took the gun away." He concluded, "For God's sake, son, don't let that happen again."

Powell later checked his gun and discovered it had not been fired. He had dropped it in his tent. Miller had fabricated the story to give him a scare.

Powell concluded, "His example of intelligent leadership was not lost on me. Nobody ever got to the top without slipping up. When someone stumbles, I don't believe in stomping on him. My philosophy is: pick 'em up, dust 'em off, and get 'em moving again."

The man who makes no mistakes
does not normally make anything.

Clearly Right or Wrong

A truthful witness gives honest
testimony, but a false witness tells lies.

PROVERBS 12:17 NIV

Four high school boys skipped their first-period class one morning in order to take a joyride around town. When they all came in late, they apologized profusely to the teacher, claiming they had a flat tire on the way to school. They gave a long litany of complications they had experienced in repairing it.

The teacher smiled sympathetically and then explained that they had missed a quiz given during the first period. "Can't we make it up?" one of the boys asked. Another chimed in, saying, "It wasn't our fault." A third added, "Surely, you can't hold a flat tire against us."

The teacher said, "Well, all right." She then told the boys to take empty seats in the four corners of the room, take out paper and pencil, and answer this one question: "Which tire was flat?"

There's no substitute for telling the truth. Sometimes we think that if we only tell a little white lie, we really aren't hurting anybody. But in fact, we are hurting ourselves. By telling lies of any size, we are developing a pattern of mixing black with white. Eventually, we will see only gray and be unable to discern between right and wrong.

Remember, lies never travel alone. If you tell one, you have to continue lying to maintain that first lie. One small fib can grow into a lie of gargantuan proportions! Keep your life simple—just tell the truth.

What ARE THE GRAY AREAS IN MY LIFE IN WHICH I HAVE TROUBLE DISCERNING RIGHT FROM WRONG?

If you tell the truth, you don't
have to remember anything.

Truth and Compassion

The LORD detests lying lips, but he delights in men who are truthful.
PROVERBS 12:22 NIV

How CAN AN HONEST LOOK AT MYSELF HELP ME GROW AND FULFILL MY POTENTIAL?

One morning, a young mother went out shopping only to encounter her son on the town streets. Angry that her son had skipped school, she demanded that he tell her why he wasn't in class. She listened patiently to his explanation and then replied, "I'm not accusing you of telling a lie, but I have never heard of a school that gives time off for good behavior."

At the opposite end of the spectrum was the dentist who said to his patient, hypodermic needle in hand, "You might feel a little sting. On the other hand, it might feel as though you've been kicked in the mouth by a mule."

As much as we might say we always want to be told the truth, sometimes the truth hurts. But it never hurts as much as being told a lie.

Telling the truth includes being honest about ourselves—about our own nature, our sins, and our faults. It means confessing that we aren't perfect and that we don't always do what is right before God or in relationship to others. When we lie about ourselves, we become self-deprecating and rarely seek ways to grow and fulfill our potential.

Tell the truth to others and especially to yourself! Honesty is still the best policy.

---

*A half-truth is usually
less than half of that.*

Clay in the Potter's Hand

After this manner therefore pray ye. . . . Thy kingdom come. Thy will be done in earth, as it is in heaven.

MATTHEW 6:9-10

During a prayer meeting one night, an elderly woman pleaded, "It really doesn't matter what You do with us, Lord, just have Your way with our lives." Adelaide Pollard, a rather well-known itinerant Bible teacher, overheard her prayer. At the time, she was deeply discouraged because she had been unable to raise the money she needed to go to Africa for missionary service. She was moved by this woman's sincere request, and when she went home that evening, she meditated on Jeremiah 18:3-4: "Then I went down to the potter's house, and, behold, he wrought a work on the wheels. And the vessel that he made of clay was marred in the hand of the potter: so he made it again another vessel, as seemed good to the potter to make it." Before retiring, Adelaide took pen in hand and wrote her own prayer, in the form of a hymn:

> Have Thine own way, Lord! Have Thine own way! Thou art the potter, I am the clay. Mold me and make me after Thy will, while I am waiting, yielded and still.

> Have Thine own way, Lord! Have Thine own way! Search me, and try me, Master, today! Whiter than snow, Lord, wash me just now, as in Thy presence humbly I bow.

When we yield our lives to the hand of the potter, He can make us into useful vessels for His kingdom. We must simply trust in His loving touch to mold us and shape us.

I HAVE REFUSED TO YIELD MY LIFE TO THE HAND OF THE POTTER WHEN IT COMES TO . . .

Don't ask God for what you think is good; ask Him for what He thinks is good for you.

Identifying Divine Love

To offer ourselves as a model for you,
so that you would follow our example.

2 THESSALONIANS 3:9 NASB

How CAN I
SHOW LOVE
TO THE
DISEASED
AND
IMPOVERISHED?

The Supervisor's Prayer: Lord, when I am
wrong, make me willing to change; when
I am right, make me easy to live with. So
strengthen me that the power of my example
will far exceed the authority of my rank.

Bishop Fulton Sheen, perhaps best known for his radio sermons on the *Catholic Hour* broadcast and his *Life Is Worth Living* weekly telecast, once recalled the following incident as the most memorable experience in his life:

> I visited a leper colony in Africa. I brought with me 500 small silver crucifixes to give to each victim of the dread disease. The first leper who came up to me had only a stump of his left arm. . . . The right arm and hand were full of those telltale white open sores of leprosy. I held the crucifix a few inches above that hand and let it drop into the palm. At that moment there were 501 lepers in the camp, and the most leprous of them all was myself. I had taken the symbol of Redemption, of Divine Love for man . . . and had refused to identify myself with all that that symbol implied. . . . Seeing myself in the full shame of refusing to identify myself with this victim, I looked at the crucifix in the putrid mass of his hand and realized that I, too, must become one with suffering humanity. Then I pressed my hand to his hand with the symbol of Love between us and continued to do it for the other 499 lepers.

God's love is not only for those who are worthy, for none of us are worthy. God's love is for the broken-hearted, the diseased, and the impoverished. Those who are most unlovable need God's love the most.

Think Before You Speak

*Self-control means controlling
the tongue! A quick retort
can ruin everything.*

PROVERBS 13:3 TLB

A little girl named Mary had come home from a tough day at school. She stretched herself out on the living-room sofa to have her own private pity party. "Nobody loves me," she moaned to her mom and brother. "The whole world hates me!"

Her brother, occupied with his Nintendo, hardly looked her way as he passed on an encouraging word. "That's not true, Mary," he said. "Some people don't even know you."

Mary, no doubt, was not amused. She probably wished her brother had heeded the advice of William Penn, founding leader of the colony that became Pennsylvania. He had these rules for conversation:

> Avoid company where it is not profitable or necessary, and in those occasions, speak little, and last. Silence is wisdom where speaking is folly, and always safe. Some are so foolish as to interrupt and anticipate those who speak instead of hearing and thinking before they answer, which is uncivil, as well as silly. If thou thinkest twice before thou speakest once, thou wilt speak twice the better for it. Better to say nothing than not to the purpose. And to speak pertinently, consider both what is fit, and when it is fit, to speak. In all debates, let truth be thy aim, not victory or an unjust interest; and endeavor to gain, rather than to expose, thy antagonist.

If we stop and think before we speak, we may sometimes find we really have nothing worthwhile to say. On the other hand, we should always speak positive words of encouragement; they bring life to the hearer and blessings to the speaker.

What
NEGATIVE OR
CONDESCEND-
ING WORD
DO I REGRET
HAVING SAID
RECENTLY?

Not only to say the right thing in the right place, but far more difficult, to leave unsaid the wrong thing at the tempting moment.

Faithful Risks

*The soul of the sluggard desireth,
and hath nothing: but the soul of
the diligent shall be made fat.*

PROVERBS 13:4

What
OPPORTUNITY
REQUIRING
A STEP OF
FAITH AM
I FACING
RIGHT NOW?

A man once went with a friend for a ride out in the country. They drove off the main road and through a grove of orange trees to a mostly uninhabited piece of land. A few horses grazed there amidst a couple of old shacks. Walter stopped the car and began to vividly describe the things he was going to build on the land. He wanted his friend, Arthur, to buy some of the acreage surrounding his project. Walter explained to his friend, "I can handle the main project myself. It will take all my money, but . . . I want you to have the first chance at this surrounding acreage, because in the next five years, it will increase in value several hundred times."

Who in the world is going to drive twenty-five miles for this crazy project? His dream has taken the best of his common sense, Arthur thought to himself. He mumbled something about a tight money situation and promised to look into the deal later. "Later will be too late," Walter cautioned. "You'd better move on it right now." However, Arthur failed to act.

And so it was that Art Linkletter turned down the opportunity to buy the land that surrounded what was to become Disneyland, the land his friend Walt Disney had tried to talk him into buying.

Most opportunities, whether financial or emotional investments, require a step of faith. Nothing worth doing is easy. Opportunities must be acted upon; they will not act upon you.

*The doors of opportunity are
marked "Push" and "Pull."*

Uncommon Courtesy

Treat others the same way,
you want them to treat you.

LUKE 6:31 NASB

We often refer to courtesy as "common courtesy," but these days, it is far from common. How many people do you know who follow the most basic common courtesies like saying "please" and "thank you," or arriving at appointments on time?

A father once remarked about his three children: "My children may not be the brightest children in their class. They may not be the most talented or the most skilled. They may not achieve great fame or earn millions of dollars. But by my insisting that they have good manners, I know they will be welcome in all places and by all people." How true!

Good manners are like a calling card. They open doors that are otherwise shut to those who are rude, crude, or unmannerly. They bring welcome invitations and, quite often, return engagements. They cover a multitude of weaknesses and flaws. They make other people feel good about themselves, which often causes them to extend kindness and generosity they might not otherwise exhibit. Good manners are a prerequisite for good friendships, good business, and good marriages. They hold the keys to success!

Always say "thank you," "excuse me," and
"please" when you have done a favor
and when you are apologizing.

I CAN EXTEND "COMMON COURTESY" TO OTHERS IN MY EVERYDAY LIFE BY...

The Value of a Mistake

Pride only breeds quarrels, but wisdom is found in those who take advice.

PROVERBS 13:10 NIV

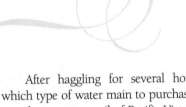

What GOOD ADVICE SHOULD I HEED IN MY LIFE?

After haggling for several hours about which type of water main to purchase for their city, the town council of Pacific Vista remained deadlocked. One member suggested, "Let's appoint a committee to confer with the city engineer at Los Angeles to find out which type they have found to be most successful over the years. If we can profit by another city's mistakes, I think we should do so."

Leaping to his feet, an angry councilman—obviously full of civic pride but with little discretion—replied, "Why should we have to profit by the mistakes of Los Angeles? Gentlemen, I contend that Pacific Vista is a big enough town now to make its own mistakes!"

Most of us are surrounded by good advice at any given time.

- The books in our libraries are full of it.
- Preachers proclaim it weekly.
- People with highly varied experiences and backgrounds abound with it.
- Schools give access to it; labs report it.
- Commentators and columnists gush with it.

But all the good advice in the world is worth little if it isn't heeded. Be one of the wise—value good advice and apply it!

Isolation is the worst possible counselor.

Freed by Needs, Not Frozen by Fear

Be strong and of a good courage, fear not,
nor be afraid of them: for the LORD
thy God, he it is that doth go with thee;
he will not fail thee, nor forsake thee.

DEUTERONOMY 31:6

On a summer morning as he was fixing his breakfast, Ray Blankenship looked out his window to see a young girl being swept along in the rain-flooded drainage ditch beside his Ohio home. Blankenship knew that farther downstream, the ditch disappeared with a roar underneath the road and then emptied into the main culvert.

Ray dashed from his house and raced along the ditch, trying to get ahead of the flailing child. Finally, he hurled himself into the deep, churning water. When he surfaced, he was able to grab the girl's arm. The two tumbled end over end and then, within about three feet of the yawning culvert, Ray's free hand felt something protruding from the bank. He clung to it desperately, the tremendous force of the water threatening to sweep him and the child away.

By the time a fire-department rescue team arrived, Blankenship, amazingly, had pulled the girl to safety. Both were treated for shock. In that heroic moment, Ray Blankenship was at an even greater risk than most people knew—Ray couldn't swim!

Fear can be paralyzing. Today let your courage respond to the needs you see, not to the fear you feel.

Do the thing you fear and
the death of fear is certain.

If I GENUINELY BELIEVED THAT GOD WOULD NEVER FAIL ME, I WOULD NEVER BE PARALYZED BY THE FEAR OF . . .

Laboring Not in Vain

*The LORD said to him, "This is the land
I promised on oath to Abraham, Isaac and
Jacob. . . .I have let you see it with your eyes,
but you will not cross over into it."*

DEUTERONOMY 34:4 NIV

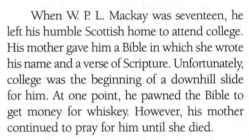

Specific

WAYS I
CAN PRAY
FOR THE
SPIRITUAL
WHOLENESS
OF MY
CHILDREN
(OR OTHER
LOVED ONES)
INCLUDE:

_____

_____

_____

_____

_____

_____

_____

_____

_____

_____

_____

_____

_____

_____

_____

When W. P. L. Mackay was seventeen, he left his humble Scottish home to attend college. His mother gave him a Bible in which she wrote his name and a verse of Scripture. Unfortunately, college was the beginning of a downhill slide for him. At one point, he pawned the Bible to get money for whiskey. However, his mother continued to pray for him until she died.

Eventually, Mackay became a doctor. While working in a hospital, he encountered a dying patient who repeatedly asked for his "book." After the man died, Mackay searched the hospital room to find what book it was that had been so important to him. He was surprised to find the same Bible he had once pawned!

Mackay took the Bible to his office and stared at the familiar writing of his mother. He thumbed through the pages, reading the many verses his mother had underscored in hopes her son might heed them in his life. After many hours of reading and reflection, Mackay prayed to God for mercy. The physician later became a minister, and the Bible he once had treated so callously became his most precious possession.

You may not live to see how your children will turn out. But you can trust that nothing you do for their spiritual wholeness will have been in vain! When you turn your children over to the Lord in prayer, you can rest in the knowledge that they will always be in His hands.

*Every mother is like Moses.
She does not enter the promised land.
She prepares a world she will not see.*

Going against the Grain

*Have not I commanded thee? Be strong
and of a good courage; be not afraid,
neither be thou dismayed: for the LORD
thy God is with thee whithersoever thou goest.*

JOSHUA 1:9

At one point during his youth, baseball great, Jackie Robinson, began to run with a neighborhood gang. In later years, he recalled that while he had wished for a better life as a boy, he did not understand that gang membership was not the way to achieve it. An older friend finally came to Jackie and made him see how much he was hurting his hard-working mother as well as limiting himself. Robinson said, "He told me that it didn't take guts to follow the crowd, that courage and intelligence lie in being willing to be different."

Jackie listened, left the gang, and traded his wishbone for a backbone. He began to develop his physical potential, and within a few short years, he became a sensational athlete. Starring in football, basketball, baseball, and track at UCLA, he was the first person at the university to win athletic awards in all four sports. He went on to play pro football with the Los Angeles Bulldogs before being drafted for World War II duty. After the war, he signed with the Brooklyn Dodgers. Not only did Jackie Robinson become the first black baseball player in the major leagues, but he was also voted rookie of the year.

Many a dreamer has failed to see his dreams become a reality, because he never quit dreaming long enough to start working. Don't quit dreaming. Put your dreams into motion by setting goals and working toward them. Dreams coupled with hard work result in accomplishment.

The PRACTICAL GOALS I CAN SET THAT WILL PUT MY DREAMS INTO MOTION ARE...

*Many a good man has failed
because he had his wishbone where
his backbone should have been.*

Ship Versus Shore

He who ignores discipline despises himself, but whoever heeds correction gains understanding.

PROVERBS 15:32 NIV

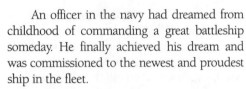

I CAN BRING
HONOR AND
PROSPERITY
TO MYSELF
AND OTHERS
BY BEING
WILLING
TO CORRECT
MY . . .

An officer in the navy had dreamed from childhood of commanding a great battleship someday. He finally achieved his dream and was commissioned to the newest and proudest ship in the fleet.

One stormy night, the captain was on duty on the bridge when he spotted a strange light rapidly closing in on his own vessel. As his ship plowed through the giant waves, the light rose and fell just above the horizon of the sea. He ordered his signalman to flash a message to the unidentified craft, "Alter your course ten degrees to the south."

Within seconds a reply came, "Alter your course ten degrees to the north." Determined that his ship would never give way to any other, the captain snapped a second order, "Alter your course ten degrees—I am the captain!" The response was beamed back, "Alter your course ten degrees—I am Seaman Third Class Smith." By this time the light was growing brighter and larger.

Infuriated, the captain grabbed the signal light himself and signaled, "Alter your course. I am a battleship." The reply came back quickly, "Alter your course. I am a lighthouse."

We should always be willing to "give way" to others. Arrogantly steaming on can be disastrous and costly, but heeding correction can bring honor and prosperity.

The best way to be successful is to follow the advice you give others.

A Student of Character

He that walketh with wise men
shall be wise: but a companion
of fools shall be destroyed.

PROVERBS 13:20

A scorpion, being a very poor swimmer, once asked a turtle to carry him across the river on his back. "Are you mad?" exclaimed the turtle. "You'll sting me while I'm swimming, and I'll drown."

The scorpion laughed as he replied, "My dear turtle, if I were to sting you, you would drown and I would go down with you. Now what would be the point of that? I won't sting you. It would mean my own death!"

The turtle thought about the logic of the scorpion's argument for a moment, then said, "You're right. Hop on!" The scorpion climbed aboard and halfway across the river, he gave the turtle a mighty sting.

As the turtle began to sink to the bottom of the river with the scorpion on its back, it moaned in dismay, "After your promise, you still stung me! Why did you do that? Now we're both doomed!"

The drowning scorpion sadly replied, "I couldn't help it. It's my nature to sting."

Know a person's character before you make them a close friend. Your life is the stage on which their character—good or bad—will be played out.

Your companions are like the buttons
on an elevator. They will either take
you up or they will take you down.

What
CHARACTER
TRAITS DO I
LOOK FOR IN
A FRIEND?

A good man leaveth an inheritance to his children's children: and the wealth of the sinner is laid up for the just.

PROVERBS 13:22

How CAN I BE SURE THAT I HAVEN'T LIVED—OR LOVED— IN VAIN?

If I can throw a single ray of light across the darkened pathway of another; if I can aid some soul to clearer sight of life and duty, and thus bless my brother; if I can wipe from any human cheek a tear,

I shall not have lived my life in vain while here.

If I can guide some erring one to truth, inspire within his heart a sense of duty; if I can plant within my soul of rosy youth a sense of right, a love of truth and beauty; if I can teach one man that God and Heaven are near,

I shall not then have lived in vain while here.

If from my mind I banish doubt and fear, and keep my life attuned to love and kindness; if I can scatter light and hope and cheer, and help remove the curse of mental blindness; if I can make more joy, more hope, less pain,

I shall not have lived and loved in vain.

If by life's roadside I can plant a tree, beneath whose shade some wearied head may rest, though I may never share its beauty, I shall yet be truly blest—though no one knows my name, nor drops a flower upon my grave,

I shall not have lived in vain while here.

—Anonymous

The measure of a man's character is not what he gets from his ancestors, but what he leaves his descendants.

Directed Discipline

He who withholds his rod hates
his son, but he who loves him
disciplines him diligently.

PROVERBS 13:24 NASB

A grandfather once found his grandson, Joey, jumping up and down in his playpen, crying at the top of his voice. When Joey saw his grandfather, he stretched out his chubby hands and cried all the louder, "Out, Gamba, out!"

Naturally, the grandfather reached down to lift Joey out of his predicament, but as he did, Joey's mother said, "No, Joey, you are being punished—so you must stay in your playpen."

The grandfather felt at a loss as to what to do. On the one hand, he knew he must comply with the mother's efforts to discipline her son. On the other hand, Joey's tears and uplifted hands tugged at his heart. Love found a way! If Gamba couldn't take his grandson out of the playpen, he could climb in and join him there!

Discipline in its finest form is "directing a child toward a better way." Discipline goes beyond punishment by instilling the desire to never repeat the misdeed, but instead a better choice. The desire to do right is born of love— the love of the child for the parent, and more importantly, the love of the parent shown to the child.

How CAN I TEACH MY CHILDREN TO MAKE THE BEST CHOICES IN LIFE?

Too much love never spoils children.
Children become spoiled when we
substitute "presents" for "presence."

Productivity with a Purpose

*Martha was cumbered about much serving,
and came to him, and said, Lord, dost thou not
care that my sister hath left me to serve alone?
bid her therefore that she help me. And Jesus
answered and said unto her, Martha, Martha,
thou art careful and troubled about many
things: But one thing is needful: and Mary
hath chosen that good part, which shall
not be taken away from her.*

LUKE 10:40-42

Do I
NEED TO
REALIGN MY
PRIORITIES
THIS WEEK
SO I CAN
BE OF HELP
TO OTHERS?

In April 1973, the Park Center YMCA in Midland, Texas, asked for volunteers to help repair seventeen run-down homes in the city. The effort was so successful that Midlanders made it an annual event. After volunteers had completed repairs on one home, the owner opened her front door and exclaimed, "It's just like Christmas in April." The phrase stuck.

"Christmas in April" has not only made hundreds of homes in the West Texas oil town more livable, but it has helped bring the city together. Men and women, young and old, black, Hispanic, and white build community spirit as they scrape, caulk, plaster, paint, hammer, and roof together. "It's a blessing to us as well as to those we help," one volunteer said. "There's no better way to get to know someone than to sit up on a roof with him all day."

Midlanders have learned how to be both busy and productive by coming together to help others. An old maxim says: "Many hands make light work." In most instances, work need not be left undone or goals sacrificed. Priorities simply need to be realigned.

---

*Don't mistake activity for achievement.
Busyness does not equal productiveness.*

Six Little Words—One Big Message

Ask, and it shall be given you;
seek, and ye shall find; knock,
and it shall be opened unto you.

LUKE 11:9

Sir Winston Churchill took three years getting through the eighth grade because he had trouble learning English. It is somewhat ironic that years later, Oxford University asked him to speak at their commencement exercises! He arrived for the event with his usual props—a cigar, a cane, and a top hat. As he approached the podium, the crowd rose in appreciative applause.

With great dignity, Churchill settled the crowd as he stood confidently before his admirers. He then removed his cigar from his teeth and carefully placed his top hat on the lectern. Looking directly at the eager audience, with authority ringing in his voice, he cried, "Never give up!" Several hushed seconds passed. He rose to his toes and shouted again, "Never give up!"

His words thundered across the audience. A profound silence enveloped the crowd as Churchill reached for his hat and cigar, steadied himself with his cane, and descended the platform. His oration was finished.

Churchill's six-word commencement speech was no doubt the shortest and most eloquent address ever given at Oxford. His message was one every person present remembered for the rest of their lives.

No matter what obstacles you face in life, always remember Churchill's admonition: "Never give up!"

What HAVE I BEEN TEMPTED TO GIVE UP ON RECENTLY?

Perseverance is a great element of success;
if you only knock long enough and
loud enough at the gate, you are
sure to wake up somebody.

Even in the Little Things

*A truthful witness gives honest
testimony, but a false witness tells lies.*
PROVERBS 12:17 NIV

I CHOOSE TO
BE TRUTHFUL
ABOUT ALL
THE LITTLE
THINGS IN
MY LIFE,
INCLUDING...

Four young men once competed to become head of the trust department at the bank where they worked. After considering the merits of each applicant, the board of directors made its decision. They decided to notify the young man of his promotion, which included a substantial raise in salary, at a meeting scheduled after lunch.

During the noon hour, the young man they had selected went to the cafeteria for lunch. One of the directors was several people behind him in the line. The director saw the young man select his food and a small piece of butter. As soon as he flipped the butter onto his plate, however, he shuffled some food on top of it to hide it from the cashier. Thus, he avoided paying for it.

That afternoon the directors met to notify the young man of his promotion, but prior to bringing him into the room, the incident was related to the entire board. Rather than give the young man the promotion, they called him in to discharge him from the bank. They had concluded that if he was willing to lie to a cashier about a small bit of butter on his plate, he would be just as willing to lie about what was in the bank's accounts.

Lying isn't a matter of degree. A lie is a lie. The truth is the truth. You can bank on it!

---

*Sin has many tools, but a lie is
the handle which fits them all.*

Possessing Life

A man's life consisteth not in the abundance of the things which he possesseth.

LUKE 12:15

With the national coffers depleted from costly wars, King Frederick William III of Prussia found his nation seriously short of funds as it attempted to rebuild. He refused to capitulate to his enemies, and he couldn't face disappointing his people. After considerable thought, he asked the women of Prussia to bring their gold and silver jewelry to be melted down and used as exchange for the things the nation desperately needed. As each woman brought her jewelry, she was given a "decoration" of bronze or iron as a symbol of the king's gratitude. On the decoration was inscribed, "I gave gold for iron, 1813."

The response was overwhelming. The women came to prize their gifts from the king more than their jewels! The decorations were proof that they had sacrificed for their king. In fact, in the early nineteenth century it became highly unfashionable for Prussian women to wear jewelry, but quite fashionable to wear a cross of iron. It was from this trend that the Order of the Iron Cross was established.

The meaning of life does not lie in the possession of things, but rather in using those things to bring true meaning to life!

Measure wealth not by the things you have, but by the things you have for which you would not take money.

What ADORNMENTS IN MY LIFE PROVE THAT I HAVE SACRIFICED FOR MY KING?

A Tenth of a Percent

Blessed is that servant, whom his lord when he cometh shall find so doing.
LUKE 12:43

I CAN "GO FOR THE TOP" IN MY DAILY WALK WITH THE LORD BY . . .

One responsibility that we all have is the responsibility to do our best, which is to strive toward perfection. Consider the implications of giving only a 99.9-percent performance in the following areas:

- Two million documents would be lost by the Internal Revenue Service this year.

- Twelve babies would be given to the wrong parents each day.

- Some 291 pacemaker operations would be performed incorrectly.

- Twenty thousand incorrect prescriptions would be written.

- About 114,500 mismatched pairs of shoes would be shipped by shoe manufacturers.

None of us will ever achieve perfection in every area of our lives. However, neither do any of us have an excuse for failing to try to do our jobs with 100-percent accuracy. As the owner of the Ritz-Carlton Hotels said after his enterprise received the prestigious Malcolm Baldrige National Quality Award, "Quality is a race with no finish line."

"Giving it your best" means "going for the top" every time, regardless of the result.

✆

Responsibility is the thing people dread most of all. Yet it is the one thing in the world that develops us, gives us manhood . . . fibre.

Turning Worry into Prayer

Be careful for nothing; but in every thing by prayer and supplication with thanksgiving let your requests be made known unto God.

PHILIPPIANS 4:6

A businessman once made a worry chart on which he recorded all of his worries. After a year he tabulated the results. He found that 40 percent of the things he had worried about were now unlikely to happen; 30 percent were worries about past decisions he had made which he could not change now; 12 percent dealt with other people's opinions of him; and 10 percent were worries about his future health, only about half of which he could presently do anything about. In all, he concluded that only about 8 percent of his worries over the previous year had been legitimate.

What is it that you are worried about today? Most days? Keeping a worry chart might be a good way of discovering what it is that truly concerns you and what things aren't really worth worrying about at all.

A comparative way of measuring one's worries would be to use a prayer chart. What is it that you pray about the most? When asked to catalogue their prayers, many people find that they actually spend very little time praying about the things that concern them the most!

Convert your worry time into prayer time. It's not only a more productive activity but a healthier and more enjoyable one.

My LIST OF PERENNIAL WORRIES, WHICH TODAY I CHOOSE TO GIVE TO GOD:

When we depend on man, we get what man can do; when we depend on prayer, we get what God can do.

Building Families of God

As for me and my house,
we will serve the LORD.
JOSHUA 24:15 RSV

How CAN I
MAKE SURE
MY SPOUSE
AND I AGREE
ON THE
BASICS OF
RAISING OUR
CHILDREN?

You can do everything else right as a parent,
but if you don't begin with loving
God, you're going to fail.

In *Fit to Be Tied*, Bill and Lynne Hybels write:

> There is a cruel, ungodly world out there that wants to eat our kids for lunch. Our son was offered drugs when he was ten years old and taunted by friends to "have sex" with a fourth-grade girl. In the halls of her suburban high school, our daughter is daily bombarded with profanity and sexual innuendoes, with immoral lifestyles and alluring temptations. Never before have our children and yours so needed the advantage of being led by parents with shared values and beliefs; there is power in a unified front. But you can't fake that. Kids pick up on the discrepancies. So, what do they do when they sense that the two primary authority figures in their lives don't agree on the basics? What do they believe? What do they have to go on? What can they grab on to and say, "This must be true"? How can they determine right from wrong?

> The only way to present a united front is to marry someone who has the same Lord—someone who cherishes the same treasure, trusts the same blueprint, and taps the same strength. Only then can you share the same values and establish a home where children can get the kind of guidance they need.

Control or Be Controlled

He that is soon angry dealeth foolishly.

PROVERBS 14:17

A little girl was once in a bad mood. She took her frustration out on her younger brother, at first just teasing him, but eventually punching him, pulling his hair, and kicking him in the shins. The boy could take it all and even return a few blows, until the kicking began. That hurt! He went crying to his mother, complaining about what his sister had done.

The mother came to the little girl and said, "Mary, why have you let Satan put it into your heart to pull your brother's hair and kick his shins?"

The little girl thought it over for a moment and then answered, "Well, Mother, maybe Satan did put it into my heart to pull Tommy's hair, but kicking his shins was my own idea."

Not all of the evil in the world comes directly from Satan. Much of it comes from the heart of man. What we do with our anger, hatred, and frustration is subject to our will. We can choose how we will respond to stress or the behavior of others. Our challenge is to govern our emotions; otherwise, they will rule in tyranny over us.

❦

*A man is never in worse company
than when he flies into a rage
and is beside himself.*

I CAN BETTER
GOVERN MY
EMOTIONS
BY . . .

117

*Though a righteous man falls
seven times, he rises again.*

PROVERBS 24:16 NIV

What

GREAT THING

CAN I

ATTEMPT FOR

GOD, EVEN IF

IT MEANS

RISKING

FAILURE?

After Dwight Eisenhower won the Republican nomination for president from Robert Taft in 1952, a reporter asked Taft about his goals. He replied, "My great goal was to become president of the United States in 1953."

The reporter smirked and said, "Well, you didn't make it, did you?"

Taft responded, "No, but I became senator from Ohio!"

Imagine a target like the type used for playing darts. The bull's-eye is usually worth one hundred points. The concentric rings are labeled 80, 60, 40, and 20. Bull's-eyes are rare; players most often hit the lesser-valued rings. But nearly every dart player will tell you that if he doesn't aim for the bull's-eye, he scores lower than he would otherwise. And the person who doesn't throw at all scores zero!

A person once said, "I would rather attempt to do something great for God and fail, than to do nothing and succeed." Another has said, "Shoot for the moon. Even if you don't make it, you'll land among the stars."

———

*The man who wins may have been
counted out several times, but
he didn't hear the referee.*

Right Courage

Take up the full armor of God, so
that you will be able to resist in the
evil day, and having done everything,
to stand firm. Stand firm therefore.

EPHESIANS 6:13-14 NASB

Napoleon called Marshall Ney the bravest man he had ever known. Yet Ney's knees trembled so badly one morning before a battle that he had difficulty mounting his horse. When he was finally in the saddle, he shouted contemptuously down at his limbs, "Shake away, knees. You would shake worse than that if you knew where I am going to take you."

Courage is not a matter of not being afraid. It is taking action even when you are afraid!

Courage is more than sheer bravado, shouting, "I can do this!" and launching out with a do-or-die attitude over some reckless dare. True courage is exhibited when a person chooses to take a difficult or dangerous course of action because it is the right thing to do. Courage is looking beyond yourself to what is best for others.

The source of all courage is the Holy Spirit, our Comforter. It is His nature to remain at our side and help us. When we welcome Him into our lives and He compels us to do something, we can confidently trust Him to be right there, helping us get the job done!

Is THE HOLY SPIRIT COMPELLING ME TO DO SOMETHING THAT WILL TAKE GENUINE COURAGE?

Courage is resistance to fear—mastery
of fear—not the absence of fear.

APRIL 21

Not that I speak in respect of want:
for I have learned, in whatsoever state
I am, therewith to be content.

PHILIPPIANS 4:11

How HAVE
I ALLOWED
SELF-PITY
AND DESPAIR
TO PARALYZE
ME
EMOTIONALLY?

Contentment isn't getting what we want but
being satisfied with what we have.

In a matter of seconds, Vickie's life was shattered. A trapeze artist, she lost control of the flybar one day and careened headfirst into the net. She broke her neck between the fifth and sixth cervical vertebrae and was paralyzed, becoming a quadriplegic.

Three years after the accident, she had fallen into deep despair and self-pity and was determined to take her life. Her attempt failed, and she ended up in a psychiatric hospital. On the fourth anniversary of her fall, she and her husband separated. Bitterness set in.

One day a Christian home health aide was assigned to Vickie. Mae Lynne introduced her to Jesus Christ and the Bible. Vickie learned how to "stand firm" in her faith and "walk" in obedience to God.

A minister faithfully taught her for two years. Then Vickie began her own ministry of encouragement by writing a dozen letters each week to prison inmates and others with disabilities. She now says, "Quadriplegics aren't supposed to have this much joy, are they?"

Vickie still uses a wheelchair, becomes dizzy at times, experiences occasional respiratory problems, and needs an attendant's care. However, she has deep inner strength because of her relationship with Jesus. The joy of the Lord is her strength. Now others describe her as "a fountain of smiles."

Even in extremely difficult circumstances, when we take our eyes off of our own problems and begin helping others with theirs, our despair and self-pity are replaced with God's joy and peace.

An Attitude of Gratitude

There is that maketh himself rich, yet hath nothing: there is that maketh himself poor, yet hath great riches.

PROVERBS 13:7

Fulton Oursler told a story of an old nurse who was born a slave on Maryland's eastern shore. She had not only attended Fulton's birth, but that of his mother. He credits her for teaching him the greatest lesson he ever learned about thankfulness and contentment. Oursler recalled:

I remember her as she sat at the kitchen table in our house; the hard, old, brown hands folded across her starched apron, the glistening eyes, and the husky old whispering voice, saying, "Much obliged, Lord, for my vittles."

"Anna," I asked, "what's a vittle?"

"It's what I've got to eat and drink—that's vittles," the old nurse replied.

"But you'd get your vittles whether you thanked the Lord or not."

"Sure," said Anna, "but it makes everything taste better to be thankful."

For many people, poverty is not a condition of the pocketbook, but a state of mind. Do you think of yourself as being rich or poor today? What do you value and count as wealth in your life? If you are able to list things that are not material in nature, you are wealthy indeed!

What SMALL THING DO I MOST NEED TO BE THANKFUL FOR TODAY?

A man is rich according to what he is, not according to what he has.

A Covey of Quarrels

Be ye kind one to another, tenderhearted,
forgiving one another, even as God for
Christ's sake hath forgiven you.

EPHESIANS 4:32

How CAN
I PROMOTE
TEAMWORK
AND A
SPIRIT OF
HELPFULNESS
IN MY OWN
SPHERE OF
INFLUENCE?

An old legend tells of a covey of quail that lived in a forest. They would have been happy except for their enemy, the quail catcher. He would imitate their call, and then when they gathered together, he would throw a net over them, stuff them into his hunting basket, and carry them off to market.

One wise quail said, "Brothers, I have a plan. When the fowler puts his net over us, we should each put our head into a section of the net and begin to flap our wings. Together, we can lift the net and fly away with it." All agreed. The next day they did just that, escaping successfully. After several days the fowler's wife asked him, "Why don't you have any quail to take to market?" He replied, "The trouble is that all the birds work together and help one another escape."

Awhile later, one quail began to fight with another. "I lifted all the weight on the net. You didn't help at all," he cried. The other quail became angry, and before long, the entire covey was quarreling. The fowler saw his chance. He imitated the cry of the quail and cast his net over them. Preoccupied with their quarreling, they didn't even attempt to help one another lift the net. Sometimes pointing out the faults of others can mean our own downfall.

Quarrels are the weapons of the weak.

Beautiful Silence

*A wise man will hear, and will increase
learning; and a man of understanding
shall attain unto wise counsels.*

PROVERBS 1:5

Helen Keller was left deaf and blind by an incurable childhood illness. A patient and persistent teacher, Anne Sullivan, taught her to read through her remaining senses: touch, smell, and taste. At the close of her autobiography, Helen Keller writes:

"Fate—silent, pitiless—bars the way. Fain would I question his imperious decree; for my heart is undisciplined and passionate, but my tongue will not utter the bitter, futile words that rise to my lips, and they fall back into my heart like unshed tears. Silence sits immense upon my soul. Then comes hope with a smile and whispers, 'There is joy in self-forgetfulness.' So I try to make the light in other people's eyes my sun, the music in others' ears my symphony, the smile on others' lips my happiness."

Silence can be used to nurture pouting, anger, and hatred. However, far better uses for silence are reflecting, meditating, and listening. It is only when we are truly silent before the Lord that we can hear His still, small voice speaking to our souls.

In THE SILENCE OF THIS MOMENT, I HEAR THE LORD'S STILL SMALL VOICE TELLING ME...

*The first step to wisdom is silence;
the second is listening.*

Ideas + Action = Change

All hard work brings a profit, but
mere talk leads only to poverty.

PROVERBS 14:23 NIV

What

IDEA + WHAT
ACTION WILL
= MUCH-
NEEDED
CHANGE IN
MY LIFE?

Many people remember President Theodore Roosevelt as an avid hunter and sportsman. Few, however, know of his conservation efforts, which left behind a far greater legacy.

After a hunting trip to the Dakota region in 1887—years before he was president—Roosevelt returned to his East Coast home, reporting that trees were being carelessly cut down, animals were being slaughtered by "swinish game-butchers," and the wilderness was in danger. He expressed great shock at how quickly this region that he loved was being stripped of its glory. The big game was gone, the ponds were drying up, the beavers were disappearing, and the grasslands were becoming desert.

Roosevelt did more than talk. He founded the Boone & Crockett Club, dedicated to the preservation of American wilderness. Largely through the club's influence, legislation was passed to care for Yellowstone National Park, to protect sequoia trees in California, to set aside nature reserves for bird and sea life, and to limit the shooting of big game. Laws also were passed to regulate hunting practices.

Merely hoping for change rarely brings it about. Work, however, usually does!

He who is waiting for something to turn up
might start with his own shirtsleeves.

Money Isn't Everything

Be not deceived; God is not mocked:
for whatsoever a man soweth,
that shall he also reap.

GALATIANS 6:7

Long ago there was a wealthy noble-woman who had grown tired of life. She had everything one could wish for except happiness and contentment. She said, "I am weary of life. I will go to the river and there end my life."

As she walked along, she suddenly felt a little hand tugging at her skirts. Looking down, she saw a frail, hungry-looking little boy who pleaded, "There are six of us. We are dying for want of food!" The noblewoman thought, *Why should I not relieve this wretched family? I have the means, and it seems I will have no more use for riches when I am gone.*

Following the little boy, she entered a scene of misery, sickness, and want. She opened her purse and emptied its contents. The family members were beside themselves with joy and gratitude. Even more taken with their need, the noblewoman said, "I'll return tomorrow, and I will share with you more of the good things that God has given to me in abundance!"

She left that scene of want and wretched-ness, rejoicing that the child had found her. For the first time in her life, she understood the rea-son for her wealth. Never again did she think of ending her life, which was now filled with meaning and purpose.

The greatest use of wealth is to give it away. Self-centeredness can never bring happiness. When we look to meeting the needs of others, we find soul-satisfaction that all the wealth in the world could never obtain.

Who IS MOST IN NEED OF A PORTION OF MY WEALTH— HOWEVER LIMITED IT IS—TODAY?

Those who bring sunshine to the lives of others cannot keep it from themselves.

Active Listening

The ear that heareth the reproof
of life abideth among the wise.

PROVERBS 15:31

Today I
CHOOSE TO
LISTEN FOR
THE VOICE
OF GOD
BY . . .

An American Indian was once visiting New York City. As he walked the busy Manhattan streets with a friend from the city, he suddenly stopped, tilted his head to one side, and said, "I hear a cricket."

"You're crazy," his friend said. The Cherokee answered, "No, I hear a cricket. I do! I'm sure of it."

The friend replied, "It's the noon hour. People are jammed on the sidewalks, cars are honking, taxis are whizzing by—the city is full of noise. And you think you can hear a cricket?"

"I'm sure I do," said the visitor. He listened even more intently and then walked to the corner. Spotting a shrub in a large cement planter, he dug into the leaves underneath it and pulled out a cricket. His friend was astounded. The man said, "The fact is, my friend, that my ears are different than yours. It all depends on what your ears have been tuned to hear. Let me show you." He reached into his pocket, pulled out a handful of loose change, and dropped the coins on the pavement. Every head within a half-block turned. "See what I mean?" he said, picking up the coins. "It all depends on what you are listening for."

Listen today for those things that will make you wise. Heed those things that prepare you for eternity.

❧

A good listener is not only popular
everywhere, but after awhile
he knows something.

Loyal Friends

*Not forsaking the assembling of ourselves
together, as the manner of some is;
but exhorting one another: and so much
the more, as ye see the day approaching.*

HEBREWS 10:25

Few sights evoke as much attention and awe as that of a large flock of Canadian geese winging their way in a V-formation to the North or South. They signal the changing of seasons and speak of the value of teamwork.

What many don't know is that when a goose becomes ill or wounded, it never falls from formation alone. Two other geese also drop out of formation and follow the ailing goose to the ground. One of them is usually the mate of the wounded bird, since geese mate for life and are extremely loyal to their mates. Once on the ground, the healthy birds help protect him and care for him as much as possible, even to the point of throwing themselves between the weakened bird and possible predators. They stay with him until he is either able to fly again or dies. Then, and only then, do they launch out. In most cases, they wait for another group of geese to fly overhead, and join them, adding to the safety and efficiency of their numbers.

If only human beings would care for one another this well! Stick by your friends when they need your help.

*Remember the banana—when it
left the bunch, it got skinned.*

Which ONE OF MY FRIENDS IS WOUNDED AND NEEDS MY ATTENTION RIGHT NOW?

APRIL 29

Thou, O man of God, flee these things;
and follow after righteousness, godliness,
faith, love, patience, meekness.

1 TIMOTHY 6:11

What KIND
OF SPOUSE
DO I ASPIRE
TO BE?

In Thornton Wilder's play, *The Skin of Our Teeth*, the character Mrs. Antrobus says to her husband, "I didn't marry you because you were perfect. . . . I married you because you gave me a promise."

She then takes off her ring and looks at it, saying, "That promise made up for your faults and the promise I gave you made up for mine. Two imperfect people got married, and it was the promise that made the marriage."

In every marriage, no matter how well the two people know one another, great mysteries remain. Most often, each person comes to the marriage:

- not fully knowing himself or herself.

- not fully knowing about life.

- not fully knowing about his or her spouse.

What is unknown is far greater than what is known!

Becoming a faithful, loving spouse not only takes courage and faith, but patience and a desire to keep learning and growing. Better than asking, "What kind of spouse do I desire to have?" is the question, "What kind of spouse do I aspire to be?"

Success in marriage is more
than finding the right person.
It's becoming the right person.

Winning at Losing

Them that honour me I will honour.

1 SAMUEL 2:30

The moment was a tense one. Rosalie Elliott had made it to the fourth round of a national spelling contest in Washington. The eleven-year-old from South Carolina had been asked to spell the word "avowal." In her soft southern accent, she spelled the word, but the judges were not able to determine if she had used an "a" or an "e" as the next-to-the-last letter. They debated among themselves for several minutes as they listened to tape-recording playbacks. The crucial letter, however, was too blurred by her accent to decipher. Finally, the chief judge put the question to the only person who knew the answer.

"Was the letter an 'a' or was it an 'e'?" he asked Rosalie. By this time, surrounded by whispering young spellers, Rosalie knew the correct spelling of the word. Still, without hesitation, she replied that she had misspelled the word and walked from the stage.

The entire audience stood and applauded, including some fifty newspaper reporters. The moment was a heartwarming and proud one for her parents. Even in defeat, she was a victor. Indeed, more has been written about Rosalie Elliott over the years than about the now-forgotten winner of the event!

Being a person of truth, even when it counts against us, will bring us great honor.

Would I HAVE THE INTEGRITY TO BE AS TRUTHFUL AS ROSALIE IN A SIMILAR SITUATION?

Honor is better than honors.

Laughter—Good for the Soul

A happy heart makes the face cheerful,
but heartache crushes the spirit.

PROVERBS 15:13 NIV

The LAST
TIME I HAD
A GOOD,
HEARTY
LAUGH WAS
WHEN . . .

A little girl was eating her breakfast one morning when a ray of sunlight suddenly appeared through the clouds and reflected off the spoon in her cereal bowl. She immediately put it into her mouth. With a big smile, she exclaimed to her mother, "I just swallowed a spoonful of sunshine!"

A spoonful of sunshine just may be the best "soul food" a person can have in a day. A prominent surgeon once wrote, "Encourage your child to be merry and to laugh aloud. A good, hearty laugh expands the chest and makes the blood bound merrily along. A good laugh will sound right through the house. It will not only do your child good, but will be a benefit to all who hear and be an important means of driving the blues away from a dwelling. Merriment is very catching and spreads in a remarkable manner, few being able to resist the contagion. A hearty laugh is delightful harmony; indeed it is the best of music."

An old poem advises: "If you are on the Gloomy Line, the Worry Train, or the Grouchy Track, get a transfer! It's time to climb aboard the Sunshine Train and sit in one of its Cheerful Cars."

The most wasted of all days is that
on which one has not laughed.

Careful Response

Do not forsake wisdom, and she will protect you. . . . When you walk, your steps will not be hampered; when you run, you will not stumble.

PROVERBS 4:6,12 NIV

A mother of six walked into her house one day to see all of her children huddled together in a circle. When she approached them to investigate what had evoked such intense interest, she could hardly believe her eyes.

To her horror, in the middle of the circle of children were several baby skunks. She immediately screamed at the top of her voice, "Children! Run, run, run! Out, out, out!"

At the sound of their mother's alarmed voice, each child quickly grabbed a baby skunk and headed for the door. The panic, of course, set off the instinctual danger alarm in the skunks, and each of them quickly dispelled its horrible scent. Each child and the house itself were doused with an aroma that lingered for weeks, despite vigorous scrubbing and the use of strong disinfectants.

How we react to a situation often has greater negative consequences than the situation itself! Don't make matters worse by overreacting. Choose to act rather than react, taking sufficient time to choose a course of action based upon calm reason and thoughtful prayer.

Hindsight explains the injury that foresight would have prevented.

How HAVE I OVERREACTED LATELY, CAUSING MORE HARM THAN GOOD?

Decorating with Personality

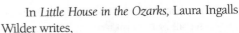

*Better a meal of vegetables where there
is love than a fattened calf with hatred.*

PROVERBS 15:17 NIV

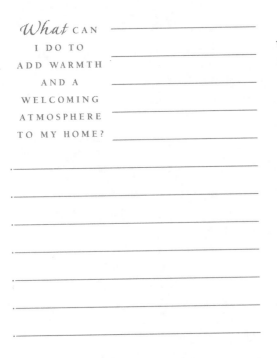

What CAN
I DO TO
ADD WARMTH
AND A
WELCOMING
ATMOSPHERE
TO MY HOME?

In *Little House in the Ozarks,* Laura Ingalls Wilder writes,

> I spent an afternoon a short time ago with a friend in her new home. The house was beautiful and well-furnished with new furniture, but it seemed bare and empty to me. I wondered why this was until I remembered my experience with my new house. I could not make the living room seem homelike. I would move the chairs here and there and change the pictures on the wall, but something was lacking. Nothing seemed to change the feeling of coldness and vacancy that displeased me whenever I entered the room.
>
> Then, as I stood in the middle of the room one day wondering what I could possibly do to improve it, it came to me that all that was needed was for someone to live in it and furnish it with the everyday, pleasant thoughts of friendship and cheerfulness and hospitality.

A homey atmosphere is not a matter of the right decor; it emanates from the thoughts and feelings of the people who occupy a home. Those who are kind, generous, and even-tempered create feelings of warmth and welcome. Today determine to decorate your home with warmth and hospitality.

*A house is made of walls and beams;
a home is made of love and dreams.*

Who's Holding You Up?

*Cast your cares on the LORD
and he will sustain you.*

PSALM 55:22 NIV

Many years ago, a young woman who felt called into the ministry was accepted into a well-known seminary. There were only two other women enrolled there, and her presence seemed to make her male classmates uncomfortable. She felt isolated, yet on display at the same time. To make matters worse, many of her professors were doing their best to destroy her faith rather than build it up. Even her private devotions seemed dry and lonely.

At Christmas break she sought her father's counsel. "How can I be strong in my resolve and straight in my theology with all that I face there?" she asked.

Her father took a pencil from his pocket and laid it on the palm of his hand. "Can that pencil stand upright by itself?" he asked her.

"No," she replied. Then her father grasped the pencil in his hand and held it in an upright position. "Ah," she said, "but you are holding it now."

"Daughter," he replied, "your life is like this pencil. But Jesus Christ is the One who can hold you." The young woman took her father's pencil and returned to seminary.

Whatever difficulties you may encounter today, remember that God holds you in His loving hands. His strength will hold you up and enable you to face anything that comes your way.

*It is impossible for that man
to despair who remembers
that his Helper is omnipotent.*

Surrounded BY THE LOVING HANDS OF GOD, I CAN STAND UP STRAIGHT IN THE MIDST OF . . .

Change through Praise

A man hath joy by the answer of his mouth: and a word spoken in due season, how good is it!

PROVERBS 15:23

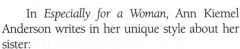

Whom DO
I NEED TO
AFFIRM
TODAY?

In *Especially for a Woman*, Ann Kiemel Anderson writes in her unique style about her sister:

Jan taught third grade once. A long time ago. One bright-eyed boy would stand at her desk. Watch her. Talk to her. All the while wrapping his finger around a piece of her hair into a little curl. He thought Jan was the shining star in the night. Over and over, however, he did poorly in his work assignments & daily quizzes.

One day Jan stopped, looked at him, and said, "Rodney, you are very smart. You could be doing so well in school. In fact, you are one of my finest students. . . ." before she could continue to tell him that he should be doing much better in school . . . he looked up at her with sober, large eyes:

"I did not know that!"

From that moment on, Rodney began to change. His papers were neater. Cleaner. His spelling improved. He was one of her top students. All because she affirmed him. She told him something no one ever had before. It changed his life.

Nobody ever became ill or died from receiving too much genuine praise and encouragement. But who can count the wounded hearts, weary souls, and troubled minds that have resulted from their lack! Give an encouraging word today to someone who needs it. Remember that what you sow, you will also reap!

We should seize every opportunity to give encouragement. Encouragement is oxygen to the soul.

Puffed-up Pride

*It is more blessed to give
than to receive.*

ACTS 20:35

At a church meeting, a wealthy man stood up to give his testimony. "I'm a millionaire," he said, not at all humbly. "I attribute it all to the rich blessings of God in my life. I came from a wonderful family. He gave me abundant intelligence and good business sense. I worked hard. On the night after I received my first paycheck, I went to a church meeting. The speaker was a missionary who told about his work. I gave everything I had to God. I believe that God blessed that decision, and that is why I am a rich man today."

He smiled broadly at the congregation, then sat down. After a few seconds of silence, a tiny elderly woman sitting in the pew behind him leaned forward and said, "I dare you to do it again."

Pride is the very antithesis of a good heart. As one missionary discovered when he attempted to translate the word "pride" for a tribe noted for its mutuality of sharing, it can be a difficult concept to define. Yet, it is universally recognized. The missionary finally attached an air pump to a bicycle tire and, while pointing first to one head and then another, began to pump until the tire inflated to several times its size and at last burst. Everyone in the village nodded in understanding!

A sure antidote for a prideful heart is to remember who is the source of all blessing. God gives freely all good things for us to enjoy.

What
BLESSING
FROM GOD
HAVE I
WRONGLY
TAKEN
CREDIT FOR?

If there be any truer measure of a man than by what he does, it must be by what he gives.

Handsome in Character

The LORD seeth not as man seeth; for man looketh on the outward appearance, but the LORD looketh on the heart.

1 SAMUEL 16:7

What KIND
OF LEGACY
DO I WANT
TO LEAVE
BEHIND?

Abraham Lincoln had a disarming and engaging ability to laugh at himself, especially about his physical appearance. When Senator Stephen A. Douglas once called him a "two-faced man," President Lincoln responded, "I leave it to my audience. If I had another face, do you think I would wear this one?"

Another time he told a group of editors about meeting a woman riding on horseback in the woods. "She looked at me intently, and said, 'I do believe you are the ugliest man I ever saw.' Said I, 'Madam, you are probably right, but I can't help it.' 'No,' said she, 'you can't help it, but you might stay at home.'"

Although his likeness is widely recognized, Lincoln is not known primarily for his appearance, but rather for his courageous stance in favor of the restoration of the Union and the abolition of slavery. He is often held as an example of remarkable determination, dedication, and compassion. These qualities are what mark Lincoln as one of America's greatest presidents.

So much is made of outward appearance and material possessions in our culture today. We do well to remember that it is our inner attributes that create a lasting reputation and leave behind a legacy of character for future generations to follow.

⸻⸺⸻

Fads come and go; wisdom and character go on forever.

Your Own Song

*The heart of the righteous weighs
its answers, but the mouth
of the wicked gushes evil.*

PROVERBS 15:28 NIV

Birds sing—never having to apologize for their songs.

Dogs bark and kittens meow—never having to say, "I'm sorry for what I just said."

Lions roar and hyenas howl—never having to retract their statements as being untrue.

The fact is that the members of the animal kingdom are what they are, and they are true in their expression of what they were created to be.

However, as human beings, we are sometimes embarrassed by our own words, feeling apologetic because we've been caught in an awkward moment. Or we recognize that we have been critical of another's performance and spoken the wrong words at the wrong time.

The blue jay doesn't criticize the robin. The kitten doesn't make snide remarks about the puppy. The lion doesn't ridicule the hyena. In like manner, we should not put down others. We can never fully understand, never fully appreciate, and never fully emulate any other person. We were all created uniquely, with differing gifts, talents, and personality traits.

Stick to singing your own song today, while appreciating the uniqueness of those around you. In so doing, you can easily avoid putting your foot in your mouth!

Instead OF PUTTING DOWN OTHERS, I CAN APPRECIATE THEIR UNIQUENESS BY . . .

———

People with tact have less to retract.

Constructive Criticism

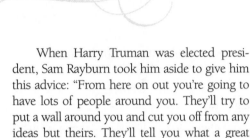

*If you profit from constructive criticism you
will be elected to the wise men's hall of fame.
But to reject criticism is to harm yourself
and your own best interests.*

PROVERBS 15:31-32 TLB

I HAVE
FOUND
MYSELF
FEELING
RESENTFUL
WHEN MY
LOVED ONES
DON'T
APPRECIATE
MY . . .

When Harry Truman was elected president, Sam Rayburn took him aside to give him this advice: "From here on out you're going to have lots of people around you. They'll try to put a wall around you and cut you off from any ideas but theirs. They'll tell you what a great man you are, Harry. But you and I both know you ain't."

In commenting on this quote, a psychologist once noted that many people find themselves gravitating toward those who continually flatter them and praise their work, only to feel a growing resentment toward their own spouse and family members because they fail to share the same enthusiasm for their many positive attributes. "I try to point out to them," the psychologist says, "that they are fantasizing about what the perfect home life should be like and concluding that the workplace is the true reality of their lives. The truth, however, is that our work is often the place where we live veiled lives of fantasy, and home is the genuine reality check."

Criticism is always tough to swallow, but in the end, it does us far more good than a diet of flattery. In either case, we should surround ourselves with and value those who speak the truth to us—good or bad.

❧

*The trouble with most of us is
that we would rather be ruined
by praise than saved by criticism.*

God's Perfect Timing

*He hath said, I will never
leave thee, nor forsake thee.*

HEBREWS 13:5

Because of cerebral palsy, Leslie was born mentally retarded and without eyes. Vegetable-like, he was completely unresponsive to sound or touch, and at the age of six months, he was not expected to live. A nurse named May Lemke was asked if she could care for him at home until he died. She did—for more than thirty years.

When May accepted baby Leslie, she accepted him as just that, a baby—no different from others—to be taught and loved. She cared for him year after year, but he never moved or responded in any way. Even so, she never stopped talking and singing to him or praying for him. She filled their home with music, but still, he showed no response. She and her husband bought an old, used piano and put it in his bedroom. She pushed his fingers against the keys. With quiet faith, she knew God would someday help Leslie break out of his prison. She rejoiced when he began to walk at age sixteen.

Several years later, May and her husband were awakened one night by the sound of *Tchaikovsky's Piano Concerto No. 1*. Startled, they arose to find Leslie at the piano with a smile glowing on his face. Shortly thereafter, he began to talk, cry, and sing. At age twenty-eight, he began to talk in earnest. May's prayers were answered—in God's timing and in God's way.

We may sometimes think our prayers are falling on deaf ears and our efforts are failing to change things, but take courage from Leslie's story. It may sound cliché, but never give up! Have patience. God is always working behind the scenes, even when you can't see the evidence. Eventually, it will be seen.

I HAVE CONFIDENCE GOD IS WORKING BEHIND THE SCENES RIGHT NOW WITH REGARD TO . . .

⸺◆⸺

*When I come to the end of my rope,
God is there to take over.*

Completing the Masterpiece

If God be for us,
who can be against us?
ROMANS 8:31

I NEED TO
BELIEVE
THAT GOD
WILL
CREATE A
MASTERPIECE
OUT OF MY
EFFORTS
TO . . .

Wishing to encourage her young son's progress at the piano, a mother bought tickets to a performance by Ignace Paderewski. When the night arrived, the two found their seats near the front of the concert hall. The boy stared in wide-eyed amazement at the majestic grand piano on the stage. The mother began talking to a friend, who was sitting nearby, and failed to notice her son slip out of his seat. As the house lights dimmed and the spotlight came up on the piano, the woman gasped as she saw her son on the piano bench, innocently picking out "Twinkle, Twinkle, Little Star."

Before the woman could retrieve her son, the famous concert pianist appeared on stage and quickly moved to the keyboard. "Don't quit—keep playing," he whispered to the boy. Leaning over, Paderewski reached down with his left hand and began filling in a bass part. Then with his right arm, he reached around the other side, encircling the child, to add a running obligato. Together, the old master and the young novice mesmerized the crowd.

No matter how insignificant or "amateurish" you may feel today, the Master has these words for you: "Don't quit—keep playing." He will add whatever is needed to turn your efforts into a masterpiece.

God plus one is always a majority!

Prayer in the Home

Let the heart of them rejoice that seek the LORD. Seek the LORD, and his strength: seek his face evermore.

PSALM 105:3-4

Parents today often use dozens of excuses to justify not taking their children to church or having a family devotional time, but if that urge strikes you, remember the family of Lydia Murphy. She moved with her parents to Shawnee, Kansas, in 1859, and she writes of their first night in their new home: "The family Bible rested in the center of the room. We gathered around the table, seated on boxes and improvised chairs, while the usual evening family prayers were held after the reading of a chapter of the Scriptures. During the fifty years of his Kansas citizenship, this morning and evening Scripture reading and prayer was not once omitted in my father's house."

The Murphys had been devout Methodists, but the nearest Methodist church was ten miles away. Therefore, they secured the services of a circuit-riding Methodist minister and opened their own home for worship, welcoming neighbors of all denominations. Within months their home had become the center of both the social and religious life of the community. Services were held every two weeks on Saturday. At other times neighbors took turns reading the Scriptures, leading prayer, and teaching Sunday school!

A child who watches his parents spend time with God has a sense of security that nothing else can establish. As you sit in the presence of God, make room for your children.

What CAN I REALISTI- CALLY DO TO BUILD FAMILY WORSHIP TIME INTO OUR DAY—OR EVEN OUR WEEK?

Happy is the child . . . who sees mother and father rising early, or going aside regularly, to keep times with the Lord.

A Powerful Witness

God so loved the world, that he gave his only begotten Son, that whosoever believeth in him should not perish, but have everlasting life.

JOHN 3:16

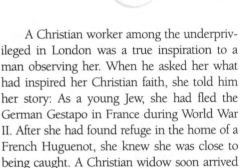

How MUCH PERSONAL SACRIFICE AM I WILLING TO MAKE FOR THE SAKE OF THE GOSPEL?

A Christian worker among the underprivileged in London was a true inspiration to a man observing her. When he asked her what had inspired her Christian faith, she told him her story: As a young Jew, she had fled the German Gestapo in France during World War II. After she had found refuge in the home of a French Huguenot, she knew she was close to being caught. A Christian widow soon arrived and told her that she must flee to a new place immediately. The girl replied, "It's no use, they will find me anyway. They are so close behind." The widow said, "Yes, they will find someone here, but go with these people to safety. I will take your identification papers."

The young girl understood the widow's plan. The Gestapo would think the widow was a fleeing Jew. She asked, "Why are you doing this?" The widow responded, "It's the least I can do. Christ has already done that and more for me." Sure enough, the widow was imprisoned in the Jewish girl's place, and within six months she died in a concentration camp.

The Jewish woman may have been able to outrun the Gestapo, but she could not outrun what this woman had done for her. Personal sacrifice is the greatest legacy a person can leave behind.

The strongest evidence of love is sacrifice.

Stargazing

Peter . . . walked on the water toward Jesus.
But when he looked around at the high
waves, he was terrified and began to sink.

MATTHEW 14:29-30 TLB

During the darkest days of the Civil War, the hopes of the Union had nearly been extinguished. When certain goals seemed unreachable, the leaders of the Union turned to President Abraham Lincoln for solace, guidance, and hope. Once when a delegation called at the White House and detailed a long list of crises facing the nation, Lincoln told this story: "Years ago a young friend and I were out one night when a shower of meteors fell from the clear November sky. The young man was frightened, but I told him to look up in the sky past the shooting stars to the fixed stars beyond, shining serenely in the firmament, and I said, 'Let us not mind the meteors, but let us keep our eyes on the stars.'"

When times are troubled or life seems to be changing too fast, keep your inner eyes of faith and hope on those things that you know to be lasting and sure. Don't limit your gaze to what you know or who you know, but focus on whom you know. A relationship with God alone is the supreme goal. God never changes. He cannot be removed from His place as the King of Glory.

Lately "METEORS" HAVE DISTRACTED ME; I NEED TO KEEP MY INNER EYES OF FAITH ON GOD WITH REGARD TO . . .

Obstacles are those frightful things you
see when you take your eyes off the goal.

Answered Prayer

Faith without works is dead.
JAMES 2:26

How CAN I
KEEP MYSELF
FROM
GETTING
AHEAD OF
GOD WHEN I
THINK I'VE
PLACED
SOMETHING
IN HIS
HANDS?

A little girl really seemed to believe in the power of prayer. Her parents were frequently amazed at the boldness with which their daughter prayed and in her unswerving confidence that God had not only heard her prayers but was in the process of answering them in the way she desired.

One day her older brother made a little trap to catch sparrows, and the girl found this offensive. She felt sorry for the birds that might be caught and was angry and upset that her brother would do such a thing. When he failed to respond to her arguments and pleas, she informed him and her entire family, "I'm going to pray about this."

Three nights later, her face seemed almost radiant as she said her bedtime prayers, voicing with absolute faith her belief that the traps would be futile and that no birds would be harmed. After she had finished her prayer, her mother asked, "Child, how can you be so positive about this?"

The little girl smiled and said, "Because I went out three days ago and kicked the trap to pieces."

While it may be unwise to take matters into our own hands, we are always wise to put everything into God's hands.

Pray as if everything depended on God,
and work as if everything
depended upon man.

Empathy over Ideas

Now these three remain:
faith, hope and love. But the
greatest of these is love.
1 CORINTHIANS 13:13 NIV

In 1873, a Belgian Catholic priest named Joseph Damien De Veuster was sent to minister to lepers on the Hawaiian Island of Molokai. He arrived in high spirits, hoping to build a friendship with each of the lepers. However, people shunned him at every turn. He built a chapel, began worship services, and poured his heart out to the lepers, but all seemed futile. No one responded to his ministry, and after twelve years of struggling, Father Damien decided to leave. Dejected, as he stood on the dock waiting to board the ship, he looked down at his hands and noticed some mysterious white spots on them. Feeling some numbness, he knew immediately what was happening—he had contracted leprosy!

Father Damien returned to the leper colony and to his work. Word spread quickly, and within hours hundreds gathered outside his hut, fully identifying with his plight. On the following Sunday, he received an even bigger surprise. When he arrived at the chapel, it was full! Father Damien began to preach from the empathy of love rather than the distance of theology, and his ministry became enormously successful.

People need your empathy, not your sympathy. Those who receive your love today will be much more interested in hearing about your faith tomorrow.

The measure of a man is not how great his faith is, but how great his love is.

Have I BEEN SHARING GENUINE EMPATHY OR MERELY EXHIBITING SYMPATHY TOWARD OTHERS?

Jumping In

I know whom I have believed, and am persuaded that he is able to keep that which I have committed unto him against that day.

2 TIMOTHY 1:12

Even
THOUGH I
CANNOT SEE
WHAT GOD IS
DOING, I'M
TAKING A
LEAP OF
FAITH WITH
REGARD
TO . . .

During the terrible days of the Blitz in World War II, a father held his young daughter's hand as they ran from a building that had been struck by a bomb. A large hole had been left in the front yard by a shell explosion several days earlier. Seeking shelter as quickly as possible, the father jumped into the hole and then held up his arms for his young daughter to follow.

Terrified by the explosions around her and unable to see her father in the darkness of the hole, she cried, "I can't see you, Papa!"

The father looked up at his daughter, silhouetted against the night sky lit with white tracer lights and tinted red by burning buildings, and called out, "But I can see you, my darling. Jump!"

The little girl jumped, not because she could see her father, but because he could see her. She trusted him to tell her the truth and do what was best for her.

We may not be able to clearly discern where our Heavenly Father is leading us, but we can trust that God knows what's best for us. We may not know what God has "up His sleeve," but we can trust His arms to be everlasting.

———— ⦿⦿⦿ ————

Faith is not belief without proof,
but trust without reservation.

Locked Inside Paper Walls

As he thinketh in his heart, so is he.

PROVERBS 23:7

A new prison was built in British Columbia to replace Fort Alcan, the old prison that had been used to house inmates for hundreds of years. After the prisoners were moved into their new quarters, they became part of a work crew. They were to strip the old prison of lumber, electrical appliances, and plumbing that might be reused. Under the supervision of guards, the inmates began tearing down the old prison walls.

As they did, they were shocked at what they found. Although massive locks had sealed heavy metal doors and two-inch steel bars had covered the windows of the cells, the walls of the prison had actually been made out of paper and clay that had been painted to resemble iron! If any of the prisoners had given a mighty heave or hard kick against a wall, they might have easily knocked a hole in it, allowing them to escape. For years they had huddled in their locked cells, regarding escape as impossible. Nobody had even tried to escape, because they thought it was impossible.

Today many people are prisoners of fear. They never attempt to pursue their dreams, because the thought of reaching them seems impossible. But with God, all things are possible. How do you know you can't succeed if you don't try?

Whether you think you can or think you can't, you're right.

What IS THE "IMPOSSIBLE" DREAM THAT I'M AFRAID TO PURSUE?

Killed by Kindness

The LORD that delivered me out of the paw of the lion, and out of the paw of the bear, he will deliver me out of the hand of this Philistine.

1 SAMUEL 17:37

What "GIANT" IN MY LIFE NEEDS TO BE FELLED BY AN ACT OF KINDNESS AND FAITH ON MY PART?

When confronted with a Goliath-sized problem, which way do you respond: "He's too big to hit," or like David, "He's too big to miss."

One day the Pahouins brought a giant native in chains to Albert Schweitzer's hospital. In a fit of madness, N'Tschambi had killed a woman. Reaching down to help the man to the landing, Schweitzer saw fear and sadness in his face. When others refused his order to remove the man's chains, he did it himself. He then explained sedatives to N'Tschambi, and the fearful man gratefully accepted them. That night he slept without nightmares for the first time.

N'Tschambi became a model patient, and soon Schweitzer gave him periods of freedom outside his room, to which he often voluntarily returned if he became agitated. Still, he tackled any task he was given with a fierce energy that frightened the staff. One day Schweitzer gave him an axe and asked him to help him make a clearing. N'Tschambi drew back in alarm, stating he was afraid to touch the axe for fear of what he might do with it. Schweitzer replied, "If I'm not afraid, why should you be?" Then as the entire hospital watched, the two went into the jungle. Hours later, they returned, N'Tschambi's big body dripping with sweat but his face lit up with a radiant smile. The giant inside him had been felled by kindness and the faith another human being had placed in him!

Albert Schweitzer was able to defeat his "giant" because he knew the same simple truth that David knew when he faced Goliath: When God is on your side, it is impossible to fail!

Soothing Words

Pleasant words are a honeycomb,
sweet to the soul and
healing to the bones.
PROVERBS 16:24 NASB

It takes just as much energy to say a positive word as it does a negative one. In fact, it may actually take less. Research has shown that when we speak positive words—even in difficult circumstances or troubling situations—we become relaxed. As we relax, the flow of blood to the brain increases. A well-oxygenated brain can think more creatively, make wise decisions, find reasonable solutions, and generate pertinent answers.

Positive words ease relationships and create an atmosphere of peace that is conducive to rest, relaxation, and rejuvenation—all of which are necessary for good health.

A continual flow of negative words causes relationships to suffer, which creates an atmosphere of disharmony and makes for fitful sleep and frayed nerves—none of which are healthy!

Contrary to popular thought, negative words do not release tension. They keep the body in a state of tension, constricting muscles and blood vessels, which often causes irrational behavior.

One of the best things we can do for our overall health is to carefully monitor our speech habits!

If I COULD CHANGE ONE NEGATIVE SPEECH HABIT THAT GIVES ME THE MOST TROUBLE, IT WOULD BE...

Good words are worth much and cost little.

Measuring Up

I warn everyone among you. . . . [not to have an exaggerated opinion of his own importance], but to rate his ability with sober judgment.

ROMANS 12:3 AMP

Have
I BEEN
GROWING—OR
SHRINKING—
SPIRITUALLY?

A little boy struggled to rehang the growth chart that had come off the inside of his closet door. He finally got it hung as straight as he could. Then he backed up against it, placed a ruler against his head, and reached up to mark the place on the chart where the ruler touched. "I've grown ten inches," he cried in joy as he ran to the kitchen to tell his mother. "I'm four feet eleven inches tall!"

His mother knew that something must be amiss, so she followed him back to his room. She quickly realized what had happened. The boy had hung the chart so that the bottom of it touched the floor, instead of hanging it six inches above the floor as called for on the chart's instructions. He had also held the ruler at an angle.

The boy was disappointed when his mother adjusted the chart and then remeasured him. "If you hadn't measured yourself," she asked, "wouldn't you have been happy with growing an inch and a half? That's a lot for just one summer." The boy thought for a moment and then said, "Well, at least I didn't shrink."

When measuring our spiritual growth, we should leave the measuring up to God. Only He has the proper chart to measure us against, and He's big enough to hold the ruler straight!

The most difficult secret for a man to keep is the opinion he has of himself.

The Source of Our Supply

Behold, I stand at the door, and knock: if any man hear my voice, and open the door, I will come in to him, and will sup with him, and he with me.

REVELATION 3:20

Once there was a saintly man who lived, by his own choice, on the edge of poverty. He distributed equally all the money he earned between himself and the poor. The man's adult son was among those who found it extremely difficult to make ends meet, so the man gave him just enough to keep body and soul intact and continued to help others who found themselves in dire need. One day the father was asked why he paid so little attention to his own son's personal needs while the bulk of his attention went to others. "You could help your son much more," his critic said, "if you would help strangers less."

"Ah," the man replied wisely, "but if I were to meet all my son's requirements, would he perhaps forget the necessity of relying upon the Lord? Would he begin to see me as the source of all his supply, rather than his Heavenly Father? If that became the case, I would not be helping my son at all!"

God forbid that we should find ourselves feeling totally self-sufficient. Pride lurks in that dark corner of emotion. Once pride takes over, we see little reason to invite the Lord to do His work in our lives. Take inventory, and invite God into the affairs of your life.

I AM MOST APT TO TRY TO BE SELF-SUFFICIENT WHEN IT COMES TO...

God intervenes in the affairs of men by invitation only.

Scheduled Delays

He that is slow to anger is better than the mighty; and he that ruleth his spirit than he that taketh a city.

PROVERBS 16:32

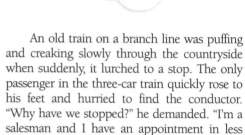

I FIND I
BECOME
MOST
FRAZZLED
AND
FRUSTRATED
WHEN . . .

An old train on a branch line was puffing and creaking slowly through the countryside when suddenly, it lurched to a stop. The only passenger in the three-car train quickly rose to his feet and hurried to find the conductor. "Why have we stopped?" he demanded. "I'm a salesman and I have an appointment in less than an hour in the next town. Surely this old train can make it through a pasture!"

The conductor smiled, "Nothing to worry about, sir. Just a cow on the tracks. Gotta wait her out." The salesman returned to his seat, fuming and fidgeting until the train began to creep forward again about ten minutes later. It chugged along for a mile or two and then ground to a halt once again.

This time the conductor found the salesman. "Don't worry," he said. "We'll be on our way shortly. It's just a temporary delay." The exasperated salesman asked, "What now? Did we catch up to the cow again?"

What the salesman didn't know was that the schedule for this particular train had been set as to allow for temporary delays and cows on the track! The salesman easily made it to his appointment, but he was worn to a frazzle by his frustration and worry.

Practice patience. Allow for delays. You'll enjoy life's journey more.

⸺⟨❦⟩⸺

Patience is the ability to keep your motor idling when you feel like stripping your gears.

Making History

I am the light of the world: he that
followeth me shall not walk in darkness,
but shall have the light of life.

JOHN 8:12

John Woolman, a twenty-three-year-old clerk in a dry-goods shop, was busy adding up the day's receipts when his employer approached him with another man at his side and said, "John, I've sold Nancy to this gentleman. Draw up a bill of sale for her." As Woolman prepared to do so, something seemed to paralyze his arm. He could not write a word. He declared to his employer, a fellow Quaker, "I believe slave-keeping to be a practice inconsistent with the Christian religion."

The incident deeply troubled Woolman and shortly thereafter, he wrote a pamphlet, "Some Considerations on the Keeping of Negroes," which was printed by Benjamin Franklin in 1754. Although he became a tailor and orchard keeper, Woolman spent part of every year traveling to preach against slavery. He petitioned the Rhode Island legislature to abolish the slave trade. On a personal level, he stopped eating sugar and wearing indigo-dyed clothes produced as the result of slave labor.

Eventually, Woolman traveled to England in his crusade and there, his campaign of writing and speaking resulted in Parliament outlawing the slave trade in 1807 and abolishing slavery in all British colonies by 1933.

One man who will listen to God and follow His guidance can change history.

❦

Our grand business in life is not to
see what lies dimly at a distance,
but to do what lies clearly at hand.

The ONE LAW OR PRACTICE IN THIS COUNTRY THAT I WOULD LIKE TO HELP CHANGE IS . . .

Destined to Fly

Knowing this, that the trying of your faith worketh patience. But let patience have her perfect work, that ye may be perfect and entire, wanting nothing.

JAMES 1:3-4

How IS GOD
PREPARING
ME FOR MY
DESTINY
IN LIFE?

An old legend says that God first created birds without wings. Sometime later God made wings and said to the birds, "Come, take up these burdens and bear them." The birds hesitated at first but soon obeyed. They tried picking up the wings in their beaks but found them too heavy. Then they tried picking them up with their claws but found them too large. Finally, one of the birds managed to get the wings hoisted onto its shoulders where it was possible to carry the burdens.

To the amazement of the birds, the wings began to grow, and they soon had attached themselves to their bodies. One of the birds began to flap his wings, and others followed his example. Before long, one of the birds took off and began to soar in the sky above!

What had once been a heavy burden now became the very thing that enabled the birds to go where they could never go before and at the same time, truly fulfill the destiny of their creation.

The duties and responsibilities you count as burdens today may be part of God's destiny for your life, the means by which your soul is lifted up and prepared for eternity.

---

*Don't be afraid of pressure.
Remember that pressure is what
turns a lump of coal into a diamond.*

A Wish for a Leader

Whatever is born of God overcomes the world; and this is the victory that has overcome the world—our faith.

1 JOHN 5:4 NASB

Earl Reum has written these thought-inspiring words about experience:

I wish you could know how it feels "to run" with all your heart and lose—horribly!

I wish that you could achieve some great good for mankind, but have nobody know about it except for you.

I wish you could find something so worthwhile that you deem it worthy of investing your life within it.

I hope you become frustrated and challenged enough to begin to push back the very barriers of your own personal limitations.

I hope you make a stupid mistake and get caught red-handed and are big enough to say those magic words: "I was wrong."

I hope you give so much of yourself that some days you wonder if it's worth all the effort.

I wish for you a magnificent obsession that will give you reason for living and purpose and direction and life.

I wish for you the worst kind of everything you do, because that makes you fight to achieve beyond what you normally would.

I wish you the experience of leadership.

What IS THE MOST IMPORTANT LESSON I HAVE LEARNED FROM RECENT FAILURES?

_____

Experience is not what happens to a man, it's what a man does with what happens to him.

155

Set Free

Be ye kind one to another, tenderhearted,
forgiving one another, even as God for
Christ's sake hath forgiven you.

EPHESIANS 4:32

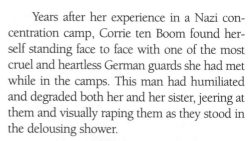

My
UNWILLING-
NESS TO
FORGIVE HAS
KEPT ME A
PRISONER
TO...

———

"I can forgive, but I cannot forget," is
only another way of saying, "I will not
forgive." Forgiveness ought to be like a
canceled note—torn in two, and burned up,
so that it never can be shown against one.

Years after her experience in a Nazi concentration camp, Corrie ten Boom found herself standing face to face with one of the most cruel and heartless German guards she had met while in the camps. This man had humiliated and degraded both her and her sister, jeering at them and visually raping them as they stood in the delousing shower.

Now he stood before her with an outstretched hand, asking, "Will you forgive me?" Corrie said,

I stood there with coldness clutching at my heart, but I know that the will can function regardless of the temperature of the heart. I prayed, "Jesus, help me!" Woodenly, mechanically I thrust my hand into the one stretched out to me and I experienced an incredible thing. The current started in my shoulder, raced down into my arm, and sprang into our clutched hands. Then this warm reconciliation seemed to flood my whole being, bringing tears to my eyes. "I forgive you, brother," I cried with my whole heart. For a long moment we grasped each other's hands, the former guard, the former prisoner. I have never known the love of God so intensely as I did in that moment!

When we forgive, we set a prisoner free— ourselves!

Healed by Helping

I am come that they might have life,
and that they might have
it more abundantly.

JOHN 10:10

One bleak winter morning, Jim was overwhelmed by a sense of failure. He couldn't stop thinking, *My life is worthless. I don't fit.* At the age of forty-three, he had lost his job. Alcohol had wreaked havoc on his life, and although he had been without a drink for some months and was involved in Alcoholics Anonymous, he didn't see that he had any hope for the future. The image of the shotgun in the attic began to fill his thoughts. Abruptly, he roused himself and said, "I'll go see Ted."

Ted was Jim's AA sponsor, a crusty, straight-talking farmer. Jim drove to Ted's house and found him sitting by his wood-burning stove. Ted seemed genuinely pleased to see Jim and began telling him how things were going on the farm—which wasn't good. They talked for nearly two hours, with Jim doing most of the listening. On the way home, Jim realized that he had made it through the day. Seeing Ted had saved his life. To his surprise, a week later it was Ted who stood at an AA meeting and revealed, "A week ago, my life seemed hopeless. I had lots of troubles. Then another recovering alcoholic stopped by and cheered me up and gave me a reason to keep going."

God is truly the faithful author of our lives. He orders our steps to accomplish His purpose and to bless and keep us.

———

People, places, and things were never
meant to give us life. God alone
is the author of a fulfilling life.

The AUTHOR OF MY LIFE KEEPS ME GOING EVEN WHEN I FEEL LIKE . . .

Where Anger Leads

Starting a quarrel is like breaching
a dam; so drop the matter
before a dispute breaks out.

PROVERBS 17:14 NIV

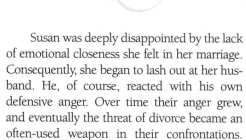

What ROAD
HAS MY
ANGER LED
ME DOWN
RECENTLY?

Susan was deeply disappointed by the lack of emotional closeness she felt in her marriage. Consequently, she began to lash out at her husband. He, of course, reacted with his own defensive anger. Over time their anger grew, and eventually the threat of divorce became an often-used weapon in their confrontations. Finally, Susan's husband moved out, and she filed for divorce.

The divorce proceedings were bitter. They fought all the way through it. When they met to sign the final papers, they stopped to look at each other, and Susan saw in his eyes the same feelings she was experiencing—feelings of longing, yet resignation. She thought, *I don't want to divorce him, and I don't think he wants to divorce me.*

She voiced her thoughts to her husband, and for a moment it appeared that he might also soften and admit that he still cared. Instead, he said in a dull monotone, "We've come this far. I guess we should finish it." Susan left the courtroom realizing she had never really wanted a divorce. She just wanted her husband to listen.

Don't allow anger to lead you anywhere, especially down a road you truly don't want to travel.

It isn't hard to make a mountain out
of a molehill. Just add a little dirt.

A Friend

A friend loves at all times, and
a brother is born for adversity.

PROVERBS 17:17 NIV

A friend is someone you are comfortable with, someone whose company you prefer. A friend is someone you can count on.

A friend is one who believes in you—someone with whom you can share your dreams. In fact, a real friend is a person you want to share all of life with—and the sharing doubles the fun.

When you are hurting and you can share your struggles with a friend, it eases the pain. A friend offers you safety and trust. . . .

A friend will laugh with you, but not at you—a friend is fun.

A friend will pray with you—and for you.

My friend is someone with whom I can share my ideas and philosophies, someone with whom I can grow intellectually. . . .

My friend is one who hears my cry of pain, who senses my struggle, who shares my lows as well as my highs.

My friend does not always say I am right, because sometimes I am not. . . .

My lover, my friend—this is what a marriage partner should be.

—Colleen Evans

How CAN I TRULY BE MY SPOUSE'S BEST FRIEND?

Friendship improves happiness
and abates misery by doubling
our joy and dividing our grief.

Being Right

Reckless words pierce like a sword, but the tongue of the wise brings healing.

PROVERBS 12:18 NIV

Whom DO
I NEED TO
APOLOGIZE
TO TODAY?

In looking over a café menu, a woman noticed that both a chicken-salad sandwich and a chicken sandwich were listed. She decided to order the chicken-salad sandwich, but absentmindedly wrote "chicken sandwich" on her order slip. When the waiter brought the chicken sandwich, she protested immediately, insisting the waiter had erred.

Most waiters would have picked up the order slip and shown the customer the mistake she had made. But instead, he expressed regret at the error, picked up the sandwich, returned to the kitchen, and a moment later placed a chicken-salad sandwich in front of the woman.

While eating her sandwich, the woman picked up her order slip and noticed the mistake she had made. When it was time to pay for the meal, she apologized to the waiter and offered to pay for both sandwiches. The waiter said, "No, ma'am. That's perfectly all right. I'm just happy you've forgiven me for being right."

Love always overlooks a fault and doesn't place blame. Like the waiter, rather than correcting or arguing with someone who says you're wrong, simply fix the problem. And like the woman, when you realize you're in the wrong, apologize quickly. God will always see to it that the truth is revealed.

Tact is the art of making a point without making an enemy.

Instant Relief

*A merry heart doeth
good like a medicine.*

PROVERBS 17:22

Norman Cousins was once asked by a group of physicians to meet with cancer patients at a hospital. He told the story of how he had lost a quarter in a pay phone. "Operator," he said, "I put in a quarter and didn't get my number." She said, "Sir, if you give me your name and address, we'll mail the coin to you."

He recited a long litany of all the steps and expense involved in returning his coin that way and concluded, "Now, operator, why don't you just return my coin and let's be friends?"

She repeated her offer and then asked if he had pushed the coin-return plunger. He hadn't, but when he did, the phone box spewed out close to four dollars worth of change!

The operator said, "Sir, will you please put the coins back in the box?" Cousins replied, "If you give me your name and address I will be glad to mail you the coins."

The veterans exploded with cheers as Cousins told his story. Then one of the physicians asked, "How many of you came into this room in pain?" More than half raised their hands. "How many of you in the past few minutes had less or no pain?" The same people once again raised their hands.

Laughter is one of the best pain medications ever!

❦

*Laughter is a tranquilizer
with no side effects.*

The ONE THING OR PERSON GUARANTEED TO MAKE ME LAUGH IS . . .

One Family's Heritage

Pray without ceasing.
1 THESSALONIANS 5:17

What KIND
OF MEMORIES
WILL MY
CHILDREN
HAVE WHEN
I'M GONE?

_____

_____

_____

_____

_____

_____

_____

_____

_____

_____

_____

If you have no prayer life yourself, it is rather a useless gesture to make your child say his prayers every night.

The actor known as Mr. T gave an unusual tribute to his mother. He said that he wanted to recognize "her hands, her feet, and her knees."

He called attention to his mother's feet because they had taken her across town to do domestic work. Her hands and knees were used to scrub floors and toilets. He also said,

> She used her feet to walk against my sickness when my body was ill and racked with pain. It was my mother who walked the floor with me, on her feet all night long, talking to God; then she would get down on her knees to pray some more, still holding me in her hands. I guess the only payment she ever wanted was for me to grow up and carry on her teachings . . . to share, to love, to be kind and always take God with me wherever I go. . . . She always said, "Don't be bitter, don't hate, don't hold grudges, and never forget to pray."

It's so hard to try to describe my mother's endurance, her patience, her love, her feelings for her family, her spiritual convictions, her right to be, her loyalty, and her pride in parenthood. I will just say that my mother was God-sent.

Feet to walk, hands to carry, knees to bend in prayer. What a legacy for any mother to leave a child!

Little Acts, Big Changes

*By this shall all men know that
ye are my disciples, if ye
have love one to another.*

JOHN 13:35

In *Les Misérables,* Victor Hugo tells of Jean Valjean, whose only crime was the theft of a loaf of bread to feed his sister's starving children. Valjean served nineteen years for this crime before being turned out on the streets, penniless. Hardened and unable to find work as a former convict, Valjean finally makes his way to the home of a good, old bishop, who gives him supper and a bed for the night. He serves Valjean using his best silver platters and candlesticks, which Valjean recognizes as highly valuable.

Yielding to temptation, Valjean steals the bishop's silver plates and slips away from his home but is soon caught and returned by watchful police. When shown the silver plates, the bishop says to the apprehending policeman, "Why, I gave them to him." And then turning to the thief, Valjean, he adds, "And Jean, you forgot to take the candlesticks." A shocked and eternally grateful Valjean accepts the candlesticks as more than valuable silver pieces, but as expressions of love beyond measure. The bishop's act brought about a true repentance and changed life.

Who knows who might be impacted by your act of kindness today? What seems little to you may be great in the eyes of a person in need of love.

I COULD GO ABOVE AND BEYOND BY SHOWING AN UNCONDITIONAL ACT OF KINDNESS TO . . .

It's good to be a Christian and know it, but it's better to be a Christian and show it.

Say More with Silence

In the multitude of words there wanteth not sin: but he that refraineth his lips is wise.

PROVERBS 10:19

I NEED TO LEARN TO BE QUIET IN SITUATIONS WHERE . . .

When Western Union told Thomas Edison to name his price for the ticker he had invented, he asked for several days to consider it. His wife suggested $20,000, but he thought such an amount was exorbitant.

At the appointed time, he went to the meeting still unsure what the price should be. When the official asked, "How much?" He tried to say $20,000, but the words just wouldn't come out of his mouth. The official finally broke the silence and asked, "Well, how about $100,000?"

Often silence allows others to say something better than we could have said it ourselves. By keeping quiet, others will have a greater interest in our thoughts. Then when we have an interested audience, our words will have greater impact.

The Bible tells us that even a fool may be thought of as wise when his mouth is kept shut (Proverbs 17:28). In that sense, silence can keep us from embarrassing ourselves. People may think we are smarter than we really are!

When you feel moved to express an opinion, weigh the impact of your words and keep this thought in mind, *The less said, the best said.* We can't get in trouble for what we don't say! Like Edison, we might even benefit from our silence.

I regret often that I have spoken; never that I have been silent.

Something Out of Nothing?

A fool finds no pleasure in understanding but delights in airing his own opinions.

PROVERBS 18:2 NIV

A pompous city man turned farmer was showing a young boy his vast acreage. As they drove through field after field, the man bragged incessantly about his accomplishments—how he had started from scratch as a young man and worked his way up through the business world. He told how he had earned far more money than had been necessary to purchase the land and how he had invested thousands upon thousands of dollars to transform the formerly worthless farm into the agricultural paradise they were exploring. He told of the amazing yield of his crops and the lushness of the new spring planting.

Finally, he pointed toward the stacked hay, the full granary, and the boxes of produce and declared, "And I grew it all by myself, sonny. Started with nothing, and now look at it!"

"From nothing?" echoed the duly impressed lad.

"That's right," said the man. "From nothing."

"Wow," the young boy said, pausing to reflect for a few seconds. "My dad farms, but he needs seed to grow his crops."

Before we become too impressed with our own accomplishments, we would be wise to remember that without God, we can never achieve anything of lasting significance on our own.

———

A man wrapped up in himself makes a very small package.

I MUST NEVER LOSE SIGHT OF THE FACT THAT GOD IS RESPONSIBLE FOR MY SUCCESS IN . . .

Saving Face

Here is how to measure it—the greatest love is shown when a person lays down his life for his friends.

JOHN 15:13 TLB

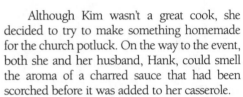

How CAN
MY SPOUSE
AND I
BECOME
BETTER
FRIENDS?

Marriage must exemplify friendship's highest ideal, or else it will be a failure.

Although Kim wasn't a great cook, she decided to try to make something homemade for the church potluck. On the way to the event, both she and her husband, Hank, could smell the aroma of a charred sauce that had been scorched before it was added to her casserole.

When they arrived at the potluck, Kim's casserole was placed on the table along with the other dishes. Before anyone came to the table, Kim spooned a bit of the casserole out for Hank to taste. The look on his face confirmed her worst nightmare. What would her new friends think of her now?

Before anyone else came to the table, Hank picked up Kim's casserole and announced to the group that he was going to make a pig out of himself and eat Kim's casserole all by himself. He noted that there were plenty of other hot dishes, salads, and desserts for the rest of them—but after all, he asked, how often did he get his favorite dish?

Hank sat in a corner courageously eating most of the casserole, enough for four people, before anyone else could taste it. They laughed about it later, and Kim told her friends for years, "I knew then I had married a man I would do my best to keep forever."

Is your spouse your best friend? Recommit yourself today to nurture your friendship with your mate. Spend time together talking and doing things you both enjoy. Remember what attracted you to one another in the beginning of your relationship. Focus on those things and overlook the faults you've discovered. God will bless your efforts, and your love for one another will be increased.

You've Got a Fan

These things I have spoken unto you, that in me ye might have peace. In the world ye shall have tribulation: but be of good cheer; I have overcome the world.

JOHN 16:33

Babe Ruth hit 714 home runs during his baseball career, but on one particular day toward the end of his career, the Braves were playing the Reds in Cincinnati, and the great Bambino was no hero. He dropped the ball and threw badly. In one inning alone, his errors were responsible for most of the five runs scored by Cincinnati.

As the Babe walked off the field and headed toward the dugout after the third out, a crescendo of boos rose to greet him. Then a boy jumped over the railing and ran out onto the field. With tears streaming down his face, he threw his arms around the legs of his hero.

Ruth didn't hesitate for a second. He picked up the boy, hugged him, then set him down and patted his head. The cries from the crowd abruptly stopped. A hush fell over the entire park. In that brief moment, the fans saw two heroes on the field: Ruth, who in spite of his own dismal day cared about the feelings of a young fan, and a small boy, who cared about the feelings of another human being.

No matter how you perform on the playing field of life, the Lord has a hug waiting for you. He is your number one fan.

We are never defeated unless we give up on God.

DO I CARE ABOUT THE FEELINGS OF OTHERS EVEN WHEN MY DAY ISN'T GOING WELL?

Sweet Toil

*He also that is slothful in his work is
brother to him that is a great waster.*

PROVERBS 18:9

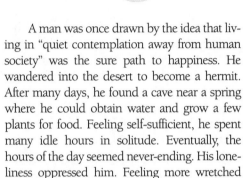

My
ATTITUDE
TOWARD
WORK THESE
DAYS CAN
BEST BE
CHARACTER-
IZED AS . . .

A man was once drawn by the idea that living in "quiet contemplation away from human society" was the sure path to happiness. He wandered into the desert to become a hermit. After many days, he found a cave near a spring where he could obtain water and grow a few plants for food. Feeling self-sufficient, he spent many idle hours in solitude. Eventually, the hours of the day seemed never-ending. His loneliness oppressed him. Feeling more wretched than holy, he cried, "Father God, let me die. I am weary of this life." Exhausted, he fell asleep and dreamed that an angel stood before him, saying, "Cut down the palm tree that grows near the spring and turn its fibers into a rope."

The hermit awoke and with great effort and many hours of toil, he felled the palm and made a coil of rope from its fibers. Again the angel appeared to him, saying, "I've seen you smiling every day as you worked. I can tell you are no longer weary of life. Go back into the world with your rope and find employment with it. Let it remind you toil is sweet."

Work not only benefits the mind and wallet, but the body, emotions, and soul. Work keeps all parts of the human machine in order. Just as machines rust out faster than they wear out, so, too, with people.

---

*One thing you can learn by watching
the clock is that it passes time by
keeping its hands busy.*

Holding On

*Love never fails [never fades out or
becomes obsolete or comes to an end].*

1 CORINTHIANS 13:8 AMP

A family sailing trip almost turned into tragedy when gale-force winds and towering waves threatened to swamp their vessel. Their frantic call to the coast guard brought two ships to their rescue. Unfortunately, the first ship had only a rope ladder, too dangerous to be used in such rough seas. Then the nine-hundred-foot tanker, the *James N. Sullivan,* arrived. It shielded the sailboat until, after several hours of maneuvering, a set of stairs could be lowered from the side of the tanker to the sailboat.

Using a tethered safety line, Bob and Sherry made it to the tanker in good order, as did their two young children. Then it was Grandmother Laurie's turn. Grandfather Dave passed her tether to Bob, but her harness got caught when she stepped across to the stairs. As the boats pulled apart, Laurie fell into the sea. With a surge of the waves, the boats came crashing back together. Dave was afraid to look—his beloved wife of thirty-three years could not swim, and even worse, he feared she might have been crushed as the boats collided. Nevertheless, he clung to the tether, refusing to let go. Laurie later explained, "That's the only reason I'm here."

No matter how troubled the seas of life may become, hold on to the tether with your love. A life can be saved when you trust God for the impossible!

---

*There is no greater love than the love
that holds on where there seems
nothing left to hold on to.*

Right NOW, I
NEED TO
CLING
TIGHTLY TO
THE TETHER
OF GOD
THAT'S
KEEPING ME
FROM . . .

Too High to See

I say, through the grace given unto me, to every man that is among you, not to think of himself more highly than he ought to think; but to think soberly, according as God hath dealt to every man the measure of faith.

ROMANS 12:3

I NEED TO BE
PATIENT AND
WAIT ON
GOD'S
TIMING
BEFORE I
CAN . . .

A little Swiss watch had been made with the smallest of parts and greatest of skill. It ran with precision, to the great delight of its owner. Still, the watch was dissatisfied with its restricted sphere of influence on the lady's wrist. It envied the high and lofty position of the great clock on the tower of City Hall.

One day as the little watch and its owner passed City Hall, the tiny watch exclaimed, "I sure wish I could be way up there! I could serve many people instead of just one." The watch's owner looked down and said, "I know someone who has a key to the tower. Little watch, you shall have your opportunity!"

The next day, a slender thread was let down from the tower and the little watch was tied to it. The watch was pulled up the side of the tower—higher and higher it rose! Of course, when it reached the top, it could not be seen. "Oh my," said the watch. "My elevation has resulted in my annihilation!"

If you desire to trade your current small sphere of influence for a larger one—be patient. Let the Lord elevate you in His timing.

---

*The hardest secret for a man
to keep is his opinion of himself.*

Rescue Me!

Fixing our eyes on Jesus, the author and perfecter of faith, who for the joy set before Him endured the cross, despising the shame, and has sat down at the right hand of the throne of God.

HEBREWS 12:2 NASB

Can the Lord speak through a pop song? Fontella Bass thinks so. During 1990, she was at the lowest point in her life. It had been twenty-five years since her rhythm-and-blues single had hit number one on the charts. She had no career to speak of, and she was broke, tired, and cold. The only heat in her tiny house came from a gas stove in the kitchen. She had also strayed far from the church where she had started singing gospel songs as a child.

Fontella says, "I said a long prayer. I said, 'I need to see a sign to continue on.'" No sooner had she prayed than she heard her hit song, "Rescue Me," on a television commercial! To her, it was as if "the Lord had stepped right into my world!"

Fontella was unaware that American Express had been using her song as part of a commercial. Officials had been unable to locate her to pay her royalties. Not only did she receive back royalties, but also new opportunities for her to sing began to open.

She released a new album entitled "No Ways Tired," but the best news is that she renewed her relationship with God. "For so many years I tried doing it on my own, and it didn't work," she says. "Then I took it out of my hands and turned it over to Him, and now everything's happening."

When we cry out to God because we've realized the futility of our own efforts, He comes through with blessings far greater than we could have ever imagined on our own.

One TIME WHEN GOD CAME THROUGH FOR ME WITH BLESSINGS FAR GREATER THAN I COULD IMAGINE WAS WHEN . . .

Sorrow looks back. Worry looks around. Faith looks up.

Unseen Player

The fool hath said in his heart,
There is no God.

PSALM 14:1

In WHAT
AREAS OF MY
LIFE DO I
FAIL TO
RECOGNIZE
THE HAND
OF GOD?

The story is told of a colony of mice who made their home at the bottom of a large upright piano. To them, music was frequent, even routine. It filled up all the dark spaces with lovely melodies and pleasant harmonies.

At first, the mice were impressed by the music. They drew comfort from the thought that Someone made the music—though invisible to them, yet close to them. They loved to tell stories about the Great Unseen Player whom they could not see.

Then one day, an adventuresome mouse climbed up part of the way in the piano and returned with an elaborate explanation about how the music was made. Wires were the secret—tightly stretched wires of various lengths that vibrated and trembled from time to time. A second mouse ventured forth and returned telling of hammers—many hammers dancing and leaping on the wires. The mice decided they must revise their old opinions. The theory they developed was complicated, but backed up by evidence. In the end, the mice concluded that they lived in a purely mechanical and mathematical world. The story of the Unseen Player was relegated to mere myth.

But the Unseen Player continued to play nonetheless.

———

Now there's even a "dial-a-prayer"
for atheists. You call a number
and nobody answers.

A Greater Gift

*He did that which was right
in the sight of the LORD. . . .
as Joash his father did.*

2 KINGS 14:3

While a grown man was awaiting surgery in a hospital, he began talking with his father. "I sure hope I can be home by Father's Day," he said. The two recalled various Father's Day celebrations they had shared through the years, and then the son said wistfully, "I still feel awful that when I was ten years old, I didn't give you either a card or a gift."

The father replied, "Son, I remember the Saturday before that Father's Day. I saw you in a store, but you didn't see me. I watched as you picked up several cigars and stuffed them in your pocket. I knew you had no money and I suspected you were about to steal those cigars as a present for me. I felt extremely sad to think you would leave the store without paying for them. But almost as soon as you tucked the cigars in your pocket, you pulled them out and put them back in the box on the shelf.

"When you stayed outside playing all the next day because you had no present to give me, you probably thought I was hurt. You were wrong. When you put those cigars back and decided not to break the law, you gave me the best Father's Day present I ever received."

The greatest honor a parent can receive is children who serve the Lord.

———❦———

*What was silent in the father speaks in
the son, and often I have found in the
son the unveiled secret of the father.*

How CAN
I HONOR
MY PARENTS
TODAY—EVEN
IF THEY'RE
NO LONGER
ALIVE?

Hold Your Tongue

Death and life are in the power of the tongue: and they that love it shall eat the fruit thereof.

PROVERBS 18:21

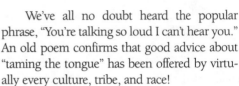

This DAY, I
WILL USE
MY TONGUE
TO BLESS
OTHERS
BY . . .

A father's words are like a thermostat that sets the temperature in the house.

We've all no doubt heard the popular phrase, "You're talking so loud I can't hear you." An old poem confirms that good advice about "taming the tongue" has been offered by virtually every culture, tribe, and race!

> "The boneless tongue,
>   so small and weak,
> Can crush and kill,"
>   declares the Greek.
> "The tongue destroys
>   a greater horde,"
> The Turk asserts,
>   "than does the sword."
> The Persian proverb wisely saith,
> "A lengthy tongue—
>   an early death!"
> Or sometimes
>   takes this form instead,
> "Don't let your tongue
>   cut off your head."
> "The tongue can speak
>   a word whose speed,"
> Say the Chinese,
>   "outstrips the steed."
> The Arab sages said in part,
> "The tongue's great storehouse
>   is the heart."
> From Hebrew
>   was the maxim sprung,
> "Thy feet should slip,
>   but ne'er the tongue."
> The sacred writer
>   crowns the whole,
> "Who keeps the tongue
>   doth keep his soul."

Tools to Make Friends

A man that hath friends
must shew himself friendly.

PROVERBS 18:24

A young family in the 1950s had just purchased their first television set. All the neighbors gathered to help them put up the antenna on the roof of their home. Since they had only the simplest of tools, they weren't making much progress.

Then a new neighbor and his wife showed up with a large toolbox filled with just about any gadget or tool one could imagine. They had everything needed to install the antenna, which was up in near record time after their arrival.

The group of volunteers immediately went inside to see what kind of reception their neighbors would get on their new television set. The picture was crystal clear! Success was theirs!

As the neighbors stood around congratulating each other on their fine work, they thanked their new neighbors for their valuable assistance. One of the women asked, "What is it that you make with such a well-equipped toolbox?"

The new neighbors smiled sincerely and replied, "Friends."

❦

The only way to have a friend is to be one.

What TOOLS
DO I HAVE
THAT COULD
HELP TURN
MY NEIGHBORS
INTO
FRIENDS?

Doing as You Are Told

Truly, truly, I say to you, he who believes in Me, the works that I do, he will do also; and greater works than these will he do; because I go to the Father.

JOHN 14:12 NASB

Although _____
I MAY NOT
KNOW GOD'S
ULTIMATE
PLAN FOR ME,
HIS PURPOSE
FOR MY LIFE
HERE AND
NOW IS...

Gladys Aylward saw herself as a simple woman who just did what God called her to do. Yet, her life was so remarkable that both a book (*The Small Woman*) and a movie (*The Inn of Sixth Happiness*) were produced about the great things God accomplished through her.

A British citizen, Aylward left her home in 1920 and sailed for China. There she bought orphans who were being systematically discarded, children who had been displaced by the political upheavals of the time and left to starve or wander on their own until placed in government warehouses. Gladys gave these children a home.

When the Japanese invaded China, she was forced to flee the mainland with a hundred children. She and her charges ended up on the island of Formosa. There she continued to devote her life to raising children who knew no other mother.

Gladys explains her amazing work for God like this: "I did not choose this. I was led into it by God. I am not really more interested in children than I am in other people, but God through His Holy Spirit gave me to understand that this is what He wanted me to do, so I did."

God has a purpose for your life. Simply follow His leading and you can accomplish it. Big or small, if it is God's plan, it will be great.

Expect great things from God.
Attempt great things for God.

Life-saving Dependency

He hath said, I will never
leave thee, nor forsake thee.
HEBREWS 13:5

The end of our human abilities is our opportunity to turn to God. But giving up our independence to depend on God isn't necessarily easy. We are often like the woman in this story reported in the *Los Angeles Times*:

> A screaming woman, trapped in a car dangling from a freeway transition road in East Los Angeles, was rescued one Saturday morning. A half-dozen passing motorists stopped, grabbed some rope from one of their vehicles, tied it to the back of the woman's car, and hung on until the fire-department rescue units arrived. A ladder was extended from below to help stabilize the car while firefighters tied the vehicle to tow trucks with cables and chains.
>
> "Every time we would move the car," said one rescuer, "she'd yell and scream. She was in pain."
>
> It took almost two-and-a-half hours for the passersby, CHP officers, tow truck drivers, and firefighters—about twenty-five people in all—to secure the car and pull the woman to safety.
>
> "It was kinda funny," L.A. County Fire Captain Ross Marshall recalled later. "She kept saying, 'I'll do it myself.'"

We may laugh at this story, but how many times have we done the same thing ourselves? God is right there, keeping us from plunging over the edge, and all the while we're saying, "I can do it myself!" Fortunately, just like the rescue workers, God helps us in spite of ourselves.

I ADMIT THAT I CAN'T DO IT MYSELF WHEN IT COMES TO . . .

_____
_____
_____
_____
_____
_____
_____
_____
_____
_____
_____
_____
_____
_____
_____

When I come to the end of my rope,
God is there to take over.

Whom Can You Trust?

*A false witness shall not be
unpunished, and he that
speaketh lies shall not escape.*

PROVERBS 19:5

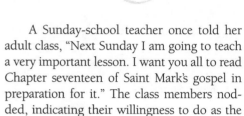

The LAST
TIME I
STRUGGLED
WITH
TELLING THE
TRUTH WAS
WHEN . . .

A Sunday-school teacher once told her adult class, "Next Sunday I am going to teach a very important lesson. I want you all to read Chapter seventeen of Saint Mark's gospel in preparation for it." The class members nodded, indicating their willingness to do as the teacher requested.

The following Sunday the teacher asked the class, "Those who read Chapter seventeen of Saint Mark's gospel during this past week, please raise your hands." Nearly all the people in the room raised their hands.

The teacher then said, "That's very interesting. The gospel of Mark has only sixteen chapters. But at least I know that my lesson is going to hit its mark. Today I'm going to teach what Jesus had to say about lying."

Perhaps the greatest punishment for lying is not that a person gets caught in the lie, but rather the "hidden" punishment that a liar can never truly believe what anyone else says.

Tell the truth! You'll suffer far less embarrassment and be much healthier emotionally. Even if complete honesty brings temporary pain, God will honor your courage and bless you for doing the right thing.

———⌘———

*The trouble with stretching the truth
is that it's apt to snap back.*

Godly Vision

Where there is no vision,
the people perish.

PROVERBS 29:18

One of the great disasters of history took place in 1271. In that year, Niccolo and Matteo Polo, the father and uncle of Marco Polo, visited the Kubla Khan, who was considered the world ruler—with authority over China, India, and the entire East.

The Kubla Khan was attracted to the story of Christianity as Niccolo and Matteo told it to him. He said to them, "You shall go to your high priest and tell him on my behalf to send me a hundred men skilled in your religion and I shall be baptized, and when I am baptized all my barons and great men will be baptized and their subjects will receive baptism, too, and so there will be more Christians here than there are in your parts."

Unfortunately, nothing was done in response to what the Kubla Khan had requested. More than thirty years later, a handful of missionaries were finally sent—too few, too late!

The West apparently did not have the vision to see the East won to Christ. The mind boggles at the possible ways the world might be different today if thirteenth-century China, India, and the other areas of the Orient had become Christian!

If you lack vision today, ask God for it. He has wonders to reveal to you that you can't yet imagine!

How CAN I PASS ON TO OTHERS THE VISION GOD HAS GIVEN ME?

Vision is the world's most desperate need.
There are no hopeless situations,
only people who think hopelessly.

Share the Warmth

Look not every man on his own things,
but every man also on
the things of others.

PHILIPPIANS 2:4

I CAN
PROVIDE
LIFE-GIVING
WARMTH TO
ANOTHER
PERSON
TODAY BY...

Sadhu Sundar Singh and a companion were traveling through a pass high in the Himalayan Mountains when they came across a body lying in the snow. They checked for vital signs and discovered the man was still alive, but barely. Sundar Singh prepared to stop and help this unfortunate traveler, but his companion objected, saying, "We shall lose our lives if we burden ourselves with him." Sundar Singh, however, could not think of leaving the man to die in the snow without even attempting to rescue him. His companion quickly bade him farewell and went on.

Sundar Singh lifted the poor traveler onto his back. With great physical exertion, made even greater by the high altitude and snowy conditions, he carried the man onward. As he walked, the heat cast off by his body began to warm the frozen man. He eventually revived, and soon they were walking side by side, each holding the other up, and in turn, each giving body heat to the other. Before long they came upon yet another traveler lying in the snow. Upon closer inspection, they discovered him to be dead, frozen by the cold. He was Sundar Singh's original traveling companion.

Don't forget that when you reach out to help others, your own problems are soon forgotten.

The best way to forget your own problems
is to help someone solve his.

A Change of Heart

If ye bite and devour one another,
take heed that ye be not
consumed one of another.

GALATIANS 5:15

After two years in the Navy, Willard Scott returned to his old job with NBC radio, but to a new supervisor. Willard found himself at odds with his new boss at every turn, and he was furious when his boss rescheduled *Joy Boys,* a comedy show he did with Eddie Walker, for the worst slot on radio—eight to midnight. Willard was braced for a "change-or-I'll-leave" confrontation when he recalled Proverbs 19:11: "The discretion of a man deferreth his anger; and it is his glory to pass over a transgression." He and Eddie decided to work themselves to the bone, and within three years they made *Joy Boys* the top-rated show in Washington—in spite of the poor time slot.

Willard says, "I learned that I, too, had been wrong. In all my dealings with my boss, I had aggravated the problem. I knew he didn't like me, and in response I was barely civil to him and dodged him as much as I could. But one day he invited me to a station party I couldn't avoid. There I met his fiancée. She was bright, alive, and down-to-earth. How could a woman like that care for anybody who didn't have something to recommend him? . . . I was able to get new insight into my boss' character. As time went on my attitude changed, and so did his." Willard and his boss became friends, and he remained at NBC.

The most effective way to deal with an enemy is to take what he throws at you and use it for your benefit. Your grateful attitude will eventually turn your enemy into a friend.

In WHAT PRACTICAL WAYS CAN I SHOW GRATITUDE TO THE PERSON I CONSIDER MY GREATEST ENEMY?

Hating people is like burning down
your own house to get rid of a rat.

The World's Way or God's Way

*Peter and the other apostles answered
and said, We ought to obey
God rather than men.*

ACTS 5:29

IS THERE
ANYTHING IN
MY LIFE THAT
CAUSES ME
TO THINK OF
THE BIBLE
LESS AND
LESS EACH
DAY?

Jenny Lind was known as "The Swedish Nightingale" during her successful career as an operatic singer. She became one of the wealthiest artists of her time, yet she left the stage at her peak and never returned.

Countless people speculated as to the reason for her leaving, and most people wondered how she could give up so much applause, fame, and money. However, she was content to live in privacy in a home by the sea.

One day a friend found her on the beach, her Bible on her knees, looking out into the glorious glow of a sunset. As they talked, the friend asked, "Madame, how is it that you ever came to abandon the stage at the height of your success?"

She answered quietly, "When every day it made me think less of this (laying a finger on her Bible) and nothing at all of that (pointing to the sunset), what else could I do?"

The world may never understand your decision to follow God. But then, perhaps God cannot understand a decision to pursue what the world offers when He has such great rewards in store for those who follow Him.

———

*Here [in the Bible] is
knowledge enough for me. . . .
Here then I am far
from the busy ways of men.
I sit down alone. Only God is here.
In His presence, I open, I read His Book.*

Contented Regardless

I will remember the works of the LORD: surely I
will remember thy wonders of old. I will meditate
also of all thy work, and talk of thy doings.

PSALM 77:11-12

For decades, Grandpa had been stubborn and crabby. His wife, children, and grandchildren seemed unable to do anything that pleased him. As far as he was concerned, life was filled with nothing but bad times and big troubles. Eventually, his family expected nothing but a gruff growl from Grandpa.

Then overnight, Grandpa changed. Gentleness and optimism marked his new personality. Positive words and compliments poured from his lips. He could even be heard giving joyful praise to the Lord. One of the family members noted, "I think maybe Grandpa found religion." Another replied, "Maybe so, but maybe it's something else. I'm going to ask him what has happened." The young man went to his grandfather and said, "Gramps, what has caused you to change so suddenly?"

"Well, son," the old man replied, "I've been striving in the face of incredible problems all my life—and for what? The hope of a contented mind. It's done no good, nope, not one bit, so . . . I've decided to be content without it."

Never count your troubles until you've counted a hundred of your blessings. By that time you will have long forgotten what your troubles even were!

Sometimes we are so busy adding up
our troubles that we forget
to count our blessings.

My GREATEST BLESSINGS ARE:

Teaching Our Children

Train up a child in the way he should go: and when he is old, he will not depart from it.

PROVERBS 22:6

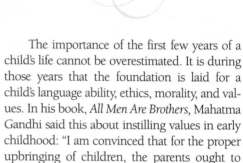

I NEED THE GRACE TO MODEL A GODLY LIFE BEFORE THE LITTLE ONES IN MY SPHERE OF INFLUENCE, INCLUDING...

The importance of the first few years of a child's life cannot be overestimated. It is during those years that the foundation is laid for a child's language ability, ethics, morality, and values. In his book, *All Men Are Brothers,* Mahatma Gandhi said this about instilling values in early childhood: "I am convinced that for the proper upbringing of children, the parents ought to have a general knowledge of the care and nursing of babies. . . . We labour under a sort of superstition that the child has nothing to learn during the first five years of its life. On the contrary, the fact is that the child never learns in after life what it does in its first five years. The education of the child begins with conception."

The famous psychoanalyst Sigmund Freud agreed. A Viennese woman once asked him, "How early should I begin the education of my child?"

Freud replied with a question of his own, "When will your child be born?"

"Born?" the woman asked. "Why, he is already five years old!"

"My goodness, woman," Freud cried, "don't stand there talking to me—hurry home! You have already wasted the five best years!"

The cure of crime is not in the electric chair, but in the high chair.

True Christian Living

Don't work hard only when your
master is watching and then shirk when
he isn't looking; work hard and with gladness
all the time, as though working for Christ,
doing the will of God with all your hearts.

EPHESIANS 6:6-7 TLB

In an extensive opinion survey, *The Day America Told the Truth,* James Patterson and Peter Kim reported some startling findings:

- Only 13 percent saw all Ten Commandments as binding and relevant.

- Ninety-one percent lied regularly, both at work and home.

- Most workers admitted to goofing off an average of seven hours a week.

- About half of the workforce admitted they regularly called in sick, even when they were well.

When they were asked what they would be willing to do for $10 million, 25 percent said they would abandon their families, 23 percent would be prostitutes for a week, and 7 percent would murder a stranger!

Lest you conclude that those surveyed were all ungodly criminals, two other surveyors, Doug Sherman and William Hendricks, found that Christians were almost as likely as unbelievers to do such things as steal from the workplace, falsify their income tax returns, and selectively obey certain laws.

To truly claim to be a Christian, a person must do far more than go to church occasionally. Practice being Christ-like 24 hours a day, 365 days a year, in all situations and in all circumstances!

During THE LAST 24 HOURS, I EXHIBITED CHRIST-LIKE BEHAVIOR WHEN I . . .

_____

_____

_____

_____

_____

_____

_____

_____

_____

_____

_____

_____

_____

_____

Merely going to church doesn't make you
a Christian any more than going to
a garage makes you an automobile.

Self-Serve

Yet a little sleep, a little slumber, a little
folding of the hands to sleep: so shall thy
poverty come as one that travelleth;
and thy want as an armed man.

PROVERBS 24:33-34

The THING I
NEED TO GET
UP AND GET
FOR MYSELF
IN LIFE
IS . . .

One day a grandfather told his grandchildren about his journey to America. He told of the trains and ship that he took from his home in Eastern Europe. He told of being processed at Ellis Island and how he had gone to a cafeteria in lower Manhattan to get something to eat. There he sat down at an empty table and waited quite some time for someone to take his order. Nobody came. Finally, a woman with a tray full of food sat down opposite him and explained to him how a cafeteria works.

She said, "You start at that end"—pointing toward a stack of trays—"and then go along the food line and pick out what you want. At the other end, they'll tell you how much you have to pay."

The grandfather reflected a moment and then said, "I soon learned that's how everything works in America. Life's a cafeteria here. You can get anything you want—even very great success—if you are willing to pay the price. But you'll never get what you want if you wait for someone to bring it to you. You have to get up and get it yourself."

The difference between where you are and where you want to be can often be summed up in one word—work.

Laziness and poverty are cousins.

Made for Success

The Lord GOD will help me; therefore shall I not be confounded: therefore have I set my face like a flint, and I know that I shall not be ashamed.

ISAIAH 50:7

Famous stage and film actress Helen Hayes believed her resolve about her own potential for success played an important role at the beginning of her career. She once said,

> Before the authors gave me the script, they observed, in a matter-of-course manner, "Of course you play piano? You'll have to sing to your own accompaniment in the piece." As these alarming tidings were in the course of being made, I caught a bewildered look in my mother's eyes, and so I spoke up before she could. "Certainly I play piano," I answered.
>
> As we left the theater, my mother sighed, "I hate to see you start under a handicap," she said. "What made you say you could play piano?" "The feeling that I will play before rehearsals begin," I said. We went at once to try to rent a piano . . . and ended by buying one. I began lessons at once, practiced finger-exercises till I could no longer see the notes—and began rehearsals with the ability to accompany myself. Since then, I have never lived too far from a piano.

What you believe about your own potential for success counts far more than what any other person may believe. Believe what God believes about you—you were created for success.

I BELIEVE THAT GOD HAS CREATED ME FOR SUCCESS IN THE AREA OF . . .

Always bear in mind that your own resolution to succeed is more important than any other one thing.

Spite at the Center

Let no corrupt communication proceed out of your mouth, but that which is good to the use of edifying, that it may minister grace unto the hearers.

EPHESIANS 4:29

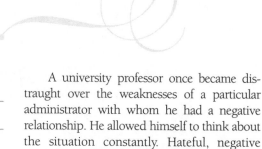

What THINGS IN MY LIFE GIVE ME JOY?

A university professor once became distraught over the weaknesses of a particular administrator with whom he had a negative relationship. He allowed himself to think about the situation constantly. Hateful, negative thoughts so preoccupied him that it affected the quality of his relationships with his family, his church, and his colleagues. He finally concluded that he needed to leave and accept a teaching appointment elsewhere.

A friend asked him, "Wouldn't you really prefer to teach at this university if the man were not here?" "Of course," the professor responded, "but as long as he is here, then my staying is too disruptive to everything in life. I have to go."

The friend then asked, "Why have you made this administrator the center of your life?" As much as the professor tried to deny the truth of this, he finally had to admit that he had allowed one individual and his weaknesses to distort his entire view of life. Still, it was not the administrator's doing. It was his own problem. From that day forward he focused on his students and his teaching, and he found new joy in his old job.

When you concentrate on running down others, usually the only one that gets run down is you.

⎯⎯ ⧉ ⎯⎯

Two things are hard on the heart—running upstairs and running down people.

What's Right, Not What's Popular

If you do not stand firm in your faith,
you will not stand at all.

ISAIAH 7:9 NIV

Former President Harry S Truman once remarked that no American president has ever escaped abuse and even libel from the press. He noted that it was quite common to find a president publicly called a traitor. Truman further concluded that the president who had not fought with Congress or the Supreme Court hadn't done his job.

What is true for the president of the United States is also true for everyone else. No matter how small a person's job may be—no matter how low he may be on a particular organizational chart or in the strata of society—there will be those who oppose him, ridicule him, and perhaps even challenge him to a fight. That is why no person can expect to accomplish anything while conducting himself as if he were trying to win a popularity contest. Rather, a person needs to chart the course he feels compelled to walk in life and then to do so with head held high and convictions intact. Recognizing that every person will eventually face the test of ridicule and criticism as he upholds his principles or defends his morals is simply a matter of taking life in stride.

Being hit isn't abnormal, but collapsing from fear of a hit isn't inevitable. Stand firm in your faith and convictions—and the Lord will stand with you!

———

If you don't stand for something,
you'll fall for anything.

Have I BEEN RUNNING IN A POPULARITY CONTEST—OR LIVING MY LIFE FOR MY HEAVENLY FATHER?

Leave It with God

Devote yourselves to prayer,
keeping alert in it with an
attitude of thanksgiving.

COLOSSIANS 4:2 NASB

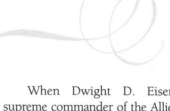

I KNOW
I CAN
TRUST GOD
WITH ANY
PROBLEM, BIG
OR SMALL,
EVEN THE
PROBLEM
OF . . .

When Dwight D. Eisenhower was supreme commander of the Allied invasion of Europe during World War II, he was faced with the responsibility of making one of the most far-reaching decisions ever posed to a single man: the decision to change the date of D-Day at the last moment. The consequences of a wrong decision were so overwhelming, in his opinion, that he felt crushed by the weight of the decision before him. Still, he was the supreme commander and the only man who could make the decision that would impact millions of lives. He later wrote: "I knew I did not have the required wisdom. But I turned to God. I asked God to give me the wisdom. I yielded myself to Him. I surrendered myself. And He gave me clear guidance. He gave me insight to see what was right, and He endowed me with courage to make my decision. And finally He gave me peace of mind in the knowledge that, having been guided by God to the decision, I could leave the results to Him."

Few decisions you face in life will ever approach the magnitude of the decision General Eisenhower faced. But whatever size problem you go up against, God wants you to trust Him enough to leave your problem in His hands.

The best advice my mother ever gave
me—don't forget to say your prayers.

First and Best

Whatsoever ye do, do it heartily,
as to the Lord, and not unto men.

COLOSSIANS 3:23

Thomas Edison, who held 1,093 patents for his inventions (which included the electric light bulb, the phonograph, and the motion-picture camera) sold the rights to many of his inventions to Western Union and other large companies to keep his workshop going. Over time others made far more money from his inventions than he did, but this didn't seem to bother him a great deal. He once said, "I don't care so much about making my fortune as I do for getting ahead of the other fellow." Edison's greatest desire was to be both the first and the best in his field, to out-invent everybody he could. He worked tirelessly, but joyfully.

Edison eventually established Menlo Park, the world's first invention factory. It was a forerunner of the private research laboratories now maintained by many large companies. At Menlo Park, Edison promised to turn out "a minor invention every ten days and a big thing every six months or so." At one point, he was working on forty-seven new ideas at once.

Other inventors may have been richer than Edison, but virtually no inventor has ever been more enthusiastic or more successful. For him, enthusiasm and employment were inextricably bound together! Find joy in your work and know that promotion comes from God.

HOW CAN I BIND MY ENTHUSIASM AND EMPLOYMENT TOGETHER— AND LEAVE THE RESULTS TO GOD?

There is a name for people who are not excited about their work—unemployed.

The Best Pursuit

The just man walketh in his integrity:
his children are blessed after him.

PROVERBS 20:7

Regardless
OF THE
PERSONAL
COST—OR
HOW FOOLISH
I MAY LOOK
TO OTHERS—I
INTEND TO
PURSUE...

In 1947, Dr. Chandrasekhar was asked to teach an advanced seminar in astrophysics at the University of Chicago. At the time he was living in Wisconsin, doing research at the Yerkes Astronomical Observatory. He faced a one-hundred-mile commute twice a week in the dead of winter to teach the class, but he nonetheless agreed enthusiastically.

However, registration for the advanced seminar was far below expectations. In fact, only two students signed up for the class. Other faculty members expected Dr. Chandrasekhar to cancel the course so as not to waste his valuable time. But he was determined to continue with the course and give his best to the two students registered.

Those students, Chen Ning Yang and Tsung-Dao Lee, made his efforts worthwhile. Ten years later, in 1957, they both won the Nobel prize for physics. In 1983, Dr. Chandrasekhar won that same award.

Ends and means are not meant to exist in conflict. God challenges us to pursue integrity and excellence, regardless of the personal cost, the effort required, or the lack of resulting public acclaim.

———✦———

The end must justify the means.

Made Whole

If we are faithless, he will remain
faithful, for he cannot disown himself.

2 TIMOTHY 2:13 NIV

When Cathy met Jim at a softball game, she thought he was the man for her—everything she was looking for! After several months of dating, Cathy was as sold on Jim as ever, except it bothered her that he found so many excuses for drinking alcohol. "I got a raise!" "My friend is getting married!" "My sister is graduating from college!"

Despite her friends' warnings and her own misgivings, Cathy married Jim. Before long, the marriage was destroyed by Jim's drinking. When the divorce was final, Cathy felt destroyed, too. By ignoring the Holy Spirit's warning and her friends' wise counsel, she had made one of the biggest mistakes a Christian can make. "I wanted to have my way instead of God's," Cathy told her pastor. "I thought I knew what was best for me."

"We all think that sometimes," Cathy's pastor said. "We forget that the One who created us knows us better than we know ourselves. But remember, Cathy, He never gives up on us! When we admit our mistakes, He always forgives us and gives us another chance."

Recovering from the bad choices we've made can be heart wrenching and difficult, but God is always right there, ready to make us whole and give us a brand-new start.

Decisions can take you out of God's will
but never out of His reach.

I NEED A BRAND-NEW START AS I RECOVER FROM THE CHOICE I MADE REGARDING . . .

Places for Love

*Be kind to one another, tenderhearted,
forgiving one another, just as God
in Christ forgave you.*

EPHESIANS 4:32 NKJV

Today I
CAN SHOW
UNCONDI-
TIONAL
LOVE AND
FORGIVENESS
TO...

_____

_____

_____

_____

_____

_____

_____

_____

_____

_____

_____

After he had been in the ministry for several years, a pastor was preparing a special sermon on the subject of love. When he went to his file cabinet to pull out the file of love material he had collected through the years, he was shocked to find that he didn't have such a file!

Thinking this to be impossible, since he knew he had collected many anecdotes and quotes about love, he began searching through the cabinet folder by folder. He fully expected to find the love folder stuck inside another folder. He searched among the folders on faith and fasting, healing and Heaven, even Christology and Christian education. But he still couldn't find one on love.

As he sat and pondered the situation, he began to think back over the sermons he had preached. He quickly realized that he had used bits and pieces of love material in preparing dozens of other sermons. He went back to the cabinet at once, and sure enough, he found parts of the love file in the folders labeled patience, kindness, humility, trust, hope, loyalty, and perseverance. The greatest amount of material on love, however, was found in his file labeled forgiveness.

The love of God touches every aspect of our lives but is in greatest operation when we forgive someone who has wronged us. God's love is unconditional. When we walk in His love, we forgive unconditionally and thereby spread His love to others.

*A happy marriage is the union
of two good forgivers.*

The Discernment of Children

Death and life are in the power
of the tongue: and they that love
it shall eat the fruit thereof.

PROVERBS 18:21

A man once told this poignant story about his own conversion experience:

My father was the senior elder in our church for many years. When I was a boy, eleven years of age, an evangelist held a series of meetings in our church. One night he asked every Christian to come forward and also asked those who desired to confess Christ to come with them. My father, of course, went up, and, as I felt the call of God, I followed after him.

Just as he reached the front he turned around, and seeing me, said, "Johnnie, you go back; you are too young." I obeyed him, as I had been taught to do, and at thirty-three I came again, but I did not know what I was coming for as clearly at thirty-three as I did at eleven.

The church lost twenty-two years of service, while I lost twenty-two years of growth because my own father, an officer in the church, had said, "Go back."

If you err at all, err on the side of your children knowing God, of their being old enough to experience God and mature enough to respond to His offer of love and forgiveness. God's offer of salvation is for all—young and old.

Have I HAMPERED ANYONE IN COMING TO KNOW THE LORD, EVEN MY OWN CHILDREN?

❦

We can either grace our children
or damn them with unrequited wounds
which never seem to heal . . . men,
as fathers you have such power!

Feud and Forgiveness

The just man walketh in his integrity:
his children are blessed after him.

PROVERBS 20:7

To WHICH
ENEMY DO I
NEED TO
EXTEND LOVE
TODAY?

A feud developed between two families who lived side by side in the mountains of Kentucky. It started when Grandpa Smith's cow jumped a stone fence and ate Grandpa Brown's corn. Brown shot the cow. A Smith boy then shot two Brown boys. In retaliation, the Browns shot one Smith. Bill Brown planned to kill a second Smith, but before he could, he was called away to war. While he was away, Bill's mother had a hard time making ends meet, since Bill's father had been one of the victims.

At Christmas, the head of the Smith clan took his family to church. Usually he stayed outside, but this year it was so cold he went inside to wait. The sermon was on Christ, the Prince of Peace, who died in our place for our sins. It struck him hard. He realized what a crime he had committed, repented, and then secretly hired a young boy to carry a basket of food to the Brown's home every day until Bill returned.

Once home, Bill set out to discover who had helped his family so generously. He followed the boy to the Smith's house where Smith met him and said, "Shoot me, Bill, if you want to. But Christ has already died for my sins and forgiven me, and I hope you'll forgive me, too." Bill did, and neighbors truly became neighbors again.

The Bible tells us to love our enemies. When we truly begin to practice God's love toward our enemies, God's love transforms them into our friends.

This world belongs to the man
who is wise enough to change
his mind in the presence of facts.

A Shadow of Truth

*Test everything that is said to be sure
it is true, and if it is, then accept it.*

1 THESSALONIANS 5:21 TLB

A group of four-year-olds was gathered in a Sunday-school class one spring. Their teacher asked them, "Does anyone know what today is?"

A little girl held up her hand and said, "It's Palm Sunday." "Wonderful!" exclaimed the teacher. "Now does anyone know what next Sunday is?" No hands went up. Finally, as if a light had just come on, the same little girl shouted, "I do! Next Sunday is Easter."

The teacher responded, "That's fantastic!" Ready to drive her point home, she asked, "Now, does anyone know what makes next Sunday Easter?"

At this the little girl jumped up and said, "Yes! Next Sunday is Easter because Jesus rose from the grave." But before the teacher could congratulate her on yet another correct answer, the little girl continued, "But if He sees His shadow, He has to go back in for seven weeks."

Listen carefully to what others tell you. Weigh everything against the truth of God's Word. Information is different from truth. Information comes in varying degrees of accuracy, whereas truth comes only in a single package labeled "the whole truth and nothing but the truth."

*Fingerprinting children is a good idea.
It will settle the question as to who used
the guest towel in the bathroom.*

What INFORMATION HAVE I BELIEVED RECENTLY THAT I NOW HAVE TO TEST AGAINST THE TRUTH?

Good from A to Z

With God all things are possible.
MATTHEW 19:26

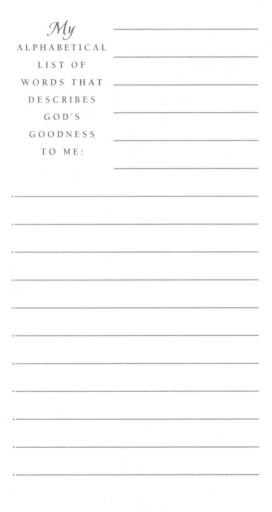

My
ALPHABETICAL
LIST OF
WORDS THAT
DESCRIBES
GOD'S
GOODNESS
TO ME:

Rachel and Jim owned a commercial building, half of which Jim used for his dental practice. For fifteen years, they had encountered no difficulty in renting out the other half. Then they lost their renter. They counted on the extra income to pay their bills. A real estate agent told them, "Forget about advertising for a while. Absolutely no one is renting."

To ease her financial worries, Rachel started swimming laps at her local YMCA pool. One day when she was feeling especially anxious, she decided to pray as she swam, using the alphabet to keep track of the number of laps. She focused on adjectives that described God, starting with the letter A. "You are the Almighty God," she prayed on lap one. "A benevolent God, a beautiful God," she prayed on the next lap, and then, "You are a caring, creative, can-do God." By the time she had completed twenty-six laps, an hour had passed and her fears were gone. She knew God would provide.

A short time later, a physical therapist called to say she had seen the "For Rent" sign in the window and asked to see the office. It was exactly what she wanted. So she and her partner rented the space. Rachel still prays while swimming laps. "After all," she says, "I've discovered God's goodness stretches from A to Z!"

When you take your eyes off of your problems and focus them on God and His incredible attributes, your worries will fade away. Remember that God's goodness stretches from A to Z!

You can accomplish more in one hour with
God than in one lifetime without Him.

The One that Got Away—For Good

*A righteous man who walks in
his integrity—how blessed
are his sons after him.*

PROVERBS 20:7 NASB

The day before bass season opened, Jimmy and his father were fishing early in the evening on a New England lake. After using worms to catch perch and sunfish, Jimmy decided to practice casting with a small, silver lure. No sooner had his lure hit the water than his pole doubled over. Jimmy knew right away that he had something huge on the line. By the time he reeled in the fish, a giant moon had risen over the lake. In the moonlight, Jimmy saw the biggest fish he had ever seen—but it was a bass. Jimmy's dad lit a match to look at his watch. It was 10 P.M., two hours before bass season opened.

"You'll have to put it back, son," he said. Jimmy protested, "There'll never be another fish as big as this one!" He looked and saw no other fishermen or boats. Still, he knew by the tone of his father's voice that there would be no discussion. He carefully worked the hook from the lip of the bass and lowered it back into the water.

Jimmy was right. He now takes his own children to that lake and in the past thirty-four years, he never has seen a bass that big. But he readily admits that any time he faces a question of ethics, he sees that fish again and has to smile! A right decision always lives fresh and sweet in the memory and encourages us to do right again and again.

*The best way to teach character
is to have it around the house.*

One
DIFFICULT
BUT RIGHT
DECISION
THAT ALWAYS
BRINGS A
SMILE TO MY
FACE WAS THE
TIME I...

Raw Determination

*As for you, be strong and
do not give up, for your
work will be rewarded.*

2 CHRONICLES 15:7 NIV

What

MOUNTAIN
MUST I
PERSEVERE IN
TRYING TO
CONQUER?

American sports fans watched in awe on Sunday, March 4, 1979, as Phil Mahre took to the giant-slalom course at Whiteface Mountain, New York. He exploded onto the slope and then settled into a powerful run down the mountainside. At gate thirty-five, tragedy struck. Phil hooked his inside ski on a pole, went flying head over heels, and crashed in a crumpled heap. The ski-team physician described the injury as "the ultimate broken ankle"—a break of both the ankle and lower leg. He put the bones back together with a three-inch metal plate and seven screws.

The question was not whether Phil would ever ski again but if he would walk again. Looking back, Phil describes the months after his injury as a time of deep despair. Still, he never entertained doubts about walking again—or skiing again.

After two months on crutches and a highly disciplined exercise program, he forced himself to walk without limping. In August, he began to ski down gentle slopes. Less than six months after the accident, he entered a race in Australia and finished second. In February 1980, less than a year after his agonizing injury, Phil Mahre took on the same mountain where he had fallen and won an Olympic silver medal.

No matter what you're going through, never give up! Keep working until you conquer your mountain.

*Never despair; but if you do,
work on in despair.*

Marking the Trouble Spots

I would have you learn this great fact: that a life of doing right is the wisest life there is. If you live that kind of life, you'll not limp or stumble as you run.

PROVERBS 4:11-12 TLB

Sara Orne Jewett has written a beautiful novel about Maine called *The Country of the Pointed Firs.* In it, she describes the path that leads a woman writer from her home to that of a retired sea captain named Elijah Tilley. On the way, there are a number of wooden stakes in the ground that appear to be randomly scattered on his property. Each is painted white and trimmed in yellow, just like the captain's house.

Once she arrives at the captain's abode, the writer asks Captain Tilley what the stakes mean. He tells her that when he first made the transition from sailing the seas to plowing the land, he discovered his plow would catch on many of the large rocks just beneath the surface. Recalling how buoys in the sea always marked trouble spots for him, he set out the stakes as "land buoys" to mark the rocks. Then he could avoid plowing over them in the future.

God's commandments are like buoys for us, revealing the trouble spots and rocky points of life. When we follow God's wisdom and steer clear of what is harmful to us, life is not only more enjoyable but also more productive.

———— ✺ ————

Wisdom is the quality that keeps you from getting into situations where you need it.

The TROUBLE SPOTS AND ROCKY POINTS IN MY LIFE ARE . . .

201

It's Impossible to Fail

Even when walking through the dark valley of death I will not be afraid, for you are close beside me, guarding, guiding all the way.
PSALM 23:4 TLB

Today, I AM RELYING ON THE LORD TO REDUCE MY UNSCALABLE MOUNTAINS TO SMALLER TASKS, SUCH AS . . .

On February 11, 1861, President-elect Abraham Lincoln left his home in Springfield, Illinois, to begin his journey to Washington, where he was to be inaugurated a month later. Lincoln had a premonition it would be the last time he would see Springfield. Standing on the rear platform of his railroad car, he bid the townspeople farewell. He closed his remarks with these words: "Today I leave you. I go to assume a task more difficult than that which devolved upon General Washington. The great God which guided him must help me. Without that assistance I shall surely fail; with it, I cannot fail."

The same is true for us. Without God's assistance, we cannot succeed, regardless of the tasks we face. We may get the dishes washed, the laundry folded, and the beds made. We may get our work done without accident or incident. We may find what we need at the market and manage to keep on schedule. But without God's help, our lives would still be a confused mess.

Does God care about what happens in our day? Absolutely! When we become overwhelmed, seeing the smallest tasks as unscalable mountains, He helps us "gather ourselves." Step by step, He shows us the way and renews our strength so we may go on.

I would rather walk with God in the dark than go alone in the light.

Hidden Value

*I heard the voice of the Lord, saying,
Whom shall I send, and who will go for
us? Then said I, Here am I; send me.*

ISAIAH 6:8

One of the items in *Ripley's Believe It or Not*
is a picture of a plain bar of iron. It is valued at
$5. The same bar of iron has a far different value,
however, if it is fashioned into different items.

- As a pair of horse shoes, it would be
  worth $50.

- Made into sewing needles, it would
  be worth $5,000.

- Formed into balance springs for fine
  Swiss watches, it would be worth
  $500,000.

The raw material is not what is important.
What's important is how the raw material is
developed!

Each of us has been given talents and abilities—some have received more, others less,
but all have received unique gifts from God. As
Christians, we also enjoy spiritual gifts that flow
from the Holy Spirit of God.

The value of these raw materials, however,
is debatable unless we develop and use our talents, abilities, and spiritual gifts as a force for
divine good in this world.

If you don't know what your abilities and
gifts are, ask God to reveal them to you. Then
ask Him to show you what He wants you to do
with them and begin doing it. Your happiness
and success in life will be found in fulfilling His
plan for your life.

*God never asks about our ability or
our inability—just our availability.*

The RAW
MATERIALS
GOD HAS
BLESSED ME
WITH CAN BE
FASHIONED
INTO . . .

Walking the Talk

Many a man claims to have unfailing love, but a faithful man who can find?

PROVERBS 20:6 NIV

I NEED TO
PUT MY
MONEY
WHERE MY
MOUTH IS
REGARDING...

Adrian Thomas had seen enough. The third-generation owner of Thomas Drug Store in Meyersdale, Pennsylvania, came to a fateful conclusion one winter day in 1992. He realized he was tired of losing friends to cancer and heart disease. For ninety-six years, his family had sold tobacco products in the front of their store and health products in the back. He just could not do both anymore.

Thomas, his employees, and family members loaded up two thousand dollars worth of cigarettes, cigars, snuff, and pipe-tobacco products into boxes and took them to a parking lot to be burned. To get the fire going, Thomas set a match to his state license to sell tobacco. Then he used the burning document to set aflame the pile of boxes.

As he watched the inventory go up in smoke, Thomas told his family and employees that he could not put dollars and cents above the health of his patrons.

Nearly everybody proclaims with their mouth the importance of doing the right thing—even if it costs them something. Adrian Thomas is one of those who put his money where his mouth was. Are you ready to put your money where your mouth is?

❦

Men are alike in their promises.
It is only in their deeds that they differ.

Working to Reach a Dream

The plans of the diligent lead to profit.

PROVERBS 21:5 NIV

The Sixty-Four-Thousand-Dollar Question was the hottest show on television in 1955. The more Joyce watched the program, the more she thought, *I could do that.* At the time, Joyce had quit her teaching job to raise her daughter, and she and her husband were living on fifty dollars a month. She didn't dream of winning the top prize—at that point, any prize would have helped greatly.

So a psychologist by training, Joyce analyzed the show. She saw that each contestant had a built-in incongruity—the Marine who was a gourmet cook, the shoemaker who was an opera buff. She was a short, blond psychologist and mother with no incongruity. She decided after some thought to become an expert in boxing! She ate, drank, and slept boxing, studying its statistics, personalities, and history. When she felt she was ready, she applied for the show, was accepted, and won and won and won until she finally won the sixty-four thousand dollar prize. The experience led her to dream of a career as a television journalist who might translate the results of psychological research into terms that people could use in their everyday lives. And once she saw that possibility, there was no stopping Dr. Joyce Brothers.

God has placed a vision on the inside of you. Sometimes all it takes to be able to see it is to begin doing something. Doing anything you desire to do, no matter how small or silly it seems (like being on a game show) can unlock that vision in your heart.

What IS THE NEXT STEP I CAN TAKE TOWARD UNLOCKING AND FULFILLING THE VISION GOD HAS GIVEN ME?

_____

Diligence is the mother of good fortune.

From Broken Bits to a Beautiful Whole

My son, give me thine heart.
PROVERBS 23:26

After GOD REASSEMBLES ME, HOW CAN I AVOID BECOMING SO FRAGMENTED AGAIN?

So many things of beauty begin as "bits and pieces"—an artist's collage, a stained-glass window, or a mosaic floor—not unlike our lives, which often seem like jigsaw puzzles containing thousands of scattered pieces.

Tragedy and pain can strike any person. When it does, we need to allow the master craftsman to put us back together according to His design, rather than trying to find all the pieces and glue ourselves together without Him.

In *The Dark Night of the Soul,* Georgia Harkness writes, "The Christian faith imparts meaning to life. A living faith that is centered in God as revealed in Christ takes our chaotic, disorganized selves, with their crude jumble of pleasures and pains, and knits them together into a steadiness and joy that can endure anything with God."

Trust God today to turn your brokenness into something of beauty and value.

God can heal a broken heart,
but He has to have all the pieces.

Brotherly Love

I have shewed you all things, how that so labouring ye ought to support the weak, and to remember the words of the Lord Jesus, how he said, It is more blessed to give than to receive.

ACTS 20:35

Two brothers farmed together. They lived in separate houses on the family farm, but each day they met in the fields to work together. One brother married and had a large family. The other lived alone. Still, they divided the harvest from the fields equally.

One night the single brother thought, *My brother is struggling to support a large family, but I get half of the harvest.* With great love in his heart, he gathered a box of things he had purchased from his earnings—items he knew would help his brother's family. He planned to slip over to his brother's shed, unload the basket there, and never say a word about it.

That same night, the married brother thought, *My brother is alone. He doesn't know the joys of having a family.* Out of love, he decided to take over a basket with a quilt and homemade bread and preserves to warm his brother's house. He planned to leave the items on his brother's porch and never say a word.

As the brothers stealthily made their way to each other's home, they bumped into one another. They were forced to admit what they were doing, and there in the darkness, they cried and embraced, each man realizing that his greatest wealth was a brother who respected and loved him.

One of the greatest joys in life comes from giving to those in need. And we always have something to give: our time, our finances, and our effort. Often the thing we take for granted may be a tremendous blessing to someone else. What do you have in your hand? Give and it will be given to you!

What BLESSING HAVE I TAKEN FOR GRANTED AND TO WHOM CAN I PASS IT ON?

———∽∿∾———

We make a living by what we get— we make a life by what we give.

Early Development

The righteousness of the blameless makes a straight way for them, but the wicked are brought down by their own wickedness.

PROVERBS 11:5 NIV

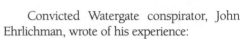

I DON'T WANT MY CHARACTER TO BE DEVELOPED TOO LATE TO DO ANY GOOD; DAILY I INTEND TO CHECK THESE QUALITIES:

Convicted Watergate conspirator, John Ehrlichman, wrote of his experience:

> When I went to jail, nearly two years after the cover-up trial, I had a big self-esteem problem. I was a felon, shorn and scorned, clumping around in a ragged old army uniform, doing pick and shovel work out on the desert. I wondered if anyone thought I was worth anything. . . . For years I had been able to sweep most of my shortcomings and failures under the rug and not face them, but during the two long criminal trials, I spent my days listening to prosecutors tell juries what a bad fellow I was. . . . I'd go back to a hotel room and sit alone thinking about what was happening to me. During that time I began to take stock. . . . I was wiped out. I had nothing left that had been of value to me—honor, credibility, virtue, recognition, profession.

But then he began to see himself and to care deeply about his own integrity, his capacity to love and be loved, and his essential worth. He concluded about the Nixon years, "In a paradoxical way, I'm grateful for them. Somehow I had to see all of that and grow to understand it in order to arrive." Sadly, the inner character Ehrlichman developed came too late to impact his political career.

Keep a daily check on your character. Of all the abilities you may possess, developing good character is the greatest.

Ability will enable a man to go to the top, but it takes character to keep him there.

Lessons from Failures

Let us fix our eyes on Jesus, the author and perfecter of our faith, who for the joy set before him endured the cross, scorning its shame, and sat down at the right hand of the throne of God.

HEBREWS 12:2 NIV

As a surgical resident in medical school, Thomas Starzl became interested in transplants. In 1958, he implanted new livers in dogs whose livers had been removed, but all died within two days of the operation. A year later he found a way to stabilize their circulation, and the dogs lived for a week after transplant surgery. In March 1963, Dr. Starzl performed the first human liver transplant, but his patient bled to death. That failure, and a hepatitis epidemic that spread through artificial kidney and transplant centers worldwide during the early 1960s, forced him to abandon his liver program.

In 1968, Starzl and others reported the results of new transplant trials to the American Surgical Association. All seven children involved in the study had survived transplants, although four died within six months—an encouraging but not stellar result. By 1975, there were only two liver programs left in the world.

Then in May of 1981, Starzl and his team found success—nineteen of twenty-two patients lived for long periods after undergoing a transplant!

Starzl was criticized, even vilified, by the medical establishment for attempting liver transplantation, but he persevered. Today liver transplants are routinely performed in hospitals around the world.

Let failure teach you, not stop you!

I DO NOT INTEND TO HAVE FAILURES ALONG THE WAY PREVENT ME FROM PURSUING . . .

_____

_____

_____

_____

_____

_____

_____

_____

_____

_____

_____

_____

_____

_____

You must have long-range goals to keep you from being frustrated by the short-range failures.

Secret Prayer Warriors

With God all things are possible.
MATTHEW 19:26

What
CHALLENG-
ING EVENTS
IN MY
ROUTINE CAN
I TURN INTO
PRIVATE
PRAYER
MEETINGS?

Claire Townsend found the weekly production meetings at the major-motion-picture studio where she worked to be extremely stressful. All morning various department heads would jockey for position. The studio had just been purchased, jobs were uncertain, and team spirit had vanished. To counteract the stress, Claire began to spend more time on her spiritual life. She began to pray again, discovering the power of God's love in her life. Even so, she dreaded this weekly battle.

Then one day during a particularly tense meeting, the thought came to her, *Pray. Pray now!* As Claire began to pray silently, she felt God's love welling up within her and moving out from her heart to every person in the room. One by one, each of her coworkers glanced in her direction, and she responded with a smile. Within minutes, the tone of the meeting had changed from confrontation to compromise. As the group relaxed, they became more creative, and Claire began to regard the meetings as an opportunity to impart God's love.

Nobody needs to know you are turning a business meeting into a prayer session, but God will. God hears your prayers, even when they're silent.

———✺———

There are moments when, whatever
be the attitude of the body,
the soul is on its knees.

Useless to Useful

Do all things without
murmurings and disputings.
PHILIPPIANS 2:14

On his way home to surprise his mother for All Souls' Day, Mishi Dobos stopped by the family's summer cottage to see what repairs he might undertake next. His eyes fell on the garden well, a solid brick structure four feet in diameter. As he leaned over to peer with a flashlight into the seventy-four-foot shaft, he failed to notice the frosty moss on the well's rim. Within seconds, he had plummeted feet first into the shaft, landing ankle-deep in soft mud.

For three days Mishi shouted for help. Then on the fourth day, while attempting to make a place to sit, he ripped a carpenter's clamp—a foot-long piece of metal with upturned ends—away from the rotting wood. Mishi thought, *What can I do with this?* Studying the walls, he saw a brick missing on one side. An idea dawned—use the clamp to chip out bricks in a staggered, upward fashion and climb out!

Mishi went to work. At best, he could remove three bricks an hour. But many bricks and a bad fall later—in all, six days and twenty-three hours after plunging into the well—Mishi swung his leg over the edge of the upper rim, the rusty carpenter's clamp in his hand.

Look around you. What normally useless object might God lead you to use in a clever, creative way? Take whatever God places in your hands, and use it as a tool for success.

———

A drowning man does not complain
about the size of a life preserver.

What
SEEMINGLY
USELESS
OBJECT IS
GOD LEADING
ME TO USE IN
A CREATIVE
WAY?

Luck and Labor

We do not want you do become lazy, but to imitate those who through faith and patience inherit what has been promised.

HEBREWS 6:12 NIV

I NEED TO
TURN MY
WHINING
INTO
WHISTLING
SO I CAN
ACCOM-
PLISH...

This following poem confirms the principle that the man who is born the luckiest is the man who doesn't believe in luck . . . but in work!

The Laggard's Excuse

He worked by day
And toiled by night,
He gave up play
And some delight.
Dry books he read
New things to learn
And forged ahead,
Success to earn.
He plodded on
With faith and pluck,
And when he won
Men called it luck.

Luck is always waiting for something to turn up. On the other hand, work, using keen eyes and a strong will, always turns something up!

Luck lies in bed and wishes the postman would bring news of an unexpected inheritance. Work springs out of bed early in the morning and lays the foundation for success with competence.

Luck whines. Work whistles.

———✦———

*Everything comes to him
who hustles while he waits.*

Tangled Threads

He will not allow your foot to slip;
He who keeps you will not slumber.

PSALM 121:3 NASB

We pray because prayer opens up the floodgates of God's infinite grace and power to flow toward a person in need. God can act without prayer, but He chooses to operate within the boundaries of human will and invitation. With each prayer, He allows us to participate in His work on earth.

Leonard Ravenhill once said about prayer, "One might estimate the weight of the world, tell the size of the celestial city, count the stars of Heaven, measure the speed of lightning, and tell the time of the rising and the setting of the sun—but you cannot estimate prayer power. Prayer is as vast as God because He is behind it. Prayer is as mighty as God because He has committed Himself to answer it."

A sign in a cotton factory read: "If your threads get tangled, send for the foreman." One day a new worker got her threads tangled. The more she tried to disentangle them, the worse the situation grew. Finally, she sent for the foreman. He asked, "Why didn't you send for me earlier?" She replied, "I was doing my best." He answered, "No, your best would have been to send for me."

When we face a tough situation, our first response should be to ask for God's help. He longs to be our helper and untangle the threads of our lives.

It is such a comfort to drop the tangles of life into God's hands and leave them there.

I OFTEN FAIL TO CALL ON GOD AND INSTEAD TRY TO DO MY BEST WHEN IT COMES TO...

Listening to Your Conscience

Herein do I exercise myself, to have always a conscience void of offence toward God, and toward men.
ACTS 24:16

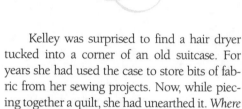

What LONG- FORGOTTEN OVERSIGHT DO I NEED TO CORRECT?

Kelley was surprised to find a hair dryer tucked into a corner of an old suitcase. For years she had used the case to store bits of fabric from her sewing projects. Now, while piecing together a quilt, she had unearthed it. *Where did this come from?* she asked herself.

After several days of trying to remember, she recalled having used it while visiting friends nearly a decade before. She had made several visits to the family and had apparently placed the borrowed hair dryer into her case inadvertently. To complicate matters, the family had asked about its whereabouts, and she had replied that she didn't have a clue!

Embarrassed, she thought, *How can I tell my friends after all these years that I have this?* However, her conscience wouldn't let the matter rest. She finally sent the hair dryer back to the family with an apology and an explanation. After many laughs, all was forgiven.

A healthy conscience is one of our greatest gifts from God. It serves to keep our lives on track and thus maintain peace in our hearts.

───※───

A quiet conscience sleeps in thunder.

Give Your Skills

The righteous give without sparing.
PROVERBS 21:26 NIV

Jonas Salk received a medical degree from New York University College of Medicine. He received an appointment to the Virus Research Laboratory at the University of Pittsburgh. He received an assignment from the army to develop a vaccine against influenza. And among the many honors he has received was a Presidential Medal of Freedom.

However, Dr. Salk is not known for what he received but for what he gave. He and his team of researchers gave their efforts to prepare an inactivated polio virus that could serve as an immunizing agent against polio. By 1952, they had created a vaccine, and in 1955, the vaccine was released for widespread use in the United States, virtually ending the ravaging, crippling effects of polio.

You will receive many opportunities in your life, and most likely a number of certificates, diplomas, or awards of various types. What will ultimately count, however, is what you do with the training you have received and the skills and traits you have developed.

Find a way to give, create, or generate something today that will benefit others. In that is not only a potential for fame and reward, but also great personal satisfaction—the reward of highest value.

No person was ever honored for what he received. Honor has been the reward for what he gave.

One THING I CAN GIVE TODAY THAT WILL BENEFIT OTHERS IS MY . . .

A Divine Inspiration

Fervent in spirit; serving the Lord.
ROMANS 12:11

Today I
CONSECRATE
TO GOD
ALONE MY
EFFORTS
AT . . .

The German sculptor Dannaker worked for two years on a statue of Christ until, to him, it looked perfect. He called a little girl into his studio, and pointing to the statue, asked her, "Who is that?" The little girl promptly replied, "A great man."

Dannaker was disheartened. He took his chisel and began anew. For six long years he toiled. Again he invited a little girl into his workshop, stood her before the figure, and said, "Who is that?" She looked up at it for a moment, and then tears welled in her eyes as she folded her hands across her chest and said, "Suffer the little children to come unto me" (Mark 10:14). This time Dannaker knew he had succeeded.

The sculptor later confessed that during those six years, Christ had revealed Himself to him in a vision, and he had only transferred to the marble what he had seen with his inner eyes.

Later when Napoleon Bonaparte asked him to make a statue of Venus for the Louvre, Dannaker refused. "A man," he said, "who had seen Christ can never employ his gifts in carving a pagan goddess. My art is henceforth a consecrated thing."

The true value of a work comes not from effort, nor its completion, but from Christ who inspires it.

———

Only passions, great passions,
can elevate the soul to great things.

Genuine Praise

Let another man praise thee,
and not thine own mouth;
a stranger, and not thine own lips.

PROVERBS 27:2

As a rookie forward with the Detroit Pistons basketball team, Grant Hill received more votes from fans who wanted to see him play in the All-Star Game than any other player in the NBA. Averaging eighteen points, five rebounds, and four assists per game, Hill was certainly an all-star talent. But his fans were responding to more than the stat sheet. In Hill, they saw a player with grace, a man who organized a summer camp for kids and called assistant coaches "sir." Hill admits of himself, "I don't carry myself like an all-star. I carry myself as if I'm a rookie trying to make it in the NBA and be as good as I can be. Look at the way I walk. I don't strut; I don't swagger."

To most sports writers and editors, Hill is perceived as a regular guy—a person who is to be admired, but someone who is down-home and easy to talk to. Hill says, "I feel I'm the best player out there, and no one can stop me. I want to beat you and embarrass you bad. But I don't want people to know that. It's like a little secret I keep to myself."

Let your fans sing your praises. It will be received as far more genuine by those who hear it, than if you had sung them yourself.

Sometimes
I SECRETLY
WISH
SOMEONE
WOULD SING
MY PRAISES
ABOUT THE
WAY I . . .

The man who sings his own praises
always gets the wrong pitch.

Cries of Hallelujah

The joy of the LORD is your strength.
NEHEMIAH 8:10

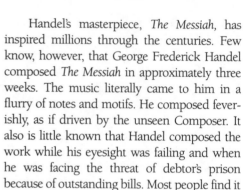

The LAST TIME I EXPERIENCED THE UNBRIDLED JOY THAT COMES WITH KNOWING CHRIST WAS WHEN...

Handel's masterpiece, *The Messiah*, has inspired millions through the centuries. Few know, however, that George Frederick Handel composed *The Messiah* in approximately three weeks. The music literally came to him in a flurry of notes and motifs. He composed feverishly, as if driven by the unseen Composer. It also is little known that Handel composed the work while his eyesight was failing and when he was facing the threat of debtor's prison because of outstanding bills. Most people find it difficult to create under stress, especially when physical or financial problems are the root of that stress. And yet, Handel did.

He credits the completion of the work to one thing: joy. He was quoted as saying that he felt as if his heart would burst with joy at what he was hearing in his mind and heart. It was joy that compelled him to write, forced him to create, and ultimately found expression in the "Hallelujah Chorus."

Handel lived to see his oratorio become a cherished tradition. He was especially pleased to see it performed to raise money for benevolent causes.

When joy is present, Jesus Christ is expressed.

*Nothing great was ever achieved
without enthusiasm.*

Passing the Test

A good name is rather to be chosen than great riches.

PROVERBS 22:1

A young lay preacher was invited at the last minute to preach a sermon at a church in his city. On impulse, he used as his text one of the Ten Commandments: "Thou shalt not steal" (Exodus 20:15). The next morning, he stepped on a bus and handed the driver a dollar bill. The driver handed him back his change and he moved to the rear of the bus. Glancing down to count the change before he pocketed it, the man noticed that the driver had given him a dime too much. His first thought was, *The bus company will never miss a dime.*

He quickly changed his mind, however, feeling conviction in his conscience that the dime didn't belong to him and he needed to return it to the driver. He made his way to the front and said, "You gave me too much change," and handed the man the dime.

To his surprise, the driver said, "Yes, I gave you a dime too much. I did it purposely. I heard your sermon yesterday, and I was watching you in my mirror as you counted your change."

The young preacher passed the test set up for him by the driver and gave a witness to his faith in the process. May all of our deeds match our words!

A good reputation is more valuable than money.

I NEED TO MAINTAIN MY INTEGRITY AND CHRISTIAN WITNESS, ESPECIALLY WHEN I'M TEMPTED TO . . .

Calling a Tail a Leg

Putting away lying, speak every man truth with his neighbour: for we are members one of another.

EPHESIANS 4:25

The MOST EFFECTIVE WAY I KNOW TO NIP GOSSIP IN THE BUD IS TO...

R.G. LeTourneau, an outstanding Christian businessman for whom LeTourneau College was named, made a fortune with a company that manufactured large earth-moving equipment. He once remarked, "We used to make a scraper known as 'Model G.' One day somebody asked our salesman what the G stood for. The man, who was pretty quick on the trigger, immediately replied, 'I'll tell you. The G stands for gossip because like a talebearer this machine moves a lot of dirt and moves it fast.'"

The trouble with gossip is not so much that it is spoken as an intended lie, but that it is heard as if it was the absolute truth. Abraham Lincoln had a favorite riddle he used to put to people: "If a man were to call the tail of a dog a leg, how many legs would the dog have?"

The usual reply was "five."

"Wrong," Lincoln would say with his wry smile. "The dog still has four legs. Calling the tail a leg doesn't make it one."

Just because a tale is repeated over and over by so-called reliable sources doesn't necessarily make it true.

He who throws dirt loses ground.

Sowing and Growing

Be thou an example of the believers,
in word, in conversation, in charity,
in spirit, in faith, in purity.

1 TIMOTHY 4:12

Many a parent moans aloud when they think of their children who are young adults and away from home: "I did everything I knew to do to be a good parent, and it looks as if nothing has worked." In fact, the good seeds that the parents have sown are still planted deeply in the soil of the child's life. It's at this point that the parent must turn to the only thing he or she can do—pray!

Pray daily. Pray persistently. Pray specifically. And above all, pray with faith that God not only hears, but that He will also answer.

A man once said to his friend, "I believe if you thought the Lord told you to jump through a stone wall, you'd jump." The friend replied, "If the Lord told me to jump through a wall, it would be my business to jump, and it would be His business to make a hole."

The same goes for parenting. The Lord tells us to do our part—to raise our children according to His commandments and to the best of the knowledge we have—and then we must trust Him to do His part in our children's lives.

You can sow, but only God can grow. Trust Him to do that work in your child's life today.

———⧌———

How to curb juvenile delinquency:
1. Take time with your children.
2. Set your children a good example.
3. Give your children ideals for living.
4. Have a lot of activities planned.
5. Discipline your children.
6. Teach them about God.

I NEED TO KNOW HOW TO DISTINGUISH BETWEEN GOD'S RESPONSIBIL- ITY AND MINE WHEN IT COMES TO . . .

Money Talks

The rich ruleth over the poor, and the borrower is servant to the lender.

PROVERBS 22:7

What
SPECIFIC
"MONEY
MESSAGE" DO
I NEED TO
HEED TODAY?

Money sends many different messages. It may say, "Hold me, and I will dry up the foundations of benevolence in your soul. Grasp me tightly, and I will focus your eyes to see nothing but my image, and transform your ears so that the soft metallic ring of coins will be louder than the cries of needy people. Hoard me, and I will destroy your sympathy for others and your love for God."

It may say, "Spend me for self-indulgence, and I will make your soul indifferent to anything other than your own pleasure. I will become your master, and you will think that I am the only mark of power and importance."

It may say, "Give me away for the benefit of others, and I will return to you in the form of abundant spiritual renewal. I will bless the one who receives and the one who gives me. I will supply food for the hungry, clothes for the poor, medicine for the sick, and send the Gospel to the ends of the earth. At the same time, I will secure joy and peace for the one who spends me in this way."

A dollar speaks in different ways to different people. It's the listener who determines which message is the most persuasive.

Money is a good servant but a bad master.

Seasons of Need

*To every thing there is
a season . . . a time to keep
silence, and a time to speak.*

ECCLESIASTES 3:1,7

In December 1994, the *Air Force Times* reported that Army soldier Joseph Cannon, who had just ended a six-year career, had not received a single military paycheck since boot camp. Officials said that Cannon's records were lost at his first duty station, and he had never complained. He missed 144 paychecks, totaling more than $103,000! It seems Cannon had lived in the barracks, eaten only in the mess halls, and when he had special needs, he had borrowed a few dollars from relatives. One observer noted, "It appears he thought his room and board were the payment the military offered, so he took it all in stride and never felt deprived or overlooked. He figured somebody 'higher up' would take care of him as long as he took care of his job."

While Cannon's example may seem a major injustice or simply an example of "ignorance gone to seed," his simple trust in authority is endearing. It takes great wisdom for most of us to discern exactly when to request more and when to accept what we have in life.

To everything there is a season. Perhaps our prayer should be: "Tell me, Lord, what season am I in?"

— ⌘ —

*There are times when silence is golden;
other times it is just plain yellow.*

IS THERE AN INJUSTICE IN MY LIFE THAT THE LORD IS TELLING ME TO SIMPLY ACCEPT?

Yes, Even These

God commendeth his love toward us,
in that, while we were yet sinners,
Christ died for us.

ROMANS 5:8

I NEED TO
REMEMBER
THAT JESUS
LOVES
EVERYONE,
EVEN...

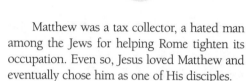

Matthew was a tax collector, a hated man among the Jews for helping Rome tighten its occupation. Even so, Jesus loved Matthew and eventually chose him as one of His disciples.

Peter had a quick temper; his emotions were easily triggered by circumstances. During the most critical hours of Jesus' life on earth, he three times denied knowing Jesus. Even so, Jesus loved Peter and empowered him to lead the early Church.

Saul wreaked havoc on the church in Jerusalem, leading raids on the homes of Christians and imprisoning the devout. He consented to the death of Stephen and was one of the official witnesses of his execution. He even requested letters of authority to extend the persecution of the Church to other cities, including Damascus. Even so, Jesus loved Saul, appeared to him in a light from Heaven, and called him to repentance.

No matter what people may have done—no matter what their character flaws—Jesus still loves them. He loved them to the point of dying on their behalf on the cross. He died for your enemy—the friend or family member who has disappointed or frustrated you. And He died for you.

Jesus is a friend who knows all
your faults and still loves you anyway.

Cleaning Day

Work instead at what is right and good, learning to trust him and love others, and to be patient and gentle.

1 TIMOTHY 6:11 TLB

At a crucial transition time in her life, a Christian woman cried out to the Lord, despairing over the lack of spiritual power in her life. Suddenly, she sensed Jesus standing beside her, asking, "May I have the keys to your life?"

The experience was so realistic that the woman reached into her pocket and took out a ring of keys. "Are all the keys here?" the Lord asked.

"Yes, except the key to one small room in my life."

"If you cannot trust Me in all the rooms of your life, I cannot accept any of the keys."

The woman was so overwhelmed at the thought of the Lord moving out of her life altogether, she cried, "Lord! Take the keys to all the rooms of my life!"

Many of us have rooms we hope no one will ever see. We intend to clean them out someday, but someday never seems to come. When we invite Jesus into these rooms, He will help us clean them out. With Him, we have the courage to throw away all the junk and fill the rooms with His love and peace and joy.

IS THERE A "ROOM" IN MY LIFE TO WHICH I'VE DENIED THE LORD ENTRANCE?

God does not give us power to imitate Him; He gives us His very self.

Improvising under Pressure

*I laboured more abundantly than
they all: yet not I, but the grace
of God which was with me.*

1 CORINTHIANS 15:10

What CAN I DO
TO ENSURE
THAT MY
CHARACTER
CAN OVER-
COME THE
UNKNOWN,
TOUGH
CIRCUMSTANCES
AHEAD?

Nicolo Paganini was a well-known and gifted nineteenth-century violinist. His most memorable concert, however, was one marked by a difficult test rather than easy success. The concert was performed with a full orchestra before a packed house in Italy. Those who heard him play say that Paganini's technique was incredible and his tone fantastic. Toward the end of the concert, Paganini was astounding his rapt audience with an intricate composition when one string on his violin suddenly snapped and hung limply from his instrument. Paganini frowned only briefly, shook his head, and continued to play, improvising beautifully.

Then to everyone's surprise, including Paganini's, a second string broke. Shortly thereafter, a third string snapped. It seemed like a slapstick comedy routine as Paganini stood before the awed crowd with strings dangling from his Stradivarius violin. Instead of leaving the stage to repair his instrument, he stood firm. He calmly completed the difficult number on the one remaining string—a performance that won him applause, admiration, and enduring fame.

Your best work may be performed under tough and unusual circumstances. So don't give up. Just keep playing!

---

*The secret of success is to be like a duck—
smooth and unruffled on top, but
paddling furiously underneath.*

Peace from Prayer

*Pray about everything; tell God your needs and
don't forget to thank him for his answers.
If you do this you will experience God's
peace. . . . His peace will keep your thoughts
and your hearts quiet and at rest.*

PHILIPPIANS 4:6-7 TLB

It was two o'clock in the morning when a weary traveler landed in Tahiti. Her flight from Hawaii had been a turbulent one, causing a delay in her arrival on the island. The stormy skies had also forced her connecting flight to a nearby island to be canceled, requiring her to make plans to spend at least a day near the airport. An hour later, she found herself standing with her luggage in a small but clean motel room, totally exhausted after more than twenty-four hours of travel. Her mind, however, refused to stop racing with concern about whom to call and what to do.

How CAN I STEADY MY EMOTIONS SO I NEVER THREATEN TO UNRAVEL?

The woman was on a short-term missionary trip to help set up a clinic on a remote South Seas island. Now she was beginning to wonder if she had heard God correctly! At that hour and as weary as she was, she felt alone at the edge of the world. Glancing down at her watch, she saw it was 11 A.M.—the time her Bible study group said they would be in prayer for her. *They're praying right now!* she thought, and suddenly, she felt deep peace and comfort. Within minutes, she was sound asleep.

When you are about to unravel inside, turn to prayer. The travel route of prayer is never misdirected or put off schedule—nor is it dangerous! On the contrary, prayer gives peace and helps us avoid danger.

———

*A day hemmed in prayer
is less likely to unravel.*

Deep Roots

I am persuaded, that neither death, nor life, nor angels, nor principalities, nor powers, nor things present, nor things to come . . . shall be able to separate us from the love of God, which is in Christ Jesus our Lord.

ROMANS 8:38-39

I CAN PUSH
MY SPIRITUAL
ROOTS
DEEPER BY . . .

Many people see abundant spring rains as a great blessing to farmers, especially if the rains come after the plants have sprouted and are several inches tall. What they don't realize is that even a short drought can have a devastating effect on a crop of seedlings that has received too much rain.

Why? Because during frequent rains, the young plants are not required to push their roots deeper into the soil in search of water. If a drought occurs later, plants with shallow root systems will quickly die.

We often receive abundance in our lives—rich fellowship, great teaching, thorough "soakings" of spiritual blessings. Yet when stress or tragedy enters our lives, we may find ourselves thinking God has abandoned us or is unfaithful. The fact is that we have allowed the easiness of our lives to keep us from pushing our spiritual roots deeper. We have allowed others to spoon-feed us, rather than develop our own deep personal relationship with God through prayer and study of His Word.

Only the deeply rooted are able to endure hard times without wilting. The best advice is to enjoy the "rain" while seeking to grow even closer to Him.

You should never let adversity get you down—except on your knees.

Time on the Bench

*Though your beginning
was insignificant, yet your
end will increase greatly.*

JOB 8:7 NASB

Most American men hear "Montana" and think of two things: a state and a star. Joe Montana is a football great by anybody's standards. Before his retirement, he led the San Francisco 49ers to four Super Bowl victories. In 16 seasons, he ran 40,551 yards, completed 3,409 passes, made 273 touchdowns, and received the highest quarterback rating (92.3) of any non-active passer in history. A town has been named after him. Teammates and opponents alike have praised his grace and skill under pressure and his ability to run a two-minute drill and turn it into a winning score.

However, at the beginning of his career, few would have thought Montana would make it big. He grew up in Monongahela, Pennsylvania, in the long shadows of former football greats such as Unitas, Blanda, and Namath. When he got to Notre Dame, he was seventh string. By the time he was a senior, he led his team to a 1979 Cotton Bowl comeback victory, but no NFL team seemed to want him. He got the interest of scouts only two days before the draft and was finally chosen in the third round—eighty-second overall selection— by San Francisco. Once there, he sat on the bench behind the starting quarterback for a season and a half!

So never give up on your dream. There's still time on the clock!

❦

Don't be discouraged; everyone who got where he is, started where he was.

Which OF
MY DREAMS
HAS MY
MEDIOCRE
TRACK
RECORD
CAUSED ME TO
GIVE UP ON?

Who Decides God's Will?

*A merry heart doeth
good like a medicine.*
PROVERBS 17:22

No MATTER
WHAT *I*
THINK, I
HAVE
DETERMINED
TO TRUST
GOD WITH
REGARD
TO...

A couple in their mid-thirties were deeply in love and eager to be married. They went to their pastor for the premarital counseling required before their wedding. He asked probing questions about their personal faith, their ability to communicate openly and honestly, their commitment to each other, their understanding of church service, their views on money, and so on. Finally, he said (half asking and half commenting), "I'm sure you are eager to get started on a family?"

"Oh, yes, we want children," the young woman said. Her fiancé nodded in agreement.

"Then I hope you have a dozen," the pastor responded enthusiastically.

The man laughed and said, "If that's God's will, I'm willing to do my part."

The young woman, however, gulped and remained silent. "Well, actually, sir," she finally said. "I discussed that with the Lord on my thirty-fifth birthday and we decided that His will is for no more than two."

Children are a blessing from the Lord, no matter how many you have. With each child, God gives you the grace you need to raise that child in the nurture and admonition of the Lord.

───❀───

*Familiarity breeds contempt—
and children.*

Beware of Whelks

Make no friendship with an angry man; and
with a furious man thou shalt not go: Lest thou
learn his ways, and get a snare to thy soul.

PROVERBS 22:24-25

Have you ever seen a whole oyster shell without an oyster in it? You may have wondered, *How did the oyster get out?* You might look for a small hole in the top of the shell. Such a hole is made by a whelk. This little ocean creature has an appendage that works somewhat like an auger. With it, the whelk bores into the oyster shell and then sucks the oyster through the hole, little by little, until it has devoured it all. Though small, a whelk—like an angry person—can do great harm.

Often, we allow another person's angry outbursts, critical remarks, or cynical comments to bore a hole into our good nature and rob us of our otherwise sunny disposition. If we aren't careful, we can become irritated to the point where genuine anger and bitterness begin to seethe within us. When that happens, we are in real danger of experiencing disease, disharmony, and discord.

One of the best things you can do is to simply avoid those people whom you find constantly irksome, continually critical, or habitually angry at life, as well as those who seem to delight in needling you. In other words, stay out of the way of whelks. You'll be healthier and happier for it!

One THING
I CAN DO TO
PROTECT MY
INNER PEACE
IS . . .

The company you keep will
determine the trouble you meet.

Hurdling the Obstacles

It is better to take refuge in the LORD
than to trust in man.

PSALM 118:8 NIV

What
ARE THE
OBSTACLES
IN MY LIFE
THAT I HAVE
BEEN UNABLE
TO SEE MY
WAY AROUND?

Trust in yourself and you are
doomed to disappointment . . . but
trust in God, and you are never
to be confounded in time or eternity.

Marian had her sights set on becoming a concert singer, a challenge that was doubly difficult because of the color of her skin. Her mother, however, had a patient trust in God. Marian later said, "Mother's religion made her believe that she would receive what was right for her to have if she was conscientious in her faith. If it did not come, it was because He had not considered it right for her. We grew in this atmosphere of faith that she created. . . . We believed as she did because we wanted the same kind of haven in the time of storm."

When Marian was denied admission to a famous music conservatory on account of her race, her mother calmly said that someone would be raised up to help her accomplish what she had hoped to do at the conservatory. That someone arrived only a few weeks later. One of Philadelphia's outstanding voice teachers, Giuseppe Boghetti, made room for her to become one of his students, and Marian Anderson was on her way to becoming one of the most magnificent singers of the twentieth century. On Easter Sunday in 1939, she sang for more than seventy-five thousand people gathered in front of the Lincoln Memorial and gave a performance never forgotten by those who were there.

Whatever obstacles lie in the path to your goal, God will be with you each step of the way. He will remove the obstacle, guide you around it, or take you over it. Be assured that God will get you there—simply trust in Him.

Uncommon Good

Seest thou a man diligent in his business? he shall stand before kings; he shall not stand before mean men.

PROVERBS 22:29

Helping the deaf to communicate was Alexander Graham Bell's motivation for his life work, perhaps because his mother and wife were both deaf. "If I can make a deaf-mute talk," Bell said, "I can make metal talk." For five frustrating and impoverished years, he experimented with a variety of materials in an effort to make a metal disk that, vibrating in response to sound, could reproduce those sounds and send them over an electrified wire.

During a visit to Washington, DC, he called on Joseph Henry, a scientist who was a pioneer in electrical research. He presented his ideas to him and asked his advice. Should he let someone else perfect the telephone or should he do it himself? Henry encouraged him to do it himself, to which Bell complained that he lacked the necessary knowledge of electricity. Henry's brief answer was, "Get it."

And so Bell studied electricity. A year later when he obtained a patent for the telephone, the patent office officials credited him with knowing more about electricity than all the other inventors combined.

Hard work. Study. Hope. Persistence. These are all "common things." They are the keys, however, to doing uncommonly well. If you need more knowledge to succeed, get it.

The secret of success is to do the common things uncommonly well.

What IS THE MOTIVATION FOR MY LIFE'S WORK?

Cut Off or Sewn In?

If it be possible, as much as lieth in you, live peaceably with all men.
ROMANS 12:18

Whom
HAVE I
UNFAIRLY
"SCISSORED"
OUT OF
MY LIFE?

In *Learning to Forgive,* Doris Donnelly writes,

Some years ago I met a family very proficient in the use of scissors. . . . The friends of each family member were under constant scrutiny to determine whether they measured up to the standards imposed by mother and father. One slip . . . resulted in ostracism from the narrow circle of "friends." . . . Anyone who did not respond immediately with profuse gratitude was eliminated from the list for the next time. Snip.

Eventually I, too, was scissored out of their lives. I never knew for sure why, but I knew enough to recognize that once I was snipped away there was no hope of my being sewn into their lives again.

Last year the mother of the family died. The father and daughters, expecting large crowds to gather to say their final farewells, enlisted the assistance of the local police to handle traffic. . . . Telegrams were sent . . . phone calls were made . . . local motels were alerted . . . yet in the end, only the husband, the daughters, their husbands, and a grandchild or two attended the services.

Cutting imperfect people out of your life is a prescription for loneliness. Who would remain? Is there anyone you could "sew" back into your life? Why not give them a call?

The bridge you burn now may be the one you later have to cross.

Who You Are in the Dark

The night is far spent, the day is at hand:
let us therefore cast off the works of darkness,
and let us put on the armour of light.

ROMANS 13:12

Herbert V. Prochnow has constructed a ten-part "Character Quiz"—an interesting checkup to see just how often we choose to be children of light:

- If you found a wallet with $1,000, would you give it to the owner if no one knew you found it?

- If you could advance yourself unfairly, would you do it if no one would ever find out?

- If the bus driver failed to collect your fare, would you voluntarily pay it?

- If there were no locks on any house, store, or bank, would you take anything if no one found out?

- If your business partner died, would you pay his relatives their fair share, if you didn't have to?

- If you were an employer, would you hire yourself at your salary?

- If you were an employer, would you like to be working for yourself?

- If you were a parent, would you like to be the child of a parent like you?

- If you had a choice, would you like to live in a community with people working in church, civic, and community affairs like you do?

- If you had to live with someone just like you for the rest of your life, would you count it a privilege?

After TAKING THIS CHARACTER QUIZ, I REALIZE I NEED TO WORK ON . . .

Do not in the darkness of night,
what you'd shun in broad daylight.

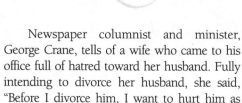

Move It!

Let us therefore follow after the things which make for peace, and things wherewith one may edify another.

ROMANS 14:19

What

ACTIONS CAN
I TAKE THAT
WILL CHANGE
MY FEELING
TOWARD...?

Newspaper columnist and minister, George Crane, tells of a wife who came to his office full of hatred toward her husband. Fully intending to divorce her husband, she said, "Before I divorce him, I want to hurt him as much as he has me."

Crane advised that she go home and act as if she really loved her husband. "Tell him how much he means to you," he said. "Praise him for every decent trait. Go out of your way to be as kind, considerate, and generous as possible. Spare no efforts to please him, to enjoy him. Make him believe you love him . . . then drop the bomb. . . . That will really hurt him."

The woman exclaimed, "Beautiful!" And she did as he had suggested with enthusiasm, acting as if she loved him. Two months later she returned to Crane, who asked, "Are you ready to go through with the divorce?"

"Divorce!" she said. "Never! I discovered I really do love him!"

Actions can change feelings. Motion can result in emotion. Love is established not so much by fervent promise as by often-repeated deeds.

Be careful that your marriage doesn't become a duel instead of a duet.

A Good Burden

Enter not into the path of the wicked,
and go not in the way of evil men.

PROVERBS 4:14

Medical missionary Dr. Lambie, formerly of Abyssinia, forded many swift and bridgeless streams in Africa. He learned from the natives the best way to make a hazardous crossing.

The danger in crossing a stream lies in being swept off one's feet and carried downstream to deeper waters or being hurled against hidden rocks. A way to avoid this is for a man about to cross a stream to find a large stone, the heavier the better, to lift it to his shoulder, and carry it across the stream as ballast. The extra weight of the stone keeps his feet solid on the bed of the stream.

In telling of this technique, Dr. Lambie drew an application to life: "While crossing the dangerous stream of life . . . we need the ballast of burden-bearing . . . to keep us from being swept off our feet."

This does not mean that we should seek out troubles or give in to our problems. It means that as we look around at others, we are to help shoulder their burdens and in return accept their help in bearing our own. It's easy to become overwhelmed in carrying your own burden. Shared burdens travel lighter.

When things go wrong,
don't go wrong with them.

Whose
BURDENS DO
I NEED TO
SHARE TODAY?

237

A Life of Learning

Apply thine heart unto instruction, and thine ears to the words of knowledge.

PROVERBS 23:12

How CAN
I DISCIPLINE
MYSELF
TO LEARN
SOMETHING
NEW EVERY
DAY?

Pat Newbury, owner of several McDonald's franchises, was concerned that some of the adults he hired were flipping hamburgers for a living because they weren't qualified to do anything else. So he began paying his high-school-aged employees to do their homework for one hour before or after their shift. To qualify, a student had to tell his manager he planned to study, do his homework in a designated booth, wear his uniform, and not smoke. "We can't testify as to what goes into their brains," Newbury has said, "but at least we know that their books are open and they are in a position to learn."

Newbury also started a program called "Golden Achiever Points." He awards employees for good grades—1,000 points for an A, 500 points for a B. The points are redeemable for merchandise, theater tickets, or money for college tuition and books. "It is critical that young people prepare for the workforce," Newbury has said. But his programs also have made good business sense. "To attract the best employees, I need to offer benefits that are sensible to them."

Never stop valuing education. Make it a point to learn something new every day. It's your ticket to a greater understanding of tomorrow's problems!

---

*A man who does not read good books
has no advantage over the man
who can't read them.*

Beauty Takes Time

*My righteousness I hold fast, and will
not let it go: my heart shall not
reproach me so long as I live.*

JOB 27:6

A man once had a friend who was a skilled potter. He often went to watch him at work as he molded the clay into various vessels. One day he asked his friend how he determined what he was going to make. The potter said he had discovered that when he was rested, he tended to make beautiful things, but when he was tired, he made more ordinary vessels.

As the potter reflected on this, he concluded that when he was relaxed, he had both the focus and the patience to make something beautiful. Oftentimes, the process of making a perfect object involved crushing an almost completed vase or bowl back into a lump so that he might start over. Beautiful objects also required that he be much more careful at each stage. When he was tired, he was less focused, less patient, and thus more apt to make mistakes and more likely to resort to making items that did not demand such precision.

So it is with our lives. Building character takes focus and patience, with attention to detail and an ability to be consistent over time. While God is ultimately our potter, we also play the role of potter in forming our own character. The more stressed we are, the less likely we are to create a character of beauty.

⸺

*Reputation is what men and women
think of us. Character is what
God and the angels know of us.*

I CAN ELIMINATE A GREAT DEAL OF STRESS IN MY LIFE BY...

Acting Out Your Faith

*Be ye followers of me, even
as I also am of Christ.*
1 CORINTHIANS 11:1

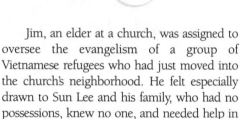

Do I WANT
OTHERS TO
THINK JESUS
IS ANYTHING
LIKE ME?

Jim, an elder at a church, was assigned to oversee the evangelism of a group of Vietnamese refugees who had just moved into the church's neighborhood. He felt especially drawn to Sun Lee and his family, who had no possessions, knew no one, and needed help in every way. Jim began by helping the family get food, and then he helped Sun Lee find a job.

Jim wanted so much to tell Sun Lee about Jesus Christ, but since he didn't speak Vietnamese and the refugees knew little English, he found it difficult to communicate. Both Jim and Sun Lee began to learn as much of each other's language as possible so they could become better friends.

One day Jim felt that he finally knew enough Vietnamese to tell Sun Lee about Jesus, but the more he talked, the more confused Sun Lee seemed to be. Finally, Sun Lee blurted out, "Is your God like you?"

Jim replied, "Oh, He's far, far greater."

Sun Lee interrupted, "If He's like you, Jim, I want to know Him."

Often, the most effective communication of the Gospel is the "word" of your deeds. Share your faith with someone today.

My business is not to remain myself, but to make the absolute best of what God made.

Enough

Wherefore, my beloved brethren,
let every man be swift to hear.

JAMES 1:19

In *Discipleship Journal*, Stephen Sorenson writes about a two-year period in which he had such severe tendonitis in both wrists that he could not even pick up his young daughter or twist open a bottle. At the same time, he was attempting to build a major addition to their home. Willy, a retired military musician came to help. Sorenson writes,

> Willy came back to our house, day after day. He dug up our septic tank, cut diseased trees, and simply spent time with us. I could sense he understood my pain and our need. One afternoon as he and I walked and talked in the woods, I discovered why.

> For most of his life Willy had lived for his music, but a devastating ear problem developed, preventing him from listening to music of any kind. As a result, rather than being put off by my injury, Willy was drawn to me because of our common ground. And before we went separate ways, Willy became a Christian.

> As I look back, I don't know if I would have taken time to talk with Willy had my wrists been well. Most likely I'd have been hammering nails or running a chain saw. So "all" I could do was listen and talk. But in God's plan that was enough.

Don't get so busy "doing" that you never have time to sit and listen. Often that's all the help a person needs.

Sometimes I'M SO BUSY "DOING" THAT I DON'T TAKE THE TIME TO SIT AND LISTEN TO...

The first duty of love is to listen.

Reaching Goals

We do not want you to become lazy, but to imitate those who through faith and patience inherit what has been promised.

HEBREWS 6:12 NIV

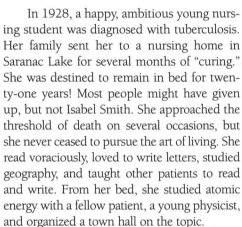

I SOMETIMES USE THE MINOR SNAGS IN MY LIFE AS AN EXCUSE TO AVOID . . .

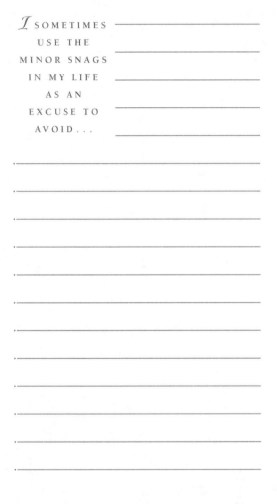

In 1928, a happy, ambitious young nursing student was diagnosed with tuberculosis. Her family sent her to a nursing home in Saranac Lake for several months of "curing." She was destined to remain in bed for twenty-one years! Most people might have given up, but not Isabel Smith. She approached the threshold of death on several occasions, but she never ceased to pursue the art of living. She read voraciously, loved to write letters, studied geography, and taught other patients to read and write. From her bed, she studied atomic energy with a fellow patient, a young physicist, and organized a town hall on the topic.

While ill, she met a kind, gentle man, also a patient at the sanitarium. She dreamed of marrying him and having a little house "under the mountains." At her lowest ebb, her dream kept her going, and in 1948, she did marry. She then wrote a book about "all the good things life has brought me." *Wish I Might,* published in 1955, earned her enough in royalties to buy her mountain retreat.

A tragic life? Hardly! Isabel Smith achieved everything she set out to achieve, even when the odds against her were a thousand to one. Even flat on her back in bed, she never quit growing, learning, and giving.

Don't let life's snags keep you from reaching your goals. Not many people spend twenty-one years of their life in bed. Imagine what you can accomplish with health and mobility!

*Do what you can with
what you have where you are.*

From Struggling to Success

Though a righteous man falls
seven times, he rises again.

PROVERBS 24:16 NIV

The difference between success and failure is often the ability to get up just one more time than you fall down!

Moses could have easily given up. He had an interrupted childhood, lived with a foster family, had a strong temper, a stammering tongue, and a crime record, but when God called to him, he said yes.

Joshua had seen the Promised Land and then been forced to wander in the wilderness for forty years with cowards who didn't believe as he did that they could possess the land. He could have given up in discouragement, but he was willing to go when God said go.

Peter had a hard time making the transition from fisherman to fisher of men. He sank while trying to walk on water, was strongly rebuked by Jesus for trying to tell Him what to do, and denied knowing Jesus in the hour Jesus needed him most. He could have seen himself as a hopeless failure. But when the opportunity came to preach before thousands on the Day of Pentecost, Peter responded.

No matter what you've done, you're not a failure until you quit trying. If you've been knocked down, get up one more time. You have nothing to lose.

Do I blame circumstances for my failures, or have I simply given up too soon?

By perseverance, the snail reached the Ark.

Happy Instead

My son, give me thine heart.
PROVERBS 23:26

Am I
SATISFIED
AND
CONTENT
WITH THE
LIFE GOD HAS
GIVEN ME?

A boy once said to God, "I've been thinking, and I know what I want when I become a man." He then proceeded to give God a long list of desires: to live in a big house with two Saint Bernards and a garden; marry a tall, beautiful, blue-eyed, woman; have three sons—one who would be a senator, one a scientist, and one a quarterback. He also wanted to drive a red Ferrari and be an adventurer who climbed tall mountains.

As it turned out, one day the boy hurt his knee while playing football. He could no longer climb trees, much less mountains. He married a beautiful and kind woman, who was short and had brown eyes. Because of his business, he lived in a city apartment, took cabs, and rode subways. He had three loving daughters, and they adopted a fluffy cat. One daughter became a nurse, another an artist, and the third a music teacher.

One morning the man awoke and remembered his boyhood dreams. He became extremely depressed, so depressed that he became ill. Close to death from a broken heart, he called out to God, "Remember when I was a boy and told You all the things I wanted? Why didn't You give me those things?"

"I could have," said God, "but I wanted to make you happy."

Remember that God only wants the best for you. Trust Him with your whole heart—He's the original heart surgeon.

*God always gives His best to those
who leave the choice with Him.*

Even Exchange?

*Ye are bought with a price: therefore
glorify God in your body, and in
your spirit, which are God's.*

1 CORINTHIANS 6:20

A saleswoman passed a particular corner each day on her way to work. For more than a week she observed a young girl trying to sell a floppy-eared puppy. The saleswoman finally said to the girl, "Honey, if you really want to sell this dog, then I suggest you clean him up, brush his coat, raise your price, and make people think they're getting something big." At noon, the saleswoman noticed the girl had taken her advice. The puppy was well-groomed and was sitting under a big sign: "Treemenndous Puppy for Sale—$5,000."

The saleswoman smiled and gulped, determined to tell the girl later that she may have overpriced the puppy. To her surprise, on the way home she saw the puppy was gone! Flabbergasted, the woman sought out the girl to ask if she had really sold the dog for $5,000.

The girl replied, "I sure did, and I want to thank you for all your help." The saleswoman stuttered, "How in the world did you do it?" The girl said, "It was easy. I just took two $2,500 cats in exchange!"

Two thousand years ago there was another great exchange. On a cross outside Jerusalem, Jesus Christ gave His life in exchange for ours. What value did He see in us? We were His prized creation, stolen for a season by our own will, but now repurchased as His beloved possession.

———

There is no father on earth who has as much love in his heart as God has for you.

IF I TRULY UNDERSTOOD HOW JESUS GAVE HIS LIFE ON THE CROSS IN EXCHANGE FOR MY SINS, I WOULD...

Preventive Medicine

The man should give his wife all that is her right as a married woman, and the wife should do the same for her husband.

1 CORINTHIANS 7:3 TLB

Do I LOVE MY SPOUSE ENOUGH TO RELEASE SOME ENDORPHINS TODAY—EVEN IF MY SPOUSE HAS MADE ME ANGRY?

This old childhood rhyme is one that many people remember:

Kiss and hug,
Kiss and hug,
Kiss your sweetie
On the mug.

While this rhyme was one children often used in ridiculing the puppy-love behavior of their older brothers and sisters, the practice of kissing and hugging actually has many healthful benefits beyond those of building a loving relationship.

A German magazine reported the results of a study conducted by a life-insurance company. The researchers discovered that husbands who kiss their wives every morning:

- live an average of five years longer.
- are involved in fewer automobile accidents.
- take 50 percent fewer sick days.
- earn 20 to 30 percent more money.

Other researchers have found that kissing and hugging release endorphins, giving the mind and body a sense of genuine well-being that translates into better health.

A kiss a day just may keep the doctor away!

*The best way to hold
a man is in your arms.*

What Makes a Man

Yea, I hated all my labour which I had taken under the sun: because I should leave it unto the man that shall be after me.

ECCLESIASTES 2:18

Dutch author and priest Henri Nouwen admits in his book, *In the Name of Jesus,* that he felt as if he was in a rut for more than twenty years of his life. With an outstanding academic résumé and a noble field of study, Nouwen seemed to have it made. Yet he said, "As I entered into my fifties . . . I came face to face with a simple question, 'Did becoming older bring me closer to Jesus?' After twenty-five years of priesthood, I found myself praying poorly, living somewhat isolated from other people, and very much preoccupied with burning issues. . . . I woke up one day with the realization that I was living in a very dark place."

Nouwen asked God to show him where He wanted him to go, and the Lord made it clear to him that he should leave his prestigious role as a distinguished professor and join the L'Arche communities for mentally handicapped people. In Nouwen's words, "God said, 'Go and live among the poor in spirit, and they will heal you.'" So he did. He faced numerous lessons—some painful, a few humiliating—but in all, he learned how to be a humble servant and a compassionate, caring friend. Nouwen came to realize that it's not work that makes a person—it's relationships.

Evaluate your life today. Do you spend too much of your time working or thinking about work? Is your family suffering from your absence, both physical and mental? Keep the eternal weight of things in mind, rather than the temporary pull of duty.

Do I SPEND TOO MUCH OF MY TIME WORKING OR THINKING ABOUT WORK, CAUSING MY FAMILY TO SUFFER?

No one ever said on their deathbed: I wish I would have spent more time at work!

Bending Your Ear

To everything there is a season . . .
a time to keep silence, and
a time to speak.
ECCLESIASTES 3:1,7

Whom DO
I NEED TO
ATTEND TO
TODAY WITH
A SHARPENED
OR BENT EAR?

_____

_____

_____

_____

_____

_____

_____

_____

_____

_____

Most communication researchers and theorists contend that the first step in effective communication is gaining attention. In order to establish lines of communication with your children, you first must "attend" to them—really see them, really hear them, really listen to them, and really feel what they feel.

The Hebrew word for "attend" has several meanings. Two of them paint vivid descriptions about the listening process:

- *A sharpened ear.* Such ears are like those of an animal listening to an unusual sound. Imagine a dog's ears being picked up or perked up to listen. That's the picture of a sharpened ear! As a parent, you are challenged to tune in to your children and listen to them with a heightened awareness.

- *A bent ear.* This is the ear that is cocked in a certain direction—the ear positioned so that it hears fully and clearly, without distortion. As a parent, put away anything that might distract you from listening to your child with your whole heart, mind, and spirit. Bend your ear in your child's direction.

This type of active listening takes effort. It can be far more draining than just talking. But it is also the foremost key to communicating with your child!

Opportunities for meaningful communication
between fathers and sons must be created.
And it's work to achieve.

Measured Words

Be not rash with thy mouth, and let not thine heart be hasty to utter anything before God: for God is in heaven, and thou upon earth: therefore let thy words be few.

ECCLESIASTES 5:2

Tom Kelly managed the Minnesota Twins to a World Series title in 1987, his first full season as their manager, and then managed them to a second world championship in 1991. Yet to watch him at work, critics have wondered if his vital signs have been stolen. Asked one sports writer, "How has T. K. managed all this, while lowering his blood pressure to the equivalent of the water pressure in your first apartment? He doesn't chew on fingernails or Rolaids or tobacco or his players. How?"

One of Kelly's trademarks is that he is a man of few words. He enjoys throwing at batting practice every day, in part because he believes that every minute he is throwing, he doesn't have to speak to the media. "I'm not really intelligent," T. K. claims. "I have a year and a half of college. But I have enough common sense to realize that I'm not intelligent. I realize that if I keep talking, I'll eventually say something dumb. So I don't give myself a lot of opportunities to open my mouth and stick my foot in it."

Tom Kelly is far from dumb. So is any person who is smart enough to limit what he or she says. A know-it-all usually doesn't know the half of it.

———

The trouble with the guy who talks too fast is that he often says something he hasn't thought of yet.

Am I WISE ENOUGH TO LIMIT WHAT I SAY TO WHAT I REALLY KNOW?

Ten Little Minutes

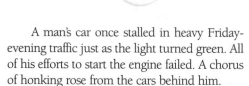

*The end of a matter is better than its
beginning, and patience is better than pride.
Do not be quickly provoked in your spirit,
for anger resides in the lap of fools.*

ECCLESIASTES 7:8-9 NIV

If I GOT UP
TEN MINUTES
EARLIER
TOMORROW,
IT WOULD
CHANGE MY
DAY BY
MAKING
ME . . .

A man's car once stalled in heavy Friday-evening traffic just as the light turned green. All of his efforts to start the engine failed. A chorus of honking rose from the cars behind him.

Feeling just as frustrated as the other drivers eager to get home for the weekend, he finally got out of his car, walked back to the first driver, and said, "I'm sorry, but I can't seem to get my car started. If you'll go up there and give it a try, I'll stay here and blow your horn for you."

The person who is chronically impatient rarely makes another person go faster or arrive earlier. Instead, the effects are nearly always negative—to others as well as to the impatient person. Accidents occur more frequently in haste. Ulcers, headaches, and other health problems develop more quickly. And relationships can become more readily strained.

Try giving yourself ten more minutes as an antidote for impatience. Get up ten minutes earlier every morning, leave ten minutes earlier, arrive ten minutes ahead of schedule, and so forth. You'll likely arrive at the end of the day feeling much more relaxed.

---

*Patience is a quality you admire
in the driver behind you and
scorn in the one ahead.*

A Worthy Note

Whatever your hand finds to do,
do it with your might.
ECCLESIASTES 9:10 NKJV

A series of illustrations in a popular magazine once depicted the life story of a "one-note musician." From frame to frame, the tale revealed how the woman followed her daily routine of eating and sleeping until the time came for the evening concert. She carefully inspected her violin, took her seat among the other violinists, arranged her music on the stand, and tuned her instrument. As the concert began, the conductor skillfully cued first one group of musicians and then another until finally, the crucial moment arrived. It was time for the one note to be played.

The conductor turned to the violinist and signaled her to sound her note. She did, and then the moment was over. The orchestra played on, and the one-note woman sat quietly through the rest of the concert—not with a sense of disappointment that she had played only one note, but with a sense of contentment and peace of mind that she had played her one note in tune, on time, and with great gusto.

Sometimes one-note people are criticized for being limited or narrow in their perspectives by those whose lifestyles require the playing of many notes. God values a job well done, so it certainly deserves our recognition and respect.

Every individual has a place to fill in the
world and is important in some respect,
whether he chooses to be or not.

Do I DO EVERYTHING WITH ALL MY MIGHT, EVEN THE SEEMINGLY INCONSEQUENTIAL THINGS?

Shine Your Light

*Be ye followers of me, even
as I also am of Christ.*

1 CORINTHIANS 11:1

How CAN
I GENUINELY
BE THE
LIGHT OF
MY CHILD'S
WORLD?

During a special program at church, a little girl was to recite the Scripture she had been assigned for the occasion. When she got in front of the crowd, however, the sight of hundreds of eyes peering at her caused her to have a bout of stage fright. She completely forgot her verse and was unable to utter a single word.

Her mother, sitting in the front row, leaned forward, and after several attempts, finally got her daughter's attention. She moved her lips and gestured, but her daughter didn't seem to comprehend what she was doing. Finally, the mother whispered the first few words of the verse she was to recite: "I am the light of the world."

The little girl's face lit up, and she smiled with confidence. "My mother is the light of the world!" she announced boldly.

Her words brought a smile to the face of every audience member, of course, and yet upon reflection, most had to admit that the little girl had declared an eloquent truth. A mother is the light of her child's world.

Let your light shine brightly today on your child's behalf!

*My mother was the source from which
I derived the guiding principles of my life.*

Tiny Steps Forward

A just man falleth seven times,
and riseth up again.

PROVERBS 24:16

Most people know that Thomas Edison conducted countless experiments with various kinds of materials in search of an effective filament to use in carbon incandescent lamps. As each fiber failed, he would toss it out the window. Ultimately, the pile of failures reached to his second-story window.

One day in 1879, some thirteen months after his first failure, he succeeded in finding a filament that would withstand the stress of an electric current. Edison casually picked up a bit of lampblack, mixed it with tar, rolled it into a thin thread, and thought, *Why not try a carbonized cotton fiber?* He worked for five hours to make a fiber, but it broke in two before he removed the mold. He used two spools of cotton thread before a perfect strand emerged, only to have it fall apart when he tried to place it in a glass tube. He continued without sleep for two days and nights before he managed to slip one of the carbonized threads into a vacuum-sealed bulb. When he turned on the current, he saw the glow of electric light that we now take for granted.

A failure doesn't signal the end of your dream. It simply brings you one step closer to the success you desire!

———— ❦ ————

Falling down doesn't make you a failure,
but staying down does.

I MAY NEVER INVENT ANYTHING, BUT I CAN CONTRIBUTE TOWARD . . .

Gift and Giver

How fair is thy love, my sister, my spouse!
how much better is thy love than wine! and
the smell of thine ointments than all spices!
SONG OF SOLOMON 4:10

I NEED A
SPIRIT OF
GENEROSITY
AND A
WILLINGNESS
TO GIVE
WHEN IT
COMES TO...

The ability to give is, in itself, a gift—a manifestation of God's goodness to a person. If you have trouble giving, ask God to give you a spirit of generosity and a willingness to give!

George MacDonald writes in *The Word of Jesus on Prayer,* "For the real good of every gift it is essential, first, that the giver be in the gift—as God always is, for He is love—and next, that the receiver know and receive the giver in the gift. Every gift of God is but a harbinger of His greatest and only sufficing gift—that of Himself. No gift unrecognized as coming from God is at its own best: therefore many things that God would gladly give us must wait until we ask for them, that we may know whence they come. When in all gifts we find Him, then in Him we shall find all things."

Choose gifts wisely. Put yourself into them—your time, your creativity, and your sensitivity to the other person's needs and desires.

When you receive a gift, look beyond its surface appearance and value the one who gave it. Receive the giver's present as an act of their love and their desire to have a relationship with you.

A wise lover values not so much the gift
of the lover as the love of the giver.

A Helpful Stranger

Though I have the gift of prophecy, and understand all mysteries, and all knowledge; and though I have all faith, so that I could remove mountains, and have not charity, I am nothing.

1 CORINTHIANS 13:2

On a bitter-cold Virginia evening, an old man waited on a path by a river, hoping for someone on a horse to carry him across. His beard was glazed with frost, and his body grew numb before he finally heard the thunder of horses' hooves. Anxiously, he watched as several horsemen appeared. He let the first pass by without making an effort to get his attention, then another and another. Finally, only one rider remained. As he drew near, the old man caught his eye and asked, "Sir, would you mind giving me a ride to the other side?"

The rider helped the man onto his horse and, sensing he was half frozen, decided to take him all the way home, which was several miles out of the way. As they rode, the horseman asked, "Why didn't you ask one of the other men to help you? I was the last one. What if I had refused?" The old man said, "I've been around awhile, son, and I know people pretty well. When I looked into their eyes and saw they had no concern for my condition, I knew it was useless to ask. When I looked into your eyes, I saw kindness and compassion."

At the door of the old man's house, the rider resolved, "May I never get too busy in my own affairs that I fail to respond to the needs of others." And with that, Thomas Jefferson turned and directed his horse back to the White House.

May you never get too busy with your own affairs that you fail to respond to the needs of others!

When PEOPLE LOOK IN MY EYES, DO THEY SEE LACK OF CONCERN OR KINDNESS AND COMPASSION?

⌘

People don't care how much you know, until they know how much you care . . . about them.

To Crown a Life

Many waters cannot quench love,
nor will rivers overflow it; if a man
were to give all the riches of his house
for love, it would be utterly despised.

SONG OF SOLOMON 8:7 NASB

How HAVE
I MADE
THE WAY
SMOOTHER
FOR THOSE
I LOVE?

Love is the filling from one's own,
Another's cup,
Love is the daily laying down
And taking up;
A choosing of the stony path
Through each new day,
That other feet may tread with ease
A smoother way.
Love is not blind, but looks abroad
Through other's eyes;
And asks not, "Must I give?"
But "May I sacrifice?"
Love hides its grief, that other hearts
And lips may sing;
And burdened walks, that other lives
May buoyant wing.
Hast thou a love like this?
Within thy soul?
'Twill crown thy life with bliss
When thou dost reach the goal.

—Author Unknown

Love gives itself; it is not bought.

Getting a Tune-Up

Let the heart of them rejoice that seek the LORD. Seek the LORD, and his strength: seek his face evermore.

PSALM 105:3-4

"You must have a good heart," one man said to his child, "if you are going to act right in this world." And then to illustrate his point, he continued, "Suppose my watch was not keeping time very well. Would it do any good if I went to the town clock and made the hands of my watch point exactly the same as those of the larger clock in the square? No, of course not! Soon my watch would be just as inaccurate as before. Rather, I should take my watch to a watchmaker or to a jewelry store that repairs watches. It is only when my watch has been cleaned and repaired that its hands will be able to keep time accurately all day long."

When we spend time in prayer, we are going to the heart maker, asking Him to clean and repair our hearts from the damage caused by sins we have committed. We are asking Him to put us right again on the inside, so that we can act right on the outside. When our children see us doing this, they are much more likely to go to the heart maker when they feel their own lives are in disarray or out of sync, rather than turn to the world and reset their souls according to its standards and priorities.

Have you visited the heart maker today?

—✦—

Example is not the main thing in influencing others. It is the only thing.

My HEART NEEDS TO BE CLEANED AND REPAIRED FROM THE DAMAGE CAUSED BY . . .

The Parts of a Successful Life

I laboured more abundantly than they all: yet not I, but the grace of God which was with me.

1 CORINTHIANS 15:10

What STANDARD DO I MEASURE MY EVERYDAY ACTIONS AGAINST?

Wallace E. Johnson, president of Holiday Inns and one of America's most successful builders, once said,

> I always keep on a card in my billfold the following verses and refer to them frequently: "Ask, and it shall be given you; seek, and ye shall find; knock, and it shall be opened unto you: For every one that asketh receiveth; and he that seeketh findeth; and to him that knocketh it shall be opened" (Matthew 7:7-8).
>
> These verses are among God's greatest promises. Yet they are a little one-sided. They indicate a philosophy of receiving but not of giving. One day as my wife, Alma, and I were seeking God's guidance for a personal problem, I came across the following verse which has since been a daily reminder to me of what my responsibility as a businessman is to God: "Study to shew thyself approved unto God, a workman that needeth not to be ashamed, rightly dividing the word of truth" (2 Timothy 2:15).
>
> Since then I have measured my actions against the phrase: "A workman that needeth not to be ashamed."

What standard do you measure your actions against?

Faith on the inside + Works on the outside = A successful life!

Picking Teams

*He that walketh with wise men
shall be wise: but a companion
of fools shall be destroyed.*

PROVERBS 13:20

In his book, *The Mind of Watergate,* psychiatrist Leo Rangell, M.D., relates what he calls a "compromise of integrity" as he analyzes the relationship between former President Richard M. Nixon and several of his closest confidants. He records a conversation between investigative committee member Senator Howard Baker and young Herbert L. Porter:

Baker: Did you ever have any qualms about what you were doing? . . . Did you ever think of saying, "I do not think this is quite right." . . . Did you ever think of that?

Porter: Yes, I did.

Baker: What did you do about it?

Porter: I did not do anything.

Baker: Why didn't you?

Porter: In all honesty, probably because of the fear of the group pressure that would ensue, of not being a team player.

There's nothing wrong with being a team player as long as you are careful about choosing your team! You will become like your friends, just as they will become like you. Therefore, choose your team cautiously and thoughtfully!

Am I ON
THE RIGHT
TEAMS IN
THE VARIOUS
SPHERES OF
MY LIFE?

The rotten apple spoils his companion.

When Silence Equals Agreement

If you do not stand firm in your faith,
you will not stand at all.

ISAIAH 7:9 NIV

HOW HAS MY
SILENCE ON A
RECENT
ISSUE LED
OTHERS TO
BELIEVE
I AGREED
WITH THEIR
UNSCRIPTURAL
POSITION?

As legend has it, a just and good man went to Sodom one day, hoping to save the city from God's judgment. He tried talking to first one individual and then the next, but no one would talk to him.

Next, he tried carrying a picket sign that had "Repent" written on it in large letters. Nobody paid any attention to his sign.

Finally, he began going from street to street and from marketplace to marketplace, shouting loudly, "Men and women, repent! What you are doing is wrong. It will kill you! It will destroy you!"

The people laughed at him, but still he went about shouting. One day someone stopped him and said, "Stranger, can't you see that your shouting is useless?" The man replied, "Yes, I see that." The person then asked, "So why do you continue?"

The man said, "When I arrived in this city, I was convinced that I could change them. Now I continue shouting because I don't want them to change me."

Speak out for those things you believe to be good and true. If you remain silent, others may take your silence as affirmation of their position.

A barking dog is often more
useful than a sleeping lion.

Clear Conscience

If our hearts do not condemn us,
we have confidence before God.

1 JOHN 3:21 NIV

Among the items in the Mark Twain Memorial in Hartford, Connecticut, are these words neatly framed: "Always do right. It will gratify some people and astonish the rest. Truly yours, Mark Twain. New York, February 16, 1901."

Conscience is what leads a person to do right. A conscience is molded from the first lessons we learn about right and wrong. If we are never taught those lessons, we fail to develop a moral conscience. If we are taught poorly or incompletely, we develop a stunted conscience. If we override our conscience and refuse to obey its advice, we develop a hardened conscience, and over time, we will live as if we don't have one. Without a conscience, our lives are lawless, immoral, and tainted—without character.

You can't see a conscience or autopsy it, but you can hear it whispering in your mind and feel it tugging at your heart. Nurture your conscience. Keep reinforcing what you know to be right. One way to do that is to read aloud the Word of God or to hear the Word of God preached.

Above all, don't take your conscience for granted. It is either healthy or becoming unhealthy. And as your conscience goes, so goes your reputation and the quality of your life.

—⦵⦵⦵—

There is one thing alone that stands
the brunt of life throughout its length:
a quiet conscience.

I CAN NURTURE MY CONSCIENCE DAILY BY...

Waiting for Victory

SEPTEMBER 10

Now thanks be unto God, which
always causeth us to triumph in Christ.

2 CORINTHIANS 2:14

I FIND IT
DIFFICULT TO
WAIT FOR
THINGS,
ESPECIALLY
WHEN IT
COMES TO...

Charlie Lewis moved to Michigan after losing the 1993 mayoral election in Hickory, Mississippi, by just one vote. He decided to enjoy the quiet life of a retiree, believing the election challenge he had requested from the courts was unlikely to succeed. Then came an unexpected phone call to return to Mississippi. The state's Supreme Court had thrown out three absentee ballots cast for Wayne Griffith, the residing mayor, wiping out his one-vote victory and making Lewis the winner by a two-vote margin—115 to 113.

"It's been more than two years," the seventy-two-year-old Lewis said in response to the news. "I guess I had forgotten about it. . . . I think that when you get to be seventy-two years old you learn how to digest things." Still, he was excited about the court's decision and the opportunities that awaited him.

Lewis became the first black mayor of the tiny town of five hundred nestled in the red clay hills of east Mississippi. "I waited for a while, but the law takes time," Lewis was quoted as saying.

Waiting may leech some of the enthusiasm out of a victory, but if the cause is just, waiting never destroys the joy of an eventual triumph.

I would rather fail in the cause
that someday will triumph than triumph
in a cause that someday will fail.

In the Service of Others

The only letter I need is you yourselves! . . .
They can see that you are a letter
from Christ, written by us . . . not one
carved on stone, but in human hearts.

2 CORINTHIANS 3:2-3 TLB

Oseola McCarty has spent most of her life helping people look nice—taking in bundles of dirty clothes and washing and ironing them. She quit school in the sixth grade to go to work, never married, never had children, and never learned to drive because there was no place in particular she wanted to go.

Her work was her life. It was her way of being a blessing to others. In fact, many black people in rural Mississippi didn't even have a job when Oseola began working.

For most of her eighty-seven years, Oseola spent almost no money. She lived in her old family home and bound her ragged old Bible with Scotch tape to keep the book of 1 Corinthians from falling out. She saved her money, most of it coming in dollar bills and change, until she had amassed a little more than $150,000. That money became what people in Hattiesburg call "The Gift." She donated her entire savings—all $150,000—to black college students in Mississippi. Miss McCarty said, "I know it won't be too many years before I pass on . . . so I planned to do this. I planned it myself." She also said, "I wanted to share my wealth with the children." Her great hope is to see a beneficiary of her gift graduate before she dies.

Oseola McCarty lives her life in service to others and looks to the future, rather than to her own day-to-day needs. She will leave a legacy written on the hearts of grateful college graduates, who can perpetuate her generosity.

What AM I SACRIFICING TODAY SO THAT I MAY LEAVE A GIFT TO OTHERS?

*Carve your name on hearts
and not on marble.*

Calm and Collected

Don't be anxious about tomorrow.
God will take care of your tomorrow
too. Live one day at a time.
MATTHEW 6:34 TLB

The THINGS
I'M
WORRYING
ABOUT TODAY
THAT
PROBABLY
WON'T EVEN
HAPPEN
INCLUDE...

Don't cross your bridges until you get
to them. We spend our lives defeating
ourselves, crossing bridges we never get to.

During the four-week siege of Tientsin, during the Boxer Rebellion in June of 1900, Herbert Hoover helped erect barricades around the foreign compound and organized all the able-bodied men into a protective force to man them. Mrs. Hoover went to work, too, helping set up a hospital, taking her turn nursing the wounded, and serving tea every afternoon to those on sentry duty. Like her husband, she remained calm and efficient throughout the crisis and even seemed to enjoy the excitement a bit.

One afternoon while sitting at home playing solitaire, resting after her work in the hospital, a shell suddenly burst nearby. She ran to the backdoor and found a big hole in the backyard. A little later a second shell hit the road in front of the house. Then came a third shell. This one burst through one of the windows of the house and demolished a post by the staircase.

Several reporters covering the siege rushed into the living room to see if she was all right and found her sitting at the card table. "I don't seem to be winning this hand," she remarked coolly, "but that was the third shell and therefore the last one for the present anyway. Their pattern is three in a row." Then she suggested brightly, "Let's go and have tea."

Staying calm in the face of danger is your best defense. Worrying about what might happen causes unnecessary stress. Those things you think might happen probably won't. So relax and remember that you're in God's hands.

One Word Counts

A word fitly spoken is like apples
of gold in pictures of silver.
PROVERBS 25:11

Consider the infamous statements listed below, and as you read, notice that they all could be corrected by changing or inserting only one word!

"Everything that can be invented has been invented," Charles H. Duell, U.S. Patent Office director, 1899.

"Who wants to hear actors talk?" H. M. Warner, Warner Brothers Pictures, © 1927.

"Sensible and responsible women do not want to vote," Grover Cleveland, 1905.

"There is no likelihood man can ever tap the power of the atom," Robert Millikan, Nobel prize winner in physics, 1923.

"Heavier-than-air flying machines are impossible," Lord Kelvin, president, Royal Society, © 1895.

"[Babe] Ruth made a big mistake when he gave up pitching," Tris Speaker, 1927.

"Gone with the Wind is going to be the biggest flop in Hollywood history," Gary Cooper.

Being just one word off makes a great deal of difference! Make your words count today.

The difference between the right word
and the almost-right word is the difference
between lightning and the lightning bug.

Do I MAKE SURE MY WORDS ARE "FITLY SPOKEN"?

Stuck in a Rut

Come out from among them, and
be ye separate, saith the Lord.
2 CORINTHIANS 6:17

AM I IN A
RUT OF MY
OWN MAKING,
AND IF SO,
WHERE AM
I GOING?

A biologist once experimented with what he called processional caterpillars. He lined up caterpillars on the rim of a flowerpot so the lead caterpillar was head-to-tail with the last caterpillar, with no break in the parade. The tiny creatures walked around the rim of the pot for a full week before they died of exhaustion and starvation. Not once did any of the caterpillars break out of the line and venture over into the plant to eat. Food was only inches away, but their follow-the-leader instinct was stronger than the drive to eat and survive!

When we find ourselves in a rut, we would be wise to ask ourselves these three questions:

- Is this rut of my own making? We tend to choose a rut because it's comfortable and requires no risk. To get out of a rut, make daring new choices!

- Who am I following? We adopt certain patterns in our lives because someone has taught them to us, directly or by example. Follow good leaders; don't simply follow the crowd.

- Where am I going? Ruts develop when we lose a sense of vision for our lives—when we are just traveling through life and not attempting to arrive at a destination. Goals take you somewhere!

A man who wants to lead the orchestra
must turn his back on the crowd.

Getting Up

A wise man's heart directs him toward the right, but the foolish man's heart directs him toward the left.

ECCLESIASTES 10:2 NASB

The story is told of two brothers who were convicted of stealing sheep. They were each branded on the forehead with the letters "ST"— Sheep Thief.

One brother immediately ran away from the area and attempted to build a new life in a foreign land. Even there, people asked him about the strange letters on his forehead. He wandered restlessly, and eventually, unable to bear the stigma, he took his own life.

The other brother took a different approach. He said to himself, *I can't run away from the fact that I stole sheep. But I will stay here and win back the respect of my neighbors and myself.*

As the years passed, he built a reputation of integrity. One day a stranger saw the old man with the letters branded on his forehead. He asked a citizen of the town what the letters stood for. The villager replied, "It happened a great while ago. I've forgotten the particulars, but I think the letters are an abbreviation of Saint."

You may get away with an evil deed and not be visibly branded, but evil deeds always brand your heart. The only true way to change a branded heart is to repent and say, "I'm sorry." Then rebuild your good reputation with your subsequent acts of kindness.

A man of honor regrets a discreditable act even when it has worked.

DO I HAVE A BRANDED HEART THAT NEEDS TO BE CHANGED?

When to Say When

*Withdraw thy foot from thy
neighbour's house; lest he be
weary of thee, and so hate thee.*

PROVERBS 25:17

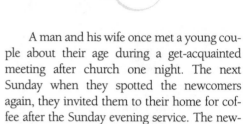

In MY
EAGERNESS
TO MAKE
FRIENDS, I
SOMETIMES
GO
OVERBOARD
BY . . .

A man and his wife once met a young couple about their age during a get-acquainted meeting after church one night. The next Sunday when they spotted the newcomers again, they invited them to their home for coffee after the Sunday evening service. The newcomers happily accepted their invitation.

Both the conversation and the coffee were warm and cozy, but the evening began to grow long. Still, the young couple—perhaps overly eager to make friends—talked on and on about their move to the city, the learning curve they were experiencing in their new jobs, the difficulty they had settling their children into new schools, their long search for a church home, the trials of finding a dentist, doctor, shoe repairman, and dry-cleaning establishment.

No matter how many times the host and hostess yawned or failed to reply, the couple had more to say. Finally, even the visiting couple began to yawn. Still, they made no move to leave.

At long last the host stood to his feet and with a wide stretch of his arms, he looked at his wife and said, "Well, darlin', let's go up to bed so these nice folks can go home!"

Your chances of being asked back are better when you don't wear out your welcome.

———∽∾∽———

*The art of being a good guest is
knowing when to leave.*

Stirring Up Trouble

*A man that beareth false witness
against his neighbour is a maul,
and a sword, and a sharp arrow.*

PROVERBS 25:18

A trumpeter was once captured by the enemy. "Please spare me," he pleaded with his captors. "I have no gun. I am not guilty of any crime. I have not killed a single one of your soldiers. I only carry this poor brass trumpet and play it when I'm told to."

"That is the very reason for putting you to death," his captors said. "For while you do not fight yourself, your trumpet stirs up all the others to battle. It causes many others to kill!"

So it is with our criticism of others. We may not hate, mistrust, or avoid the person we criticize, but our criticism can cause others to exhibit those feelings.

There was once a woman to whom gossip and criticism were so utterly distasteful that whenever a visitor brought up something negative about a person, she would say, "Come, let's go and ask if this is true." The talebearer was always so shocked that he or she would beg to be excused. But the determined woman would insist on escorting the reluctant soul to the subject of the tale to verify its truth or to hear the other point of view. After awhile, no one repeated a tale or voiced a criticism in her presence.

Build up your friends. Don't tear them down!

Pick your friends, but not to pieces.

I CAN HELP OTHERS TO AVOID STIRRING UP STRIFE BY . . .

269

The Bright Side

The authority the Lord gave us [is] for building you up rather than pulling you down.

2 CORINTHIANS 10:8 NIV

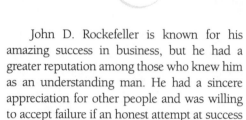

Whom
COULD I
ENCOURAGE
TODAY,
DESPITE
THEIR
OBVIOUS
FAILURE?

John D. Rockefeller is known for his amazing success in business, but he had a greater reputation among those who knew him as an understanding man. He had a sincere appreciation for other people and was willing to accept failure if an honest attempt at success had been made.

When one of his partners, Edward T. Bedford, failed in a business venture, costing Rockefeller's company a million dollars, Rockefeller responded with a statement that has become a classic in business lore. He didn't criticize Bedford, because he knew he had done his best. He did go down to Bedford's office and say, "I think it is honorable that you were able to salvage 60 percent of the money you invested in the South American venture. That's not bad; in fact, it's splendid. We don't always do as well as that upstairs."

There's little to be gained by making someone feel worse regarding something they already feel bad about. The gain lies in helping someone see the beneficial side of a failure, the positive lessons that can be learned from mistakes, and to instill hope for the future. Encourage another person today. You'll both feel, and do, better.

※

*Authority without wisdom is like
a heavy ax without an edge,
fitter to bruise than polish.*

Do What You Do

As in water face reflects face,
So the heart of man reflects man.

PROVERBS 27:19 NASB

A young man once made an appointment with a well-published author. The first question the author asked him was, "Why did you want to see me?"

The young man stammered, "Well, I'm a writer, too. I was hoping you could share with me some of your secrets for successful writing."

The author asked a second question, "What have you written?"

"Nothing," the young man replied, "at least nothing that is finished yet."

The author asked a third question, "Well, if you haven't written, then tell me, what are you writing?"

The young man replied, "Well, I'm in school right now, so I'm not writing anything at present."

The author then asked a fourth question, "So why do you call yourself a writer?"

Writers write. Composers compose. Painters paint. Workmen work. Who are you? To a great extent, what you do defines what you are and what you will become, and in turn, what you are gives rise to what you do. When what you do on the outside matches what you are on the inside, you can live with integrity.

The WORDS THAT BEST DEFINE WHO I AM AND WHAT I DO ARE:

Every man's work, whether it be
literature, or music, or pictures, or
architecture, or anything else, is
always a portrait of himself.

Taking the Initiative

Your ears shall hear a word behind you, saying, "This is the way, walk in it."

ISAIAH 30:21 NKJV

What UNCONTROL-LABLE URGE DO I HAVE TO ACCOMPLISH IN MY LIFE?

Many years ago, an intern in a New York hospital heard a surgeon bemoan the fact that most brain tumors were fatal. The surgeon predicted that someday another surgeon would discover how to save the lives of these patients. Intern Ernest Sachs dared to be that surgeon. At the time the leading expert on the anatomy of the brain was Sir Victor Horsley. Sachs received permission to study under him but felt he should prepare for the experience by studying for six months under some of the most able physicians in Germany. Then he went to England, where for two years he assisted Dr. Horsley in extensive experiments on dozens of monkeys.

When Sachs returned to America, he was ridiculed for requesting the opportunity to treat brain tumors. For years he fought obstacles and discouragement, driven by an uncontrollable urge to succeed in his quest. Today, largely thanks to Dr. Sachs, the majority of brain tumors can be cured. His book, *The Diagnosis and Treatment of Brain Tumors,* is considered the standard authority on the subject.

Just because something isn't being done doesn't mean it can't be done. Maybe you are the one to do it!

———————

Do not follow where the path may lead—go instead where there is no path and leave a trail.

272

Invest Wisely

I will very gladly spend
and be spent for you.

2 CORINTHIANS 12:15

Imagine for a moment that your bank suddenly announced this new policy:

"Every morning your account will be credited with $86,400. You can carry no balance from day to day. Every evening your account will be canceled, and whatever money you have failed to use during the day will be returned to the bank."

What would you do? Why, you'd draw out every cent of the $86,400 each day and spend it, save it, or invest it. Before long, you could be a wealthy person, indeed!

Actually, you have a bank account with a similar policy. It is called time. Every morning, you are given the prospect of 86,400 seconds. At the close of that twenty-four hour period, the moments you have failed to withdraw and invest into a good purpose are ruled off your ledger. Time carries no balance from day to day. It allows no overdrafts. Each day a new account is opened to you. If you fail to withdraw and use the day's deposit, it's your loss.

Those who truly love life use time to the maximum. Make your days count rather than counting your days!

When we love something it is of value to us, and when something is of value to us we spend time with it—time enjoying it, and time taking care of it.

I CAN BETTER
MAKE EACH
DAY COUNT
BY . . .

Hammering on Others

He that hath no rule over his own spirit is like a city that is broken down, and without walls.

PROVERBS 25:28

How CAN I BETTER CONTROL MY ANGER?

One of the most common expressions used to describe losing your temper is to "fly off the handle." This phrase refers to the head of a hammer coming loose from its handle as the carpenter attempts to use it. Several things can happen as a result:

- First, the hammer becomes useless— no longer good for work. When a person loses his temper, he loses his effectiveness. Anything he says may not be taken seriously and is likely to be unproductive.

- Second, the hammerhead—twirling out of control—is likely to cause some type of damage to anything in its path. The person who loses his temper causes damage even if he doesn't realize it—perhaps physically to people or objects in the way, and nearly always emotionally to those who feel they are the victims of this uncontrolled wrath.

- Third, the repair of both the hammer and the resulting damage takes time. The person who loses his temper may recover quickly, but the victim of a hot temper rarely recovers as quickly.

Keep your temper today. Nobody else wants it.

❦

Your temper is like a fire. It gets very destructive when it gets out of control.

To Please the Master

*Am I now trying to win the
approval of men, or of God?*

GALATIANS 1:10 NIV

A young man once studied violin under a world-renowned violinist and master teacher. He worked hard for several years at perfecting his talent, and the day finally came when he was called upon to give his first major public recital in the large city where both he and his teacher lived. Following each selection, which he performed with great skill and passion, the performer seemed uneasy about the great applause he received. Even though he knew those in the audience were musically astute and not likely to give such applause to a less-than-superior performance, the young man acted almost as if he couldn't hear the appreciation that was being showered upon him.

At the close of the last number, the applause was thunderous, and numerous "Bravos" were shouted. The talented young violinist, however, had his eyes glued on only one spot. Finally, when an elderly man in the first row of the balcony smiled and nodded to him in approval, the young man relaxed and beamed with both relief and joy. His teacher had praised his work! The applause of thousands meant nothing until he had first won the approval of the master.

Who ARE YOU MOST TRYING TO PLEASE TODAY—GOD OR MEN?

*If I were really trying to please
God instead of man, I would . . .
I don't know the secret to success, but the
key to failure is to try to please everyone.*

A Pocketful of Prayer

*Evening, and morning, and at noon,
will I pray, and cry aloud: and
he shall hear my voice.*

PSALM 55:17

I COULD
BE MORE
FAITHFUL IN
REGULARLY
PRAYING
FOR...

Like many women, Carol routinely emptied her husband's pockets before doing his laundry. She often pulled lists from his pockets, including prayer lists. Her husband rarely listed people's names, only what he was praying that the Lord would do in their lives.

One Monday a delivery woman named Betty, who picked up and delivered her husband's uniforms, came to Carol's door. Carol had never seen Betty smile before, but this day she glowed. She said, "I want to thank you for the prayers." Then she explained, "Every week I clean out the cargo pockets of your husband's fatigues. I thought that God had given up on me, but He has been speaking to me through the prayers that I find in your husband's pockets. I was starving for God and for His Word. Those scraps of paper with prayers were like food. I couldn't wait until Monday to see if I would find another message. I claimed each one as my own. Yesterday I accepted Jesus as my Savior. My new church has a group that ministers to people like me."

Only God knows the final outcome of all your prayer requests. He alone is the finisher and the great amen of what you request before His throne.

Daily prayers will diminish your cares.

Beyond the Edges

Peter answered him and said, Lord, if it be thou, bid me come unto thee on the water. And he said, Come. And when Peter was come down out of the ship, he walked on the water, to go to Jesus.

MATTHEW 14:28-29

Centuries ago when a mapmaker would run out of the known world before he ran out of parchment, he would often sketch a dragon at the edge of the scroll. This was intended to be a sign to the explorer that he was entering unknown territory at his own risk.

Many explorers, however, did not perceive the dragon as a mapmaker's warning sign but as a prophecy. They foresaw disaster and doom beyond the known worlds they traversed. Their fear kept them from pushing on to discover new lands and peoples.

Other more adventuresome travelers saw the dragon as a sign of opportunity—the doorway to a new territory worth exploring.

Each of us has a mental map containing the information we use for guidance as we explore each new day. Like the maps of long ago, our mental maps have edges, and sometimes those edges seem to be marked by dragons or fears. At times, our fears may be valid. But at other times, our fears may keep us from discovering more of this world or more about other people, including ourselves.

Don't let fear keep you from all that God desires for you to explore and to know!

Do I SEE THE UNKNOWN AS AN UNLIMITED OPPORTUNITY OR AS A DRAGON READY TO DEVOUR ME?

There is no security in life, only opportunity.

Rewarding Truth

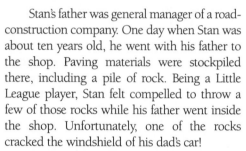

Train up a child in the way he should go: and when he is old, he will not depart from it.

PROVERBS 22:6

How CAN I EXTEND GRACE TO MY CHILDREN EVEN WHILE I'M DISCIPLINING THEM?

Stan's father was general manager of a road-construction company. One day when Stan was about ten years old, he went with his father to the shop. Paving materials were stockpiled there, including a pile of rock. Being a Little League player, Stan felt compelled to throw a few of those rocks while his father went inside the shop. Unfortunately, one of the rocks cracked the windshield of his dad's car!

No one was around, and Stan's first thought was to blame it on the poor kids who customarily passed the shop about that time each day. Still, Stan wasn't comfortable lying. When his father returned to the car, Stan was waiting there. With tears in his eyes, he told his father what had happened, fully expecting to be punished. His father surprised him, however, by calling the incident an accident. He noted that Stan could have blamed others, and he admired his honesty. Then he told his son that since he felt it was right for Stan to pay part of the damages, he would be forced to adjust Stan's weekly allowance from 25¢ a week up to 50¢ a week so Stan could pay a quarter a week toward the new windshield!

Our children are more likely to tell the truth when they are rewarded for it, rather than being severely punished for their misdeeds. God treats us with grace, and we are to treat our children in the same way. That doesn't mean they go undisciplined; it means they don't go unrewarded.

A young branch takes on all the bends that one gives to it.

Kindness—Pure and Simple

The fruit of the Spirit is love,
joy, peace, patience, kindness,
goodness, faithfulness.
GALATIANS 5:22 NIV

A number of years ago, the Advertising and Sales Executive Club sponsored a courtesy campaign in Kansas City. One thousand silver dollars were flown in from Denver. Then over a period of days mystery shoppers visited all types of stores, banks, and other places of business. They listened to telephone operators and observed bus drivers. Each day they filed a written report on the persons they found to be the most courteous.

Those chosen as the most courteous people in the city each received a silver dollar, along with a "Courtesy Pays" button and a congratulatory card. The fifteen most outstanding courteous people were guests at a banquet, where they were awarded $25 each. In all, more than a hundred people were honored.

What resulted was not only a temporary increase in the courtesy of the local residents, but awareness throughout the city that simple kindness can make a city a great place to live! The residual effect remained long after the campaign. Kansas City is still regarded as one of the friendliest cities in the nation.

It doesn't cost anything to be kind, but kindness can pay off in big ways.

Kindness is the oil that takes
the friction out of life.

Some OF THE SIMPLE ACTS OF KINDNESS I CAN EXHIBIT ON A DAILY BASIS ARE:

Instant Success?

Let us not become weary in doing good, for at the proper time we will reap a harvest if we do not give up.

GALATIANS 6:9 NIV

What ARE THE THINGS THAT CAUSE ME TO GROW WEARY AND TEMPT ME TO GIVE UP?

McCormick's father was what many might call a tinkerer. A mechanical genius, he invented many farm devices. Sadly, however, he became the laughingstock of his community for attempting to make a grain-cutting device. For years he worked on the project but never succeeded in getting it to operate reliably.

In spite of the failures of his father and the ridicule of neighbors, young McCormick took up the old machine as his own project. He also experienced years of experimentation and failure. And then one day he succeeded in constructing a reaper that would harvest grain!

Even so, jealous opposition prevented the invention from being used for a number of years. McCormick was able to make sales only after he gave a personal guarantee to each purchaser that the reaper would do the job he claimed it could do. Finally, after decades of trial and error and hoping and waiting, a firm in Cincinnati agreed to manufacture one hundred machines. Thus, the famous McCormick reaper was born.

To pick the ripest peach from the top of the tree, you have to climb up one branch at a time and not be defeated by the scrape of bark, the occasional fall, or the frequent feeling of being left dangling. Just keep climbing!

The ripest peach is highest on the tree.

The Wisdom of Youth

*He hath made us
accepted in the beloved.*

EPHESIANS 1:6

One morning, experiencing one of those irritating situations that can happen in life, a father lost his temper. He unleashed his frustration and anger on his son, who happened to be the closest target. Later in the day, while he and his son were fishing, he became convicted about what he had said and done. He began, "Son, I was a little impatient this morning."

"Uh huh," the son grunted, reeling in his line and preparing to cast again. The father continued, "Uh . . . I realize I was a little hard to be around."

Again, "Uh huh" was his son's only response. The father continued, "I . . . I want you to know that, uh . . . I feel bad about it." Then quick to justify himself he added, "But you know, Son, there are times that I'm just like that." The boy merely said, "Uh huh."

A few seconds passed, and then the boy added, "You know, Dad, God uses you to teach all of us in the family patience."

Our families have a way of nailing us with their honesty, but rather than feeling hammered, take what they say as good advice. Nobody else can help you grow into the nature of Christ as well as your family members!

Do I feel hammered when I'm nailed by someone's honesty or do I accept that person's good advice?

---

*Unless a father accepts his faults,
he will most certainly doubt his virtues.*

Working on Character

*A good name is rather to be
chosen than great riches.*

PROVERBS 22:1

What IS MY
REPUTATION
AMONG
THOSE IN MY
COMMUNITY
WHO KNOW
ME?

During a lawsuit, a witness was cross-examined regarding the statements he had made about the character and habits of the defendant. The counsel for the plaintiff said, "I believe you testified a little while ago that Mr. Smith, the defendant in this case, has a reputation for being very lazy and personally incompetent."

"No," protested the witness, "I did not say that, sir. What I said was that he changed jobs pretty often and that he seemed to get tired of work very quickly."

The lawyer persisted. "Has he or has he not a reputation in the community for being lazy?"

The witness replied, "Well, sir, I don't want to do the gentleman any injustice, and I don't go so far as to say he is lazy. But I do believe it's the general impression around the community that if it required any voluntary and sustained exertion on his part to digest his food, he would have died years ago from lack of nourishment."

Although we aren't necessarily wise to make decisions based upon what others think of us, it's a principle of life that when we work hard, do good work, and work for the good of all, others will recognize us as having reputable characters.

*If you were given a nickname descriptive of
your character, would you be proud of it?*

Gaining Wisdom

*All thy children shall be taught
of the LORD; and great shall be
the peace of thy children.*

ISAIAH 54:13

Two hunters chartered a plane to fly them into a remote region in Canada so that they might hunt for elk. When the plane returned for them a few days later, their hunt had been successful. The two hunters had six elk to show for their efforts.

When the pilot explained to them that his plane could only carry four of the elk, the hunters protested, "But the plane that we chartered last year was exactly like this one. It had the same horsepower, the weather was similar, and we took out six elk then."

Hearing this, the pilot reluctantly agreed to load all six elk. The plane struggled during takeoff and was unable to gain sufficient altitude to climb out of the valley. It crashed near the top of a mountain. To their great fortune, all three men survived.

As the hunters stumbled out of the wreckage, one of them asked the dazed pilot, "Do you know where we are?" He mumbled, "No." The other hunter, however, looked around and said confidently, "I think we're about a mile from where we crashed last year!"

Mistakes should foster wisdom. Teach your children to draw lessons from their skinned knees and bruised elbows. They'll have less pain and fewer scrapes later in life.

❦

*You cannot teach a child to take care of
himself unless you will let him try. . . .
He will make mistakes; and out of these
mistakes will come his wisdom.*

What CAN I LEARN FROM THE MISTAKES I'VE MADE RECENTLY?

A Woman of Confidence

Be patient with each other, making allowance for each other's faults because of your love.

EPHESIANS 4:2 TLB

In WHAT PRACTICAL WAYS CAN I MAKE THE DIFFERENCE BETWEEN SUCCESS AND FAILURE IN MY SPOUSE'S LIFE?

Nathaniel came home heartbroken. How could he tell his wife that he had just been fired from his job at the customhouse? The last thing he wanted her to think about him was that he was a failure, and yet he felt as if the word failure was embroidered on his chest.

To his surprise, when he told his wife what had happened, she responded with joy. "Now you can write your book!" she said optimistically.

"And what shall we live on while I am writing it?" Nathaniel replied, dejectedly.

His wife, Sophia, immediately went to a drawer, and to his amazement, she pulled out a substantial sum of money and handed it to him.

"Where did you get this?" he said in great surprise.

"I have always known you were a man of genius," Sophia said. "I knew that someday you would write a masterpiece. Every week, out of the money you gave me for the housekeeping, I saved a little bit. Here is enough to last us for one whole year."

So Nathaniel Hawthorne, buoyed by his wife's confidence, turned his hand to writing *The Scarlet Letter.*

Support and encourage your spouse, especially at his or her lowest point. You can make the difference between failure and success.

A loving spouse can see the good in you even when you can't.

Use Your Resources

Be very careful, then, how you live—
not as unwise but as wise, making
the most of every opportunity.

EPHESIANS 5:15-16 NIV

Sparky didn't have much going for him. He failed every subject in the eighth grade, and in high school, he flunked Latin, algebra, English, and physics. He made the golf team but promptly lost the most important match of the season and then lost the consolation match. He was awkward socially—more shy than disliked. While in high school, he never once asked a girl to go out on a date.

Only one thing was important to Sparky—drawing. He was proud of his artwork, even though no one else appreciated it. He submitted cartoons to the editors of his high school yearbook, but they were turned down. Even so, Sparky aspired to be an artist. After high school, he sent samples of his artwork to the Walt Disney studios. Again, he was turned down.

Still, Sparky didn't quit! He decided to write his own autobiography in cartoons. The character he created became famous worldwide—the subject not only of cartoon strips but countless books, television shows, and licensing opportunities. Sparky, you see, was Charles Schulz, creator of the "Peanuts" comic strip. Like his character, Charlie Brown, Schulz may not have been able to do many things, but he made the most of what he could do.

What you make of your life is up to you. Fill your days with activities that bring you closer to your goals.

———————

Our days are identical suitcases—
all the same size—but some people
can pack more into them than others.

What ONE SPECIFIC THING CAN I DO TODAY THAT WILL BRING ME CLOSER TO MY GOAL IN LIFE?

A Lesson at Home

So ought men to love their wives
as their own bodies. He that
loveth his wife loveth himself.
EPHESIANS 5:28

DO I TREAT
MY SPOUSE
AS I
HOPE THE
LORD WILL
TREAT ME?

Consider this:

- Children deduce their basic concept of God based upon the image of their own father—the human father is seen as a reflection of the Heavenly Father.

- Children draw their basic concepts of the Church based upon the example of their own mother—her daily nurturing, teaching, admonishing, and disciplining are internalized by her children as a reflection of these same spiritual qualities provided by the Church.

- Children draw their understanding of how God relates to the Church—and thus, how God relates to them as members of the Church—by watching how their father relates to their mother and she to him.

Your example of how you treat your spouse is a living parable to your children about how God wants to relate to them! Are you available to your spouse? Are you encouraging and supportive? Are you helpful?

Ask yourself today, "Do I treat my spouse as I hope the Lord will treat me?"

⸺◦⸺

The greatest thing a father can do
for his children is to love their mother.

What the Children See

Ye fathers, provoke not your children to wrath: but bring them up in the nurture and admonition of the Lord.

EPHESIANS 6:4

A dog once wandered to a preacher's home, and his three sons played with it, fed it, and soon became quite fond if it. It so happened that the dog had three white hairs in its tail. One day the preacher and his sons spotted an advertisement in the city newspaper about a lost dog. The stray they had taken in matched the description in the paper perfectly.

The minister later said, "In the presence of my three boys, I carefully separated the three white hairs and removed them from the dog's tail."

The real owner of the dog eventually discovered where his stray pooch had gone, and he came to claim him. The dog showed every sign of recognizing his owner, so the man was ready to take him away. At that point, the minister spoke up and asked, "Didn't you say the dog would be known by three white hairs in its tail?" The owner, unable to find the identifying feature, was forced to admit that this dog didn't fully fit the description of his lost dog, and he left.

Years passed and the minister noted with sadness, "We kept the dog, but I lost my three boys for Christ that day." His sons no longer had confidence in what their father professed to be true.

Remember that your children base their opinion of you on the choices they watch you make. Become a person of integrity—one they will admire and emulate.

Based ON THE CHOICES THEY HAVE SEEN ME MAKE, WHAT OPINION DO I THINK MY CHILDREN HAVE OF ME?

_____

No man ever really finds out what he believes in until he begins to instruct his children.

Time for Change

There is a time there for every purpose and for every work.
ECCLESIASTES 3:17

What IS MY TOP PRIORITY TODAY?

Dr. C. C. Albertson once wrote this about the use of time,

It might be wise for us to take a little inventory of our resources as to time and review our habits of using it. There are 168 hours in each week. Fifty-six of these we spend in sleep. Of the remaining 112 hours, we devote 48 to labor. This leaves 64 hours, of which let us assign 12 hours for our daily meals. . . .

We have left 52 hours, net, of conscious active life to devote to any purpose to which we are inclined.

Is it too much to say that God requires a tithe of this free time? One tenth of 52 hours is 5.2 hours. How much of this tithe of time do we devote to strictly religious uses?

If one allowed an hour for church and an hour for a Bible study or prayer meeting each week, he or she would still have 192 minutes a week—enough for nearly a half hour each day in prayer and Bible reading. Such a person would still have more than 45 hours a week for life's chores and personal fun!

The old excuse of too little time just doesn't hold water. The truth is that we always make time for those things we really want to do. What's your top priority today?

The greatest possession you have is the 24 hours directly in front of you.

Respecting Others

Don't be selfish. . . . Be humble, thinking
of others as better than yourself.

PHILIPPIANS 2:3 TLB

There's an old saying that goes, "It needs more skill than I can tell, to play the second fiddle well."

Along that line, Leonard Bernstein was once asked which instrument was the most difficult to play. He thought for a moment and said, "The second fiddle. I can get plenty of first violinists, but to find someone who can play the second fiddle with enthusiasm—that's a problem. And if we have no second fiddle, we have no harmony."

General Robert E. Lee was a man who knew the value of playing second fiddle. This great general never stopped being a true southern gentleman. Once while riding on a train to Richmond, he was seated at the rear of the car and all the other seats were filled with officers and soldiers. A poorly dressed elderly woman boarded the coach at a rural station. When no seat was offered to her, she trudged down the aisle toward the back of the car. Immediately, Lee stood up and offered her his place. Then one after another of the men arose and offered the general his seat. "No, gentlemen," he replied, "if there is none for this lady, there can be none for me!"

Genuine humility is what prompts us to give heartfelt thanks and to favor others more than ourselves.

The two most important words:
"Thank you." The most important word:
"We." The least important word: "I."

In WHAT WAYS DO I REGULARLY SHOW THAT I FAVOR OTHERS OVER MYSELF?

Finding a Purpose

Before I [God] formed thee in the belly I knew
thee; and before thou camest forth out of the
womb I sanctified thee, and I ordained thee.
JEREMIAH 1:5

I MAY NEVER
KNOW THE
WHY OF MY
TROUBLES,
BUT GOD
KNOWS WHAT
HE'S DOING
REGARDING
MY . . .

In telling her story of being paralyzed as the result of a swimming accident, Joni Eareckson wrote in *Joni,*

> I withdrew into myself and the solitude of home. After being away so long, I appreciated the old house with all its pleasant memories. Yet for some reason, I couldn't really feel at home there anymore; I felt awkward in my own home. . . .
>
> "What's the matter, honey?" Dad finally asked. . . .
>
> I sighed deeply, then said, "I guess the thing that affects me most is that I'm so helpless. I look around the house here, and everywhere I look I see the things you've built and created. It's really sad to think that I can't leave a legacy like you." . . .
>
> Dad wrinkled his forehead for a moment, then grinned again. "You've got it all wrong. These things I've done with my hands don't mean anything. It's more important that you build character. Leave something of yourself behind. Y'see? You don't build character with your hands. . . . Maybe we'll never know the why of our troubles, Joni. Look—I'm not a minister or a writer—I don't know exactly how to describe what's happening to us. But, Joni, I have to believe God knows what He's doing."

God has a purpose for every life, including yours.

There's a time when you have to explain to
your children why they're born, and it's a
marvelous thing if you know the reason.

Have or Have Not

*Not that I speak in respect of want: for
I have learned, in whatsoever state
I am, therewith to be content.*

PHILIPPIANS 4:11

The story is told of a farmer who had lived on the same farm all his life. It was a good farm with fertile soil, but with the passing of years, the farmer began to think, *Maybe there's something better for me.* He set out to find an even better plot of land to farm.

Every day he found a new reason for criticizing some feature of his old farm. Finally, he decided to sell it. He listed the farm with a real-estate broker who promptly prepared an advertisement emphasizing all the advantages of the acreage: ideal location, modern equipment, healthy stock, acres of fertile ground, high yields on crops, well-kept barns and pens, and a nice two-story house on a hill above the pasture.

When the real-estate agent called to read the ad to the farmer for his approval prior to placing it in the local paper, the farmer heard him out. When he had finished, he cried, "Hold everything! I've changed my mind. I'm not going to sell. Why, I've been looking for a place just like that all my life!"

When you start identifying the good traits of any person, situation, or organization, you are likely to find that the good often far outweighs the bad. Focus on what you have, then what you don't have will seem insignificant.

———✺———

*Contentment isn't getting what we want,
but being satisfied with what we have.*

What
POSITIVE
ASPECTS OF
MY LIFE CAN
I FOCUS ON?

Designed for Everyday Living

*That you may live a life worthy of
the Lord and may please him in every
way: bearing fruit in every good work.*
COLOSSIANS 1:10 NIV

How HAS
MY "SUNDAY
RELIGION"
SPILLED OVER
INTO MY
EVERYDAY
LIFE?

In *Growing Wise in Family Life* Charles R. Swindoll writes:

> You know what's helped us in the Swindoll home? To think of where we live as a training place, not a show-place. The home is a laboratory where experiments are tried out. It is a place where life makes up its mind. The home is a place where a child is free to think, to talk, to try out ideas. In a scene like that, God fits very comfortably into the entire conversation. And at any place where His name is inserted, it fits. . . .

> Isn't that comfortable? Ready for a shocker? It's supposed to be comfortable! Christianity is designed for everyday living. Society has made it a "Sunday religion." But true-to-life Christianity is designed for Tuesday afternoon just as beautifully as Saturday morning or Sunday evening. Thank goodness, you don't have to dress up for it. It fits after a meal as well as before bedtime.

Christianity is meant to spill over into our entire lives—to fill us to overflowing. Our faith is meant to be lived out every day of the week and in every action we take, every word we speak, and every relationship we make. It's meant to overflow from our hearts into the hearts of others.

*The measure of a man is not what he
does on Sunday, but rather who he is
Monday through Saturday.*

The Importance of Friends

*Don't be selfish. . . . Be humble, thinking
of others as better than yourself.*

PHILIPPIANS 2:3 TLB

One of the most important things we can
ever do is to be truly thankful for our friends—
and say so.

> Good friend of mine,
> Seldom is friendship such as thine;
> How very much I wish to be
> As helpful as you've been
>   to me . . .
> Of many prayer guests,
>   one thou art
> On whom I ask God to impart
> Rich blessings
>   from His storeroom rare,
> And grant to you
>   His gracious care . . .
> When I recall, from time to time,
> How you inspired
>   this heart of mine:
> I find myself inclined to pray,
> God bless my friend
>   this very day . . .
> So often, at the throne of Grace,
> There comes a picture
>   of your face:
> And then, instinctively, I pray
> That God may guide you
>   all the way . . .
> Some day, I hope
>   with you to stand
> Before the throne,
>   at God's right hand:
> And to say to you—
>   at journey's end:
> "Praise God you've been
>   to me a friend—
>   thank God for you."
> —Joseph Clark

IF I COULD
SEE MY
CLOSEST
FRIEND
BLESSED IN
ONE WAY, IT
WOULD BE . . .

A faithful friend is an image of God.

Stunted Potential

*Fathers . . . [do not be hard on
them (children) or harass them],
lest they become discouraged.*
COLOSSIANS 3:21 AMP

How CAN
I RAISE
THE CEILING
ON MY
CHILDREN'S
CREATIVITY?

For a number of years, flea circuses were quite popular. Today few people have ever seen a flea circus, much less know how fleas are trained.

When fleas are first put into a jar, they jump about wildly. Since fleas are incredible jumpers, a lid must be placed on even a large jar in order to keep the fleas contained. Still, they continue to jump, hitting their heads on the lid again and again. Over time, however, the fleas no longer jump as high as they did initially. Most of them jump to a height that is just a fraction of an inch beneath the lid.

At this point, a flea trainer can remove the lid from the jar. The fleas will continue to jump, but now they no longer jump out of the jar. The reason is simple. They have been conditioned to jump only so high. Once conditioned to jump to that height, that's all they will do! They will never aspire to jump higher.

Have you put a lid on your children's creativity? Have you built a ceiling so low that they are forever hitting their heads? Remove that lid quickly, or you may risk stunting the fulfillment of their God-given potential.

*Children are like clocks;
they must be allowed to run.*

Time for Prayer

*Devote yourselves to prayer,
keeping alert in it with an
attitude of thanksgiving.*

COLOSSIANS 4:2 NASB

Spiritual giants in every age have agreed on one thing about prayer: More is better. The founder of Methodism, John Wesley, spent one to two hours a day in private communication with God. Both Martin Luther and Bishop Francis Asbury believed a minimum of two hours of prayer a day was best. The great Scottish preacher, John Welch, regularly prayed eight to ten hours a day—and then often awoke in the middle of the night to continue his conversation with the Lord.

None of these men were ivory-tower contemplatives with nothing else to do. Asbury, for example, traveled some three hundred thousand miles, mostly on horseback, to build the American Methodist Church. Yet all advocated that people should pray as they worked.

Today many parents lead such busy lives they often think they have no time for prayer on behalf of their families. Yet the most powerful thing parents can do for their children is to pray. As you drive to work, walk from place to place, or do mundane chores, talk to God at length about each child. Thank God for your children. Listen for His advice. The change in your children and your relationship with them is likely to be remarkable, even miraculous!

How MUCH
TIME AM I
WILLING
TO DEVOTE
TO PRAYER
EACH DAY?

*The most effective thing we can do for our
children and families is pray for them.*

Hugs Help

A friend loves at all times, and a brother is born for adversity.

PROVERBS 17:17 NASB

Do I TRUST OTHERS TO HELP STEER ME THROUGH THE ROUGH COURSES OF LIFE?

A woman named Linda once was traveling from Alberta, Canada, to the Yukon. The highway was rutted and rugged, but Linda naively set out on her trip in a small run-down car. The first night on the road, she found a room at a motel near a summit. When she responded to her 5 A.M. wake-up call, she saw that the mountaintops were shrouded in early-morning fog. At breakfast, two truck drivers invited Linda to join them, and since the breakfast room was small, she did.

One of the truckers asked, "Where are you headed?" When she responded, "Whitehorse," the other driver said, "In that little car? In this fog? No way!"

"I'm going to try," Linda said bravely. "Then we'll have to hug you," one trucker said. Linda drew back. "There's no way I'm going to let you touch me!" The truckers chuckled. "Not like that," one of them said. "We'll put one truck in front of you and the other behind you. We'll get you through the mountains."

All morning long, Linda followed the two red taillights of the truck in front of her, with the reassurance of a big escort behind her. She made the trek through the treacherous passage safely.

Let your friends hug you and help you through the tough times.

A true friend never gets in your way unless you happen to be going down.

Shoulder the Burden Together

Your own friend and your father's friend, forsake them not. . . . Better is a neighbor who is near [in spirit] than a brother who is far off [in heart].

PROVERBS 27:10 AMP

A woman was in a serious automobile accident in a city far from home. She felt enclosed in a cocoon of pain, but she didn't realize how lonely she was until a forgotten friend in the city came to visit her. The friend firmly, but gently, said to her, "You should not be alone."

In the weeks that followed, this friend's advice rang in the injured woman's ears and helped her to overcome her otherwise reserved nature. When another friend called from a city several hundred miles away to say she wanted to come stay with her, the injured woman didn't say, "Don't bother," as would have been her normal response. Instead, she said, "Please come." The friend was a wonderful encouragement to her, reading the Psalms aloud when she was still too weak to read herself. Then yet another friend offered to come and help in her recovery. Again she swallowed her pride and said, "Please do." This friend stayed for several months until the injured woman was able to care for herself.

Even Jesus allowed another to help carry the cross on His way to Calvary. It's all right to ask for and receive help. You don't have to go through life alone. Let a friend help you!

The best antique is an old friend.

How HAVE I FOOLISHLY TRIED TO GO IT ALONE?

Family Etchings

The memory of the just is blessed.
PROVERBS 10:7

How CAN I MAKE MYSELF MORE REAL TO MY CHILDREN?

The bed was about forty-five years old when Elaine's mother offered it to her. Elaine decided to refinish it for her daughter's room. As she prepared to strip the wood, she noticed that the headboard was full of scratches. She deciphered one scratch as the date her parents were married. Above another date was a name she didn't recognize. A call to her mother revealed the details of a miscarriage before Elaine was born. Elaine realized the headboard had been something of a diary for her parents!

She wrote down all of the scratches she could decipher, and over lunch with her mother, she heard the stories of when her mother lost her purse at a department store, a rattlesnake was shot just as it was poised to strike her brother, a man saved her brother's life in Vietnam, her sister nearly died after falling from a swing, and a stranger stopped a potential mugging.

Elaine couldn't strip and sand away so many memories, so she moved the headboard into her own bedroom. She and her husband began to carve their own names and dates. "Someday," she says, "we'll tell our daughter the stories from her grandparents' lives and the stories from her parents' lives. And then the bed will pass on to her."

Telling our children stories of our childhood gives them a sense of who we are. It helps them realize that we were once children, too, and can identify with their pleasures and pains. It makes us seem more real to them.

*The best things you can give children,
next to good habits, are good memories.*

Consumed by Greed

*I keep under my body, and
bring it into subjection.*
1 CORINTHIANS 9:27

Eskimos use a grisly but effective means for killing the wolves that ravage their traps and dog teams.

First, the Eskimo coats a sharp knife blade with animal blood and allows it to freeze. Then he adds another layer of blood, and yet another, until the blade is completely concealed by frozen blood.

Next, the hunter places the knife in the ground with the blade up. When the wolf picks up the scent of the blood with its sensitive nose, it searches out the bait and begins licking the stick of frozen blood. The more it licks the blood, the greater its desire for more. It licks until it is eventually lapping the blade itself.

So great is the wolf's desire for more blood that it doesn't notice that the razor-sharp knife has cut its own tongue, nor does it realize that the blood it is licking is its own. Its ravenous thirst for blood causes the wolf to bleed to death. It is usually found dead at the scene, a victim of its own appetite.

In like manner, your own lusts can consume you to the point where they become your demise. What have you been craving? Today, choose wisely.

※

*I count him braver who overcomes his
desires than him who conquers his
enemies; for the hardest victory
is the victory over self.*

Lately
I'VE BEEN
CRAVING . . .

Keeping Praise Quiet

*Encourage one another and build
each other up, just as in fact
you are doing.*
1 THESSALONIANS 5:11 NIV

From WHOM
HAVE I
WITHHELD
MY PRAISE
LATELY?

It Isn't Enough

It isn't enough to say in our hearts
That we like a man for his ways,
It isn't enough that we fill our minds
With paeans of silent praise;
Nor is it enough that we honor a man
As our confidence upward mounts,
It's going right up to the man himself,
And telling him so that counts!
If a man does a work you really admire,
Don't leave a kind word unsaid,
In fear that to do so might make him vain
And cause him to "lose his head."
But reach out your hand and tell him,
"Well done," and see how his gratitude swells;
It isn't the flowers we strew on the grave,
It's the word to the living that tells.

—Anonymous

For lack of praise, many think others have drawn negative conclusions about them. You can actually wound people by withholding your praise. Let others know you think well of them. What a difference your words can make!

*Everyone has an invisible sign hanging from
his neck, saying, "Make me feel important!"*

The Attitude of Christ

Whatever you do, work at it with all your heart,
as working for the Lord, not for men. . . .
It is the Lord Christ you are serving.

COLOSSIANS 3:23-24 NIV

Legend has it that a missionary was swept overboard while traveling on high and rough seas and was subsequently washed up on a beach at the edge of a remote native village. Nearly dead from exposure and lack of food and fresh water, he was found by the people of the village and nursed back to health. He lived among them for twenty years, quietly adapting to their culture and working alongside them. He preached no sermons and made no claim of personal faith. He neither read nor recited Scripture to them.

But when people were sick, he sat with them, sometimes all night. When people were hungry, he fed them. When people were lonely, he gave a listening ear. He taught the ignorant and always took the side of the one who had been wronged.

The day came when missionaries entered the village and began talking to the people about a man named Jesus. After listening for a while to their story, the natives insisted that Jesus had already been living in their village for many years. "Come," one of them said, "we'll introduce you to Him." The missionaries were led to a hut where they found their long-lost companion.

Our actions truly do speak louder than words!

If MY ACTIONS REALLY DO SPEAK LOUDER THAN WORDS, WHAT ARE THEY TELLING PEOPLE ABOUT ME?

It is not what a man does that determines whether his work is sacred or secular, it is why he does it.

Follow the Leader

Iron sharpeneth iron; so a man sharpeneth the countenance of his friend.

PROVERBS 27:17

In WHAT WAY DO I MOST APPEAR TO IMITATE JESUS?

A missionary surgeon in one of China's hospitals restored sight to a man who had been nearly blinded by cataracts. A few weeks later, to his great surprise, forty-eight blind men showed up on the hospital's doorstep. They had all come to be cured. Amazingly, these blind men had walked more than 250 miles from a remote area of China to get to the hospital. They had traveled by holding on to a rope chain. Their guide and their inspiration was the man who had been cured.

The Christian evangelist Dr. J. Wilbur Chapman concluded from his study of the New Testament gospels that Jesus healed some forty people personally and directly. Of this number, thirty four were brought to Jesus or His attention, or Jesus was led to them by friends or family members. Only six of the forty people healed in the gospels found their way to Jesus, or He to them, without someone assisting.

In the gospels, Jesus refers to His followers as "friends." To them, He was the Friend of friends, closer even than a brother. Not only do we become like the friends with whom we associate, but when our friends are like Jesus, we find ourselves more likely to imitate Him!

*Keep company with good men
and good men you will imitate.*

Unrepentant for a Reason

A model for you, so that you would follow our example.

2 THESSALONIANS 3:9 NASB

Louisa May Alcott not only accepted her parents' values, but perpetuated them. She grew up in a generous home, even though life was plain in their house, which didn't even have a stove. A friend once observed that their extremely meager meals were often reduced from three a day to two if there was a family who might be in need. The Alcotts themselves, however, would have been the last to consider themselves poor or feel sorry for themselves.

Louisa was once invited to visit a family in Providence. With no other children in the house, she became bored after a few days. She found some dirty, ragged children who seemed like ideal playmates, and she played with them for a long time in the barn. Finding them poorly fed and hungry, she ran in haste to the pantry, which was unguarded at the time, and helped herself to figs and cakes for all. When her hostess discovered what she had done, Louisa was scolded and sent to the attic to ponder her outrageous behavior. Dear Louisa! She didn't have the faintest idea that feeding the poor was wrong. She did not cry, nor was she repentant. Rather, she was angry that her hostess had not offered more for her to take to her new friends.

Children form their perspective about money from their parents. If we behave as if we have enough, and give generously to others, our children will live the same way—and live much happier for it!

What PERSPECTIVE ON MONEY HAVE I TAUGHT MY CHILDREN?

If you want your child to accept your values when he reaches his teen years, then you must be worthy of his respect during his younger days.

An Uncompromising Man

Holding faith, and a good conscience;
which some having put away
concerning faith have made shipwreck.

1 TIMOTHY 1:19

In WHAT
WAY HAVE
I BEEN
COMPROMIS-
ING MY
PRINCIPLES?

Bubba Smith became famous not only for his performance on the football field, but perhaps even more so for his performances on television as a spokesman for a brewery. The day came, however, when Bubba swore off booze.

Actually, Bubba never did drink. Still, he sold countless kegs of beer by making clever beer commercials. He may be the first athlete ever to give up a highly lucrative, easy, and amusing job because he felt it was morally wrong. Why did he take this step?

Bubba was invited to be the grand marshal of a major university's homecoming parade, and as he rode around the field during halftime, he heard drunken college fans yelling, "Tastes great!" while others shouted, "Less filling." In Bubba's opinion, they should have been yelling, "Go, State!" or, "Get 'em, Bubba."

Bubba Smith realized in a matter of moments that he was encouraging others to do something that he himself chose not to do. When young school children began approaching him on the streets reciting his commercials verbatim, Bubba hung up his commercial career, saying simply, "I had to stop compromising my principles."

May a clear conscience always be more valuable to us than man-made rewards!

He who sacrifices his conscience to
ambition burns a picture
to obtain the ashes.

Taking God at His Word

The earnest prayer of a righteous man has great power and wonderful results.

JAMES 5:16 TLB

An old woman with a halo of silvered hair—the hot tears flowing down her furrowed cheeks—her worn hands busy over a washboard in a room of poverty—praying—for her son John—John who ran away from home in his teens to become a sailor—John of whom it was now reported that he had become a very wicked man—praying, praying always, that her son might be of service to God. The mother believed in two things, the power of prayer and the reformation of her son. God answered her prayer by working a miracle in the heart of John Newton.

John Newton, the drunken sailor became John Newton, the sailor-preacher [who wrote the words to "Amazing Grace"]. Among the thousands of men and women he brought to Christ was Thomas Scott . . . [who] used both his pen and voice to lead thousands of unbelieving hearts to Christ, among them William Cowper . . . [who] in a moment of inspiration wrote "There Is a Fountain Filled With Blood." And this song has brought countless thousands to the Man who died on Calvary. All this resulted because a mother took God at His Word and prayed that her son's heart might become as white as the soapsuds in the washtub.

—from *Spring in the Valley* by
Mrs. Charles E. Cowman

When praying for your children, keep in mind that not only will your children's lives be changed, but they will change the lives of others.

I CAN BECOME MORE FAITHFUL IN PRAYING FOR MY CHILDREN BY REMEMBERING THAT . . .

Never despair of a child. The one you weep the most for at the mercy seat may fill your heart with the sweetest joys.

Gleaming Reputations

*A good name is better
than precious ointment.*
ECCLESIASTES 7:1

I CAN BE
ON GUARD
AGAINST
DEALING
WITH
UNTRUST-
WORTHY
PEOPLE BY...

A man once went to his attorney and made this request: "I am going into a business deal with a man I do not trust. I want you to frame an airtight contract that he can't break and which will protect me from any sort of mischief he may have on his mind."

The attorney replied, "Frankly, there's no group of words in the English language that can take the place of plain honesty between men. There's nothing that can be put into a contract that will fully protect either of you if one of you plans to deceive the other."

Your name is tied to your character. If your character is bad, so will be your name. You are wise to establish a reputation of having a good name and being honest, trustworthy, and steadfast. Your name will not only follow you all the days of your life but all the days of your children's lives as well.

Before entering into a business deal or employment relationship, ask yourself:

- How has this person treated others? Talk to former associates, clients, vendors, and employees.

- How does this person talk about business? By bragging to destroy others or winning by shrewdness? If so, you are likely dealing with a schemer who uses people.

Work with those who have sterling reputations. Your own reputation is less likely to become tarnished.

*It's better to die with a good name
than to live with a bad one.*

Which One Are You?

*Be an example (pattern) for the
believers in speech, in conduct,
in love, in faith, and in purity.*

1 TIMOTHY 4:12 AMP

Although "thermostat" and "thermometer" are close in spelling, there's a world of difference between their meanings.

A thermometer tells you the temperature—whether it's cold or hot—but it does nothing about the situation it identifies. Many people are like thermometers. They readily say, "The church is unfriendly, the town is unreceptive, and the nation is sinful." They describe the atmosphere of a person, place, or institution as being "cold" or "hot." But they do little to change the situation.

Fortunately, other people are like thermostats. When a thermostat senses a room is cold, it quickly and quietly starts the machinery necessary to bring the cold room to an acceptable temperature. If a room is hot, a thermostat cues the system that cools the room.

If you don't like a situation that you face today—whether at home, at work, in your community, or in your church—choose to be a thermostat instead of just a thermometer. Make a difference that can "warm things up" or "cool things off" for the comfort of everyone.

Am I
MORE LIKE A
THERMOMETER
OR A
THERMOSTAT?

*Waste no more time arguing what
a good man should be. Be one.*

Put Your All in Everything

Whatsoever thy hand findeth
to do, do it with thy might.
ECCLESIASTES 9:10

Do I GIVE
MY ALL
TO TASKS
THAT SEEM
WORTHLESS?

In 1930, Pat O'Brien had a scene in a play called *The Up and Up* in which he had to contend with two angry people at once—a person on the phone and one at his desk. To him, playing that scene was "like fighting through Notre Dame's football line while singing 'Danny Boy.'" The play received mixed reviews, and its outlook seemed dim. O'Brien thought, *Why knock myself out on something with no future?* But then a Bible verse echoed in his memory: "Whatever your hand finds to do, do it with all your might" (Ecclesiastes 9:10 NIV). And so, at every performance, he put his all into the scene, sometimes exiting the stage wringing wet.

After the show closed, O'Brien went on to perform in a few obscure parts. Then one day he received a phone call from a man who said, "Mr. Hughes is filming the play *The Front Page* and wants you in it." O'Brien jumped at the opportunity. The film's director, Lewis Milestone, later told him why he was chosen. Milestone had gone to New York with friends, planning to see a hit show. But they were one seat short, so Lewis went to see *The Up and Up*. He said, "One scene really impressed me—the one at the desk." O'Brien's outstanding film career was launched because he gave his all to a part that had seemed worthless!

———— ∞ ————

What counts is not the number of hours
you put in, but how much
you put in the hours.

A Wealth of Wisdom

People who want to get rich fall into temptation and
a trap and into many foolish and harmful desires
that plunge men into ruin and destruction.

1 TIMOTHY 6:9 NIV

Many people think that having money would solve all their problems. Consider the words of five of the wealthiest Americans in history:

John D. Rockefeller said, "I have made many millions, but they have brought me no happiness. I would barter them all for the days I sat on an office stool in Cleveland and counted myself rich on three dollars a week." Broken in health despite his Christian beliefs, Rockefeller employed an armed guard in his latter years to ensure his personal safety.

W. H. Vanderbilt said, "The care of two hundred million dollars is too great a load for any brain or back to bear. It is enough to kill anyone. There is no pleasure in it."

Wealthy businessman John Jacob Astor was a martyr to dyspepsia and melancholy who once said, "I am the most miserable man on earth."

Automobile king Henry Ford said, "Work is the only pleasure. . . . I was happier when doing a mechanic's job."

Multimillionaire Andrew Carnegie once noted, "Millionaires seldom smile."

Money cannot satisfy the deep needs of the human heart. Learn to value your health, because all the money in the world cannot buy it.

❦

Let the nation count not wealth as wealth;
let it count righteousness as wealth.

What ARE THE DEEP NEEDS OF MY HEART THAT I TRY TO BUY WITH MONEY?

Death of a Secret

I know whom I have believed, and am persuaded that he is able to keep that which I have committed unto him against that day.

2 TIMOTHY 1:12

Have I
BEEN
HOARDING
SOMETHING
THAT I
SHOULD
SHARE WITH
OTHERS?

Time magazine ran in its January 25, 1988, issue an article about the introduction of the videocassette recorder. The article said, "The company had made a crucial mistake. While at first Sony kept its Beta technology mostly to itself, JVC, the Japanese inventor of the VHS [format], shared its secret with a raft of other firms. As a result, the market was overwhelmed by the sheer volume of the VHS machines being produced."

The result was a drastic undercutting of Sony's market share of VCRs. The first year, Sony lost 40 percent of the market, and by 1987, it controlled only 10 percent of the market with its Beta format. In the end, Sony jumped on the VHS bandwagon. While it continued for many years to make Beta-format video equipment and tapes, Sony's switch to VHS ultimately sent Beta machines to the consumer-electronics graveyard.

Even in a cutthroat business, sharing has its rewards. How much deeper, broader, and richer are the rewards of sharing those things that are spiritual and eternal in nature.

I have held many things in my hands and lost them all; but the things I have placed in God's hands, those I always possess.

More Than Getting By

Work hard so God can say to you, "Well done."
Be a good workman, one who does not need to
be ashamed when God examines your work.

2 TIMOTHY 2:15 TLB

Many people know how Helen Keller overcame the difficult physical challenge of being rendered deaf, mute, and blind after a fever as a baby, and how she eventually learned to communicate. Her life inspired millions. Mark Twain was one of her ardent admirers, and she was invited to visit every U.S. President at the White House from her childhood on.

What many people don't know, however, is how hard Helen worked as an adult. After graduating with honors from Radcliffe College, she labored to help others until her death at the age of eighty-eight. She wrote numerous articles. She gave lectures for the American Foundation for the Blind, and she helped raise a fund of some two million dollars for the foundation. On her eightieth birthday, the American Foundation for Overseas Blind honored her by announcing the Helen Keller International Award for those who gave outstanding help to the blind.

Not only are each of us called to overcome our own faults, weaknesses, and limitations, but we are asked to exercise our strengths. "Just surviving" isn't what we are challenged to do. We are destined to use our talents for God's purposes, putting all of our mind, heart, and energy to the work He sets before us.

Even a mosquito doesn't get a slap
on the back until it starts to work.

I CAN EXERCISE MY STRENGTHS TODAY BY . . .

Sowing the Seeds of Faith

All scripture is given by inspiration of God,
and is profitable for doctrine, for reproof, for
correction, for instruction in righteousness:
That the man of God may be perfect,
thoroughly furnished unto all good works.

2 TIMOTHY 3:16-17

How CAN I
PLANT THE
WORD OF
GOD IN
HEARTS AND
MINDS
AROUND ME?

The Bible—carefully read and well worn—was the most important book in Gerrit's house. His home was a house of prayer, where many tears were shed for revival in his church in Heemstede. Almost a generation later, his prayers were answered as his church became the center of an upsurge of faith in Holland, part of the Great Awakening in Europe.

When she was about eighteen years old, Gerrit's great-granddaughter had a dream about him. He was walking through a beautiful park with her, and he said, "When you sow some seed and put it in the ground, this seed will make a plant, and this plant will give seed again. . . . You, my dear Corrie, are the daughter of my grandson. . . . You are a plant, blooming from my seed. I will show you something that will never be changed. It is the Word of God." In the dream, he opened his Bible and said, "This Book will be the same forever." He then told her, "Plant the seeds from God's Book, and they will grow from generation to generation."

Corrie ten Boom did just that. She planted God's Word in hearts and minds around the world.

Information learned in textbooks is continually updated. Courses of study change. The truths of the Bible, however, are absolutes. Its promises are sure.

A knowledge of the Bible without a college
course is more valuable than a
college course without the Bible.

An Alternative to Criticism

Correct, rebuke and encourage—with
great patience and careful instruction.

2 TIMOTHY 4:2 NIV

Shortly after graduation, Joe and Lana married. One of their first marital discoveries was their different understanding of the phrase "being on time." Not wanting to end the honeymoon stage too early, Lana found herself mildly complaining about Joe's constant lateness. But Joe never took the hint, and soon her complaining turned to outright criticism.

On the surface, there may not seem to be much difference between exposing a problem and criticizing it, but in a relationship, the choice of words can bring different responses. Criticism attacks someone's personality and character. When Lana criticized Joe, she would say, "You're only thinking about yourself!"

Putting an issue on the table for discussion in a positive manner is the first step toward finding a resolution. Someone who asks gently, "Does it embarrass you when we are late?" is opening a dialogue for finding a solution to the problem. Criticism only wounds the spirit, puts the other person on the defensive, and usually ends up in an argument that doesn't solve anything.

Watch what you say! Criticism can cause a wound that takes years to heal, but a kind and gracious attitude can save you years of tears!

⋘⋙

Stack every bit of criticism
between two layers of praise.

I CAN TURN MY CRITICISM INTO ENCOURAGEMENT BY . . .

Square Pegs

Unto the pure all things are pure:
but unto them that are defiled and
unbelieving is nothing pure; but even
their mind and conscience is defiled.

TITUS 1:15

How CAN
I TEACH MY
CHILDREN
THE
IMPORTANCE
OF A CLEAR
CONSCIENCE?

One day a mother was helping her son with his spelling assignment, and they came to the words "conscious" and "conscience." She asked her son, "Do you know the difference between these two words?"

He immediately replied, "Sure, Mom. Conscious is when you are aware of something. And conscience is when you wish you weren't."

The conscience is like a sharp square peg in our hearts. When we are confronted by a situation that calls for a right-or-wrong decision, that square begins to turn. Its corner cuts into our hearts, warning us that we are facing a situation in which we must make a choice against evil and for good.

If the conscience is ignored repeatedly, however, the corners of the square are gradually worn down, and it becomes a circle that twists and turns at will. When that circle turns within our hearts, there is no inner sensation of warning. In effect, we are left without a conscience.

A sound conscience is truly a gift from God. Heed its warning signals early, and you will be spared much pain and heartache.

———⊂⊃⊃⊃———

Quite often when a man thinks
his mind is getting broader;
it's only his conscience stretching.

Too High a Price

*Encourage the young men
to be self-controlled.*

TITUS 2:6 NIV

Consider the downside of immorality when it is found out:

- Your mate experiences shame, rejection, betrayal, and heartache. No amount of repentance or asking forgiveness can soften the blow. Suspicion replaces trust.

- The innocence and trust of your children are dealt a devastating blow. Their healthy outlook on life is likely to be severely damaged.

- The heartache experienced by parents, family, and peers is indescribable. You are likely to be embarrassed in facing other Christians, especially those who have openly appreciated, respected, and trusted you.

- If you are engaged in the Lord's work, you will suffer great damage to your ministry, and a dark shadow will accompany you everywhere. Forgiveness won't erase it.

- Your fall may be perceived by others as license to do the same.

- Your own inner peace will be gone.

- Your enemies will have further reason to jeer and sneer at you.

What a high price to pay for failing to conquer one's own emotions and desires! When you are tempted today to compromise your values, practice self-control.

I NEED TO PRACTICE SELF-CONTROL IN THE AREA OF . . .

Conquer yourself rather than the world.

Be Prepared for the Battle

Make the most of every opportunity.
COLOSSIANS 4:5 NIV

This IS THE TIME FOR ME TO DEVELOP FAITH, STRENGTH, AND WISDOM IN PREPARATION FOR...

We can learn a great deal from the Alaskan bull moose. Each fall during the breeding season, the males of the species battle for dominance. They literally go head-to-head, antlers crunching together as they collide. When antlers are broken, defeat is ensured since a moose's antlers are its only weapon.

Generally speaking, the heftiest moose with the largest and strongest antlers wins. Therefore, the battle is nearly always predetermined the summer before. It is then that the moose eat nearly around the clock. The one that consumes the best diet for growing antlers and gaining weight will be the victor. Those that eat inadequately will have weaker antlers and less bulk. The fight itself involves far more brawn than brain, with more reliance on bulk than on skill.

What's the lesson for us? Spiritual battles are inevitable. We each experience seasons of attack in our lives. Whether we are victorious or fall victim depends not on our skills or brainpower, but on our spiritual strength. What we do in advance determines the outcome of the battle. Now is the time to develop enduring faith, strength, and wisdom. Now is the time for prayer, reading and memorizing God's Word, and hearing the Gospel preached! They will equip you for any future battles.

Luck is a matter of preparation meeting opportunity.

Love the Life You Have

*It is vain for you to rise up early, to take
rest late, to eat the bread of [anxious] toil—
for He gives [blessings] to His beloved in sleep.*

PSALM 127:2 AMP

At a Rotary meeting in Illinois a number of years ago, Gypsy Smith gave a stirring speech to the leading business and professional men of the city. As he prepared to close his remarks, he lifted his well-worn Bible high above his head and then asked the men in attendance, "How many of you men can recall a saintly mother and a godly father who loved this Book, read it, lived it, and seeped it into you?"

Nearly every man in the room, with moist eyes and sober expressions, raised their hands.

Then quietly and deftly, Gypsy made his final statement. "With all your influence today, how many of you are so living that your children will remember you for your faithfulness to this same Book?"

It was a tense moment; you could hear a pin drop. The point had sunk deep into the hearts of those in attendance, bringing conviction. Not a hand was raised.

If you were asked these two questions today, how would you answer them?

In all of our earning a living, may we never forget the joy of the life we have been given as a gift—a godly heritage to be perpetuated.

*Men for the sake of getting
a living forget to live.*

Lately I HAVE ALLOWED WORK TO INTERFERE WITH THINGS OF ETERNAL VALUE, SUCH AS . . .

Strength of Character

I keep under my body, and
bring it into subjection.
1 CORINTHIANS 9:27

Have

I BEEN

LIMITING

GOD'S PLAN

FOR MY LIFE?

During a homecoming football game against rival Concordia, Augsburg College was losing miserably. But late in the fourth quarter, nose guard David Stevens came off the bench and sparked a fire. He initiated or assisted in two tackles, and when a Concordia player fumbled the ball, David fell on it. As he held the recovered ball high, the crowd roared. It was an unforgettable moment for Augsburg fans!

David Lee Stevens was born to a woman who had taken thalidomide, and his feet appeared where his legs should have started. Abandoned by his mother, David was adopted by a foster family. Bee and Bill Stevens imposed strict rules of behavior on David, nurtured him, and loved him. They insisted he learn to do things for himself, and they never put him in a wheelchair. At age three, he was fitted with artificial legs. In school, David became a student leader, made good grades, organized special events, and befriended new students. In high school, he not only played football, but baseball, basketball, and hockey. He became a champion wrestler. When offered handicap license plates, he refused them, stating simply, "Those are for people who need them. I am not 'disabled.'"

What an attitude! Look past your limitations and pursue God's destiny for your life. With God, nothing is impossible!

What we do on some great occasion will
probably depend on what we already are;
and what we are will be the result of
previous years of self-discipline.

Loyalty and Vindication

He that covereth his sins shall not prosper: but whoso confesseth and forsaketh them shall have mercy.

PROVERBS 28:13

Patrick Sullivan, an Irish-American artist from Boston, moved to the village of Asolo in the Venetian Alps, where he greatly distinguished himself for his tremendous generosity. As a result, he was knighted by the king of Italy. Then Sullivan found himself in trouble. He and his friend, Count Giuseppe Samartini, were driving along a country road when their car struck a boy and fatally wounded him. The count was at the wheel. At the time Countess Samartini was seriously ill, and Sullivan, fearful that the news of the count's predicament might endanger her life, took the blame upon himself. A trial date was set.

Before the trial, the countess recovered, and Samartini went to the rescue of his friend. He claimed responsibility for the accident. His action resulted in two indictments—the count for the accident and Sullivan for willful misrepresentation.

The judge rendered this decision: The count was acquitted because the accident was unavoidable. He also set Sullivan free, declaring that his legal offense was more than compensated by his magnanimous and self-sacrificing display of friendship.

Today trust God to vindicate you.

***

Whenever a man is ready to uncover his sins, God is always ready to cover them.

HOW CAN I DISPLAY A MAGNANIMOUS AND SELF-SACRIFICING ATTITUDE IN MY RELATIONSHIPS?

Acts of Kindness

*Encourage one another day after day,
as long as it is still called "Today."*
HEBREWS 3:13 NASB

How CAN I
DISCIPLINE
MYSELF TO
BE MORE
COURTEOUS
AND
SENSITIVE TO
OTHERS ON A
DAILY BASIS?

Before he was elected as the twenty-fifth president of the United States, William McKinley served in Congress. On his way to his congressional office one morning, he boarded a streetcar and took the only remaining seat. Minutes later, a woman who appeared to be ill boarded the car. Unable to find a seat, she clutched an overhead strap next to one of McKinley's colleagues. The other congressman hid behind his newspaper and did not offer the woman his seat. McKinley walked up the aisle, tapped the woman on the shoulder, offered her his seat, and took her place in the aisle.

Years later when McKinley was president, this same congressman was recommended to him for a post as ambassador to a foreign nation. McKinley refused to appoint him. He feared that a man who didn't have the courtesy to offer his seat to a sick woman in a crowded streetcar would lack the courtesy and sensitivity necessary to be an ambassador in a troubled nation. The disappointed congressman bemoaned his fate to many in Washington, but he never learned why McKinley chose someone else for the position.

Acts of kindness can lead you to prominence. Then from a position of prominence, your kindness can extend to more people!

*You cannot do a kindness too soon,
because you never know
how soon it will be too late!*

Emergency!

*In my distress I cried unto
the LORD, and he heard me.*

PSALM 120:1

The 911 emergency system has amazing capabilities. In most places in the United States, a person need only dial those three numbers to be instantly connected to a dispatcher. On a computer screen, the dispatcher instantly sees the caller's telephone number, address, and the name under which the number is listed. Also listening in on the call are police, fire, and paramedic assistants. A caller need not say anything once the call is made. Even rasping coughs and hysterical cries can bring a quick response. The dispatcher knows where the call is coming from, and help is sent.

At times, some situations in our lives are so desperate and our pain so deep we can only muster 911 prayers to God. These could be called "SOS" prayers, and we often use the same words: "God, I need help!" God hears each one. He knows our names and every detail of our situations. Like a heavenly dispatcher, He will send precisely what is needed.

Also like a 911 dispatcher, our heavenly dispatcher may have some advice to sustain us through a crisis. Keep a listening ear and remember that help is on the way!

I NEED TO TRUST THAT GOD HEARS ME AND IS SENDING HELP WHEN I CRY OUT TO HIM ABOUT...

*Look around you and be distressed,
look within you and be depressed,
look to Jesus and be at rest.*

Eyes to the Task

I will lift up mine eyes unto the hills, from whence cometh my help. My help cometh from the LORD, which made heaven and earth.

PSALM 121:1-2

Does MY DAY-TO-DAY BEHAVIOR LINE UP WITH GOD'S WORD IN THE BIBLE?

A young man was learning to plow with a tractor. He climbed onto the seat of the tractor for his first solo run, pulled the lever that dropped the plow to the ground, and started across the field. After he had gone a few yards, he turned around to look at the furrow he was making. He became entranced by the rushing flow of topsoil along the plowshare—the rich, black soil turning over in a seemingly endless ribbon. But when he turned back to see where he was going, he realized that the wheel of the tractor had swerved a number of times. Glancing again behind him, he saw a wavering furrow, a permanent etching of his wandering eye.

The secret to pulling a straight furrow is not in watching the furrow as it is made, but in setting one's sights across the field at a distant point and keeping the nose of the tractor moving squarely toward that point. The point on which the eyes are fixed must be a fixed point, such as a tree, barn, or hilltop. Only the briefest backward glance is allowable.

The same holds true for your life of faith. Keep your eyes fixed upon Jesus, who never changes, and line up your behavior with His Word, looking back only rarely on your ministry and outreach efforts. Every day you make choices of how you will spend your time and on what you will focus. Be sure you focus on those things that line up with your life's priorities.

The way each day will look to you all starts with whom you're looking to.

Teamwork

*Be not slothful, but followers
of them who through faith and
patience inherit the promises.*

HEBREWS 6:12

The story is told of a lazy boy who went with his mother and aunt on a blueberry-picking hike into the woods. He carried the smallest pail possible. While the others worked hard at picking berries, he lolled about, chasing a butterfly and playing hide-and-seek with a squirrel. Soon it was time to leave. In a panic, he filled his pail mostly with moss and then topped it off with a thin layer of berries, so that the pail looked full of berries. His mother and aunt highly commended him for his effort.

The next morning his mother baked pies, and she made a special saucer-sized pie just for the boy. He could hardly wait for it to cool. Blueberry pie was his favorite! He could see the plump berries oozing through a slit in the crust, and his mouth watered in anticipation. However, as he sunk his fork into the flaky crust, he found mostly moss!

Many people want to experience the fullness of God's promises in their lives, but they are unwilling to do the work that goes along with the Bible's promises. Most of God's promises are "if-then" statements: "If you will listen, then I will do this," "If you will pray, then I will do this," or "If you seek, then you will find." God's promises are conditional, but He always gives us the strength, power, and grace to meet those conditions.

Am I WILLING TO DO THE WORK THAT ACCOMPANIES GOD'S PROMISES?

---

*Too many churchgoers are singing
"Standing on the Promises" when all
they are doing is sitting on the premises.*

Buoyed by God

Let patience have her perfect work,
that ye may be perfect and entire,
wanting nothing.
JAMES 1:4

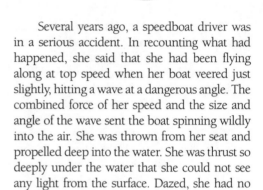

Am I LISTENING TO THE SOUND OF MANY VOICES OR THE SOUND OF THE ONE VOICE THAT MATTERS?

Several years ago, a speedboat driver was in a serious accident. In recounting what had happened, she said that she had been flying along at top speed when her boat veered just slightly, hitting a wave at a dangerous angle. The combined force of her speed and the size and angle of the wave sent the boat spinning wildly into the air. She was thrown from her seat and propelled deep into the water. She was thrust so deeply under the water that she could not see any light from the surface. Dazed, she had no idea which direction was up.

Rather than panic, the woman remained calm and waited for the buoyancy of her life vest to begin pulling her up. Then she quickly swam in that direction.

We often find ourselves surrounded by many voices, each with a different opinion, and we simply don't know which way is up. When this happens, we need to exercise patience and spend time with the Lord. The wisest course of action is to read His Word and wait for His gentle tug on our hearts to pull us toward His will. The more we read, the more confident we become, especially when His written Word and that gentle tug in our hearts come into agreement.

Remember that a few minutes, hours, days, or even months of waiting may mean the difference between sinking or swimming!

Everyone has patience.
Successful people learn to use it.

Self-Reliance?

Greater love hath no man
than this, that a man lay
down his life for his friends.

JOHN 15:13

Albert Einstein once reflected on the purpose of man's existence, writing,

> Strange is our situation here upon earth. Each of us comes for a short visit, not knowing why, yet sometimes seeming to a divine purpose. From the standpoint of daily life, however, there is one thing we do know: That we are here for the sake of others . . . for the countless unknown souls with whose fate we are connected by a bond of sympathy. Many times a day, I realize how much my own outer and inner life is built upon the labors of people, both living and dead, and how earnestly I must exert myself in order to give in return as much as I have received.

When we truly take stock of our lives, we must admit we have done nothing entirely on our own. Our thinking has been fashioned by our many teachers and mentors, including family members. Our ability to function physically is the result, in part, of our genetic code and the provision of food, water, and shelter by others. Our spiritual lives are a gift from God Himself. We are what we have received.

Our reaction to these facts motivates each of us to give to others the good things we have been fortunate enough to receive. That is what being a citizen of God's kingdom is all about!

Of THE MANY TEACHERS, MENTORS, AND FAMILY MEMBERS WHO HAVE INFLUENCED MY LIFE, I MOST APPRECIATE...

The heart is the happiest
when it beats for others.

How to Live

Make sure that your character be free from the love of money, being content with what you have; for He Himself has said, "I WILL NEVER DESERT YOU, NOR WILL I EVER FORSAKE YOU."

HEBREWS 13:5 NASB

How HAS THE FEAR OF MISFORTUNE OR THE YEARNING AFTER HAPPINESS AFFECTED MY LIFE?

Few people have undergone the trials and tribulations of Alexander Solzhenitsyn, who suffered decades of horrendous hardship as a political exile in the Siberian prison system known as the gulag. We can learn from Solzhenitsyn not only because he is a survivor, but also because he has been in a situation that few of us have ever known—an existence of near total deprivation. He has not only lived without luxuries, but without necessities.

He writes as few can in *The Prison Chronicle*:

> Don't be afraid of misfortune and do not yearn after happiness. It is, after all, all the same. The bitter doesn't last forever, and the sweet never fills the cup to overflowing. It is enough if you don't freeze in the cold and if hunger and thirst don't claw at your sides. If your back isn't broken, if your feet can walk, if both arms work, if both eyes can see, and if both ears can hear, then whom should you envy? And why? Our envy of others devours us most of all. Rub your eyes and purify your heart and prize above all else in the world those who love you and wish you well.

❦

The greedy search for money or success will almost always lead men into unhappiness. Why? Because that kind of life makes them depend upon things outside themselves.

Uplifting Others

Can two walk together,
except they be agreed?

AMOS 3:3

In both fall and spring, geese can often be seen migrating, flying in a beautiful V-shaped formation. Such a pattern may appear to us to be a thing of beauty. In fact, it is aerodynamically brilliant.

At certain intervals, relative to the strength of the headwind they are encountering, the lead goose—who does the most work by breaking the force of wind—drops back and flies at the end of the formation. A goose next in the "V" takes its place. Scientists who have studied the V-formation have calculated that it takes up to 60 percent less effort for the geese to fly this way. The flapping of wings creates an uplift of air, an effect that is greater at the rear of the formation. In essence, the geese take turns "uplifting" one another. After a turn at the point of the "V," the lead goose is allowed to rest and be "carried" by the others until it has opportunity to regain its strength and move forward in the formation to eventually take its place in the lead role again.

How fortunate we are when we become part of a circle of friends and family who cooperate and work together. All are lifted up. Is there someone today you can uplift in prayer, giving, or with heart-to-heart friendship and caring?

Success is knowing the difference
between cornering people and
getting them in your corner.

Those IN MY CIRCLE OF FAMILY AND FRIENDS THAT I NEED TO LIFT UP IN PRAYER TODAY ARE . . .

Genius

Ye have need of patience, that, after ye have done the will of God, ye might receive the promise.

HEBREWS 10:36

How CAN I BECOME THE MODEL OF PAINSTAKING PATIENCE IN MY LIFE'S WORK?

We often think of great artists and musicians as having bursts of genius. More often, they are models of painstaking patience. Their greatest works tend to have been accomplished over long periods and often during extreme hardship.

Beethoven is said to have rewritten each bar of his music at least a dozen times.

Joseph Haydn produced more than eight hundred musical compositions before writing *The Creation,* the oratorio for which he is most famous.

Michelangelo's *Last Judgment* is considered one of the twelve master paintings of the ages. It took him eight years to complete it. He produced more than two thousand sketches and renderings in the process.

Leonardo da Vinci labored on *The Last Supper* for ten years, often working so diligently that he forgot to eat.

When he was quite elderly, the pianist Ignacy Paderewski was asked by an admirer, "Is it true that you still practice every day?" He replied, "Yes, at least six hours a day." The admirer said in awe, "You must have a world of patience." Paderewski said, "I have no more patience than the next fellow. I just use mine."

Use your patience today—then the next day and the next. Your masterpiece is waiting to be completed.

Patience is bitter but its fruit is sweet.

Listen to Your Mother

> *How blessed is the man whose quiver is full of them [children]; they shall not be ashamed when they speak with their enemies in the gate.*
>
> PSALM 127:5 NASB

Lewis Smedes of Fuller Theological Seminary once said to a congregation,

May I share with you some reasons why I believe? All good reasons, none of them the really real reason. There's my family. I believe because I was brought up in a believing family. I don't make any bones about that. I don't know what would have happened to me if I had been born in the depth of Manchuria of a Chinese family. I just don't know. I do know that I was led to believe in the love of God as soon as I learned I should eat my oatmeal. We did a lot of believing in our house. We didn't have much else to do, as a matter of fact. Other kids sang "Jesus loves me this I know, 'cause the Bible tells me so." I sang, "Jesus loves me this I know, 'cause my ma told me so."

I wasn't alone. You probably heard about a reporter asking the great German theologian, Karl Barth, toward the end of his career: "Sir, you've written these great volumes about God, great learned tomes about all the difficult problems of God. How do you know they're all true?" And the great theologian smiled and said, "'Cause my mother said so!"

Families are God's primary missionary society.

Do we do "a lot of believing" in our household?

No man or woman is a failure who has helped hold a home happily together. He who has been victorious in his home can never be completely defeated.

The Good Life

You will be happy and it will be well with you.
Your wife shall be like a fruitful vine within
your house, your children like olive plants
around your table.

PSALM 128:2-3 NASB

Do I
SEE THE
BUILDING I
LIVE IN AS
A HOUSE OR
A HOME?

Even though he was single, at age thirty-two, Bill decided it was time to buy a house. He found a modestly priced four-bedroom home and began to visualize how he could use the rooms. A few months later, however, he found himself engaged to marry a woman who had three young daughters. Two years after their marriage, Bill and his wife, Dee, had a baby. The gym and TV room he had envisioned in his new home never materialized!

It took Bill and Dee four jobs to pay for the life they had chosen, and although their schedules were relentless, Bill couldn't help but conclude, "Ain't life grand?" Eventually, his stepdaughters began to leave home, and Bill once again made plans for the spare rooms in the house. But his elderly parents needed help, and Bill and Dee invited them to move in. Even in getting up at night to help his ailing father, Bill still was of the opinion, "Ain't life grand?"

After more than twenty-five years, Bill still doesn't have his dream house. What he has had, however, is two decades of a real home.

Love makes a house a home.

A Tug on the Line

*Looking unto Jesus the author
and finisher of our faith.*

HEBREWS 12:2

A twelve-year-old boy accepted Jesus Christ as his personal Lord and Savior during a weekend revival meeting. The next week, his school friends questioned him about the experience.

"Did you hear God talk?" one asked.

"No," the boy said.

"Did you have a vision?" another asked.

"No," the boy replied.

"Well, how did you know it was God?" a third friend asked.

The boy thought for a moment and then said, "It's like when you catch a fish. You can't see the fish or hear the fish; you just feel him tugging on your line. I felt God tugging on my heart."

So often we try to figure out life by what we can see, hear, or experience with our other senses. We make calculated estimates and judgments based on empirical evidence. There's a level of truth, however, that cannot be perceived by the senses or measured objectively. It's at that level where faith abounds. It is our faith that compels us to believe, even when we cannot explain to others why or how. By our faith, we only know in whom we trust. And that is sufficient.

———————

*It's not the outlook but
the uplook that counts.*

How CAN I DESCRIBE TO OTHERS THE WAY GOD INFLUENCES MY LIFE?

331

Surrounded by Good

Be content with such things as ye have.

HEBREWS 13:5

I CAN AVOID
BECOMING
BLINDED
TO THE
BLESSINGS
AROUND
ME BY...

Several years ago a newspaper cartoon was drawn of two fields divided by a fence. Both were about the same size, and each had plenty of lush green grass.

Each field had a mule whose head stuck through the wire fence, eating grass from the other's pasture. Although each mule was surrounded by plenty of grass, the neighboring field seemed somewhat more desirable—even though it was harder to reach.

In the process, the mules' heads became caught in the fence. They panicked and brayed uncontrollably at not being able to free themselves. The cartoonist wisely described the situation with one caption: "Discontent."

Like the mules, when we focus on what we don't have, we become blinded to the blessings that surround us. There is nothing wrong with desiring something greater, but to think life is easier in someone else's pasture may not be true. Besides, no matter whose pasture we are in, we will always have to deal with the attitudes of our own heart.

If there is something you desire in life, perhaps a bigger home, a better car, or even your own business, look to Jesus to help you bring it to pass. And while He is working on it, remember to find pleasure in what He's already given you!

The grass may be greener on the other side, but it still has to be mowed.

Stop! Think! Solve!

Everyone must be quick to hear,
slow to speak and slow to anger.

JAMES 1:19 NASB

Virtually every problem that frustrates or angers us has a solution! We can usually find that solution if we'll only put our emotions on hold for a while and consider the situation from another point of view.

Lance came home from work angry that one of his best supervisors had quit to take a better-paying job. He had put a great deal of time and energy into training this woman. Once he calmed his emotions, however, he began to think, *How would I feel if I were in her shoes—liking my present job but offered a better-paying one?* The next morning, Lance talked to his manager about offering the woman a small raise and a shift in her hours so she might be home when her children arrived from school. The manager agreed, and the supervisor quickly accepted the offer.

Diane became frustrated that her sons' toys seemed to be continually strewn about their room. Tired of scolding them, she calmed herself and thought, *What could I do to make picking up easier?* The next day she bought an inexpensive stack of storage containers, a preprinted chart, and a stopwatch. She made picking up toys a game the boys loved.

What's bothering you today? Rather than explode, stop and think, *How can I change things?*

———❦———

It is more important to get in the
first thought than the last word.

What CAN I DO TODAY TO CHANGE THE THINGS THAT FRUSTRATE ME THE MOST?

Seeing a Sermon

*Show me your faith without deeds, and
I will show you my faith by what I do.*
JAMES 2:18 NIV

How CAN
I BE A
WALKING
SERMON FOR
ALL TO SEE?

I'd rather see a sermon
  than hear one any day,
I'd rather one should walk with me
  than merely show the way.
The eye's a better pupil
  and more willing than the ear;
Fine counsel is confusing,
  but example always clear;
And the best of all the preachers
  are the men who live their creeds,
For to see the good in action
  is what everybody needs.
I can soon learn how to do it
  if you'll let me see it done,
I can watch your hands in action,
  but your tongue too fast may run.
And the lectures you deliver
  may be wise and true;
But I'd rather get my lesson
  by observing what you do.
For I may misunderstand you
  and the high advice you give,
But there's no misunderstanding
  how you act and how you live.
—Edgar A. Guest

*As I grow older, I pay less attention to
what men say. I just watch what they do.*

Life-changing Words

Set a watch, O LORD, before my
mouth; keep the door of my lips.

PSALM 141:3

A heart doctor was amazed at the great improvement one of his patients had made. When he had seen the woman in the hospital a few months earlier, she was seriously ill and needed an oxygen mask. He asked the woman what had happened.

The woman said,

> I was sure the end was near and that you and your staff had given up hope. However, Thursday morning when you entered with your troops, something happened that changed everything. You listened to my heart; you seemed pleased by the findings, and you announced to all those standing about my bed that I had a "wholesome gallop." I knew that the doctors, in talking to me, might try to soften things. But I knew they wouldn't kid each other. So when I overheard you tell your colleagues I had a wholesome gallop, I figured I still had a lot of kick to my heart and could not be dying. My spirits were lifted for the first time, and I knew I would live and recover.

The heart doctor never told the woman that a third-sound gallop is a poor sign that denotes the heart muscle is straining and usually failing!

Words of life can make an amazing difference to someone. How important it is to choose our words wisely!

How CAN I LIFT THE SPIRITS OF SOMEONE IN NEED TODAY?

A minute of thought is worth
more than an hour of talk.

335

Pretty Profession or Precious Gift?

What is your life? It is even a vapor that appears for a little time and then vanishes away.

JAMES 4:14 NKJV

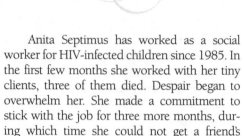

I HAVE AN INDESTRUC-TIBLE SENSE OF HOPE WITH REGARD TO . . .

Anita Septimus has worked as a social worker for HIV-infected children since 1985. In the first few months she worked with her tiny clients, three of them died. Despair began to overwhelm her. She made a commitment to stick with the job for three more months, during which time she could not get a friend's words out of her thoughts—"You have not chosen a pretty profession."

She had to admit that her friend was right. It took resolve to accept that fact and simply do what she could to help families make the most of what remained of their children's lives. She is still there.

Over the last ten years, her clinic has grown considerably. Today Anita and her staff care for more than three hundred families who have children with AIDs. They go into their homes, teach infection prevention, and help parents plan for the future. The children are regularly taken on trips to the zoo, the circus, and summer camps.

One AIDs baby wasn't expected to see her first birthday, but she recently celebrated her tenth. Such long-term clients give back to Anita what she terms as "an indestructible sense of hope"—a precious gift!

When you sow hope into the lives of others, you reap back hope into your own life. Encourage someone today!

Life is a coin. You can spend it any way you wish, but you can only spend it once.

As Important as Breathing

Is any one of you in trouble?
He should pray.

JAMES 5:13 NIV

A boy was watching a holy man praying on the banks of a river. When he had completed his prayer, the boy went over and asked, "Will you teach me to pray?"

The man studied the boy's face carefully. Then he gripped the boy's head in his hands and plunged it forcefully into the water! The boy struggled frantically, trying to free himself to breathe. When the man finally released his hold, the little boy gasped for breath, then asked, "What did you do that for?"

The holy man said, "I just gave you your first lesson." The boy asked, "What do you mean?" The holy man replied, "When you long to pray as much as you wanted to breathe, only then will I be able to teach you to pray."

We are wise to pray about even the small matters of our lives and not conserve our prayers only for times of crisis or when we face major challenges. Indeed, if we are in the habit of praying about the small problems we encounter, major problems may never arise!

—⁂—

Our prayer life never needs a bridle,
but sometimes it needs a spur.

The SMALL PROBLEMS I'M FACING NOW— THE ONES I'VE FAILED TO PRAY ABOUT— ARE...

Privilege and Honor

Ye know that ye were not redeemed with corruptible things, as silver and gold . . . but with the precious blood of Christ, as of a lamb without blemish and without spot.

1 PETER 1:18-19

The WORTHWHILE THINGS I WANT FROM LIFE—THOSE THAT WILL COST A GREAT DEAL— INCLUDE . . .

Dr. Pedro Jose Greer has become something of a legend in Miami. As an intern in 1984, Dr. Greer treated a homeless man with tuberculosis, a normally curable disease that had progressed to a fatal stage. Greer was appalled that someone in his own neighborhood could be so poor and ignorant that he failed to seek medical treatment. As the man lay dying, Greer spent four days searching the streets for the man's family, hoping the man wouldn't die alone.

Rather than merely bemoan that one case, Greer took action. He set up a clinic in a shelter, beginning with only a folding table. He took other doctors along with him. His Camillus Health Concern is now one of the largest providers of medical care for the poor in South Florida, treating forty-five hundred patients a year. Greer has won numerous awards for his humanitarian efforts. But he has never forgotten the man who died alone. Between the three days he spends at the clinic and the time he spends in private practice, he searches Miami's worst streets, looking for those who need medical care.

Greer's work costs him much, and yet he sees himself as blessed. "I've had the privilege of treating the sick and the honor of working with the poor," he says.

The truly worthwhile things in life will cost you something.

The best things in life are not free.

Adopted to Belong

*There is no respect of
persons with God.*

ROMANS 2:11

A Sunday-school superintendent was registering two new boys in Sunday school. She asked their ages and birthdays so she could place them in the appropriate classes. The bolder of the two replied, "We're both seven. My birthday is April 8, and my brother's birthday is April 20." The superintendent replied, "But that's not possible, boys." The quieter brother spoke up. "No, it's true. One of us is adopted."

"Oh?" asked the superintendent, not convinced. "Which one?" The two brothers looked at each other and smiled. The bolder one said, "We asked Dad that same question awhile ago, but he just looked at us and said he loved us both equally, and he couldn't remember anymore which one of us was adopted."

What a wonderful analogy of God's love! The apostle Paul wrote to the Romans: "Now if we are [God's] children, then we are heirs—heirs of God and co-heirs with Christ . . ." (Romans 8:17 NIV). In essence, as adopted sons and daughters of God, we fully share in the inheritance of His only begotten Son, Jesus. If our Heavenly Father can love us on equal footing with His beloved Son, surely we can love our children equally and show no partiality in the blessings—or privileges—we extend to them.

Have I EVER SHOWN FAVORITISM TO ONE OF MY CHILDREN?

*A father should never make distinctions
between his children.*

When to Give In

In the same way you married men should live considerately with [your wives], with an intelligent recognition [of the marriage relation], honoring the woman.

1 PETER 3:7 AMP

Do I EVER MAKE THE MISTAKE OF BELIEVING THAT LIFE IS FAIR?

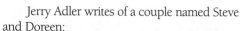

Jerry Adler writes of a couple named Steve and Doreen:

> Once, she had an angry exchange with a clerk in a bookstore who refused to give her a refund on a book she had bought a few days earlier . . . well, actually, four days earlier, which was one day more than the store allowed. But the day before was Sunday. So she was the first person in the store Monday morning, which, she thought, ought to count for something. The point, though, was that the clerk was being a total creep about it, "and Steve just stood there smiling his patient little smile. Finally, Steve offered that instead of getting my money back, we could exchange it for a book he wanted. I suppose I should have been grateful, but right at that moment I would have been happier if—$21.95 aside—he'd taken the book and shoved it sideways into the guy's mouth. . . . And I couldn't admit this to Steve, because it goes against everything I believe in. . . . I was really cold to him the rest of the day." That night he said to me, "You know, the guy was right even though he was a creep." "And after he said that, I didn't speak to him for three more days."

Life is not always fair. Giving in and agreeing is sometimes the higher path to take. Our attitude is what makes the difference between whether we view a situation as a win or a loss.

After winning an argument with his wife, the wisest thing a man can do is apologize.

An Umbrella of Love

Above all, love each other deeply, because love covers over a multitude of sins.

1 PETER 4:8 NIV

In Bible times, apartment-style homes were built atop city walls. Part of the roof extended beyond the walls to protect them from rain and sun. The word for this overhang is translated "forbear" in English. It literally means to "outroof." This is the way God commands us to love—"forbearing one another in love" (Ephesians 4:2), or to "outroof" one another—to protect those you love with your love, rather than expose them and their faults.

This does not mean we are to be blind to error or to live in a state of denial about wrongs committed around us or to us. It simply means we choose to love so much that our love overshadows the hurt those wrongs may have done. We recognize that we can never know the whole story about another person or event. We can only surmise about motives and the intent of the heart. However, we can choose not to focus on those things we don't understand and focus instead on what we can do—love.

As one old minister once told his country congregation, "God invites us to be His partner in everything but judging people." "Outroof" your family and friends with your love today.

How HAS MY LOVE OVERSHAD-OWED THE HURT CAUSED BY OTHER PEOPLE?

A good marriage is . . . a relationship where a healthy perspective overlooks a multitude of "unresolvables."

The Hole in the Water

God resisteth the proud, and
giveth grace to the humble.

1 PETER 5:5

Sometimes
I GET
CARRIED
AWAY AND
THINK I'M
INDISPENS-
ABLE TO...

Sometime, when you're feeling important!
Sometime, when your ego's in bloom;
Sometime, when you take it for granted
You're the best qualified in the room;

Sometime, when you feel that your going
Would leave an unfillable hole,
Just follow these simple instructions,
And see how it humbles your soul.

Take a bucket and fill it with water,
Put your hand in it, up to the wrist;
Pull it out, and the hole that's remaining,
Is a measure of how you'll be missed.

You may splash all you please when you enter,
You can stir up the water galore,
But stop, and you'll find in a minute
That it looks quite the same as before.

The moral in this quaint example,
Is do just the best that you can;
And be proud of yourself, but remember
There's no indispensable man.

—Anonymous

God sends no one away except
those who are full of themselves.

Faithful Followers

Let your statement be,
"Yes, yes" or "No, no."
MATTHEW 5:37 NASB

Although taken captive as children, Hananiah, Mishael, and Azariah were so wise that as adults, they were put over the affairs of the Babylonian province. Then the king they served built a golden image some one hundred feet high and placed it in their province. He invited the empire's leaders to a dedication of the image and gave a command that when a tribute of music was sounded, everyone should fall and worship the golden image. Whoever didn't do so would be thrown into a giant furnace.

The music played, and all fell on their faces—except Hananiah, Mishael, and Azariah. They were Jews and had been taught from earliest memory never to worship a graven image. Word of their refusal came quickly to the king, and in a rage, the king summoned them. The three leaders didn't hesitate in saying to the king, "We will not serve thy gods, nor worship the golden image" (Daniel 3:18).

Furious, the king commanded that the three be cast into the fire, only to find that they did not burn. They emerged unscorched! The stand these faithful men took resulted in the king decreeing that no person in the land speak anything against their God. And Hananiah, Mishael, and Azariah—whom the king called Shadrach, Meshach, and Abednego—were promoted.

If your answer is no, then make it mean something. When you stand by your word, God will stand by you.

DO I STAND BY MY WORDS, ESPECIALLY WHEN I'M DISCIPLINING MY CHILDREN?

"No" is one of the few words
that can never by misunderstood.

Who Is Your Audience?

*Daniel was preferred above the
presidents and princes, because
an excellent spirit was in him.*

DANIEL 6:3

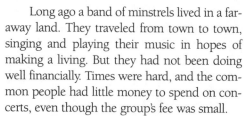

Have I
"PUNISHED"
OTHERS
BY GIVING
LESS THAN
MY BEST?

Long ago a band of minstrels lived in a far-away land. They traveled from town to town, singing and playing their music in hopes of making a living. But they had not been doing well financially. Times were hard, and the common people had little money to spend on concerts, even though the group's fee was small.

The minstrels met one evening to discuss their plight. "I see no reason for opening tonight," one said. "It's snowing, and no one will come out on a night like this." Another said, "I agree. Last night we performed for just a handful. Even fewer will come tonight."

The leader of the troupe responded, "I know you are discouraged. I am, too. But we have a responsibility to those who might come. We will go on, and we will do the best job of which we are capable. It is not the fault of those who come that others do not. They should not be punished with less than our best."

Heartened by his words, the minstrels gave their best performance ever. After the show, the old man called his troupe to him again. In his hand was a note handed to him by one of the audience members just before the doors closed behind him. Slowly the man read, "Thank you for a beautiful performance." It was signed, "Your King."

Remember that even if no one is around to see you perform, there is always one onlooker: your King.

*Every job is a self-portrait
of the person who does it.
Autograph your work with excellence.*

Bigger Than a Mountain

*Let us run with perseverance
the race marked out for us.*

HEBREWS 12:1 NIV

In the 1920s an English adventurer named Mallory led an expedition to conquer Mount Everest. His first expedition failed. So did the second. Mallory made a third attempt with a highly skilled and experienced team, but in spite of careful planning and extensive safety measures, an avalanche wiped out Mallory and most of his party. Upon their return to England, the few who had survived held a banquet to salute Mallory and those who had perished on the mountain. As the leader of the survivors stood to speak, he looked around the hall at the framed pictures of Mallory and the others who had died. Then he turned his back to the crowd and faced a large picture of Mount Everest that stood looming behind the banquet table like a silent, unbeatable giant.

With tears streaming down his face, he spoke to the mountain on behalf of his dead friends: "I speak to you, Mount Everest, in the name of all brave men living, and those yet unborn. Mount Everest, you defeated us once; you defeated us twice; you defeated us three times. But, Mount Everest, we shall someday defeat you, because you can't get any bigger and we can."

Maintain your enthusiasm. Keep persevering. Run your race until you cross the finish line!

How CAN I MAINTAIN MY ENTHUSIASM AS I RUN THE RACE OF LIFE?

*Every man is enthusiastic at times.
One has enthusiasm for thirty minutes,
another has it for thirty days—but it is
the man that has it for thirty years
who makes a success in life.*

The Origin of Happiness

The rod and reproof give wisdom:
but a child left to himself bringeth
his mother to shame.

PROVERBS 29:15

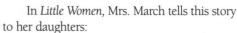

How CAN I
TEACH MY
CHILDREN
THAT
HAPPINESS
COMES FROM
WITHIN?

An infallible way to make your child
miserable is to satisfy all his demands.

In *Little Women,* Mrs. March tells this story to her daughters:

Once upon a time, there were four girls, who had enough to eat and drink and wear, a good many comforts and pleasures, kind friends and parents . . . and yet they were not contented. . . . These girls . . . were constantly saying, "If we only had this," or "If we could only do that." . . . So they asked an old woman what spell they could use to make them happy, and she said, "When you feel discontented, think over your blessings, and be grateful."

They decided to try her advice and soon were surprised to see how well off they were. One discovered that money couldn't keep shame and sorrow out of rich people's houses; another that . . . she was a great deal happier with her youth, health, and good spirits than a certain fretful, feeble old lady, who couldn't enjoy her comforts; a third that, disagreeable as it was to help get dinner, it was harder still to have to go begging for it; and the fourth, that even carnelian rings were not so valuable as good behavior. So they agreed to stop complaining, to enjoy the blessings already possessed.

Remember that the best way to bring happiness to your children is to teach them it comes from within.

Obey Your Calling

If you know that he is righteous,
you may be sure that every one
who does right is born of him.

1 JOHN 2:29 RSV

In *Dakota*, Kathleen Norris writes,

A Benedictine sister from the Philippines once told me what her community did when some sisters took to the streets in the popular revolt against the Marcos regime. Some did not think it proper for nuns to demonstrate in public, let alone risk arrest. In a group meeting that began and ended with prayer, the sisters who wished to continue demonstrating explained that this was for them a religious obligation; those who disapproved also had their say. Everyone spoke; everyone heard and gave counsel.

It was eventually decided that the nuns who were demonstrating should continue to do so; those who wished to express solidarity but were unable to march would prepare food and provide medical assistance to the demonstrators, and those who disapproved would pray for everyone. The sisters laughed and said, "If one of the conservative sisters was praying that we young, crazy ones would come to our senses and stay off the streets, that was okay. We were still a community."

God calls some to action, others to support, and still others to pray. You will be doing what is right in God's eyes if you obey His call!

Instead OF LOOKING AT WHAT OTHERS ARE DOING, I NEED TO OBEY GOD AND SERVE HIM WITH REGARD TO . . .

_____
_____
_____
_____
_____
_____
_____
_____
_____
_____
_____
_____
_____
_____
_____

My obligation is to do the right thing.
The rest is in God's hands.

Tuned In

If our hearts do not condemn us,
we have confidence before God.

1 JOHN 3:21 NIV

My MOST
PRIZED
CHARACTER
POSSESSION
IS . . .

President Woodrow Wilson was approached one day by one of his secretaries who suggested he take off from his work to enjoy a particular diversion he enjoyed. President Wilson replied, "My boss won't let me do it."

"Your boss?" the secretary asked, wondering who could be the boss of the chief executive of the United States.

"Yes," said Wilson. "I have a conscience that is my boss. It drives me to the task and will not let me accept this tempting invitation."

Our conscience should be one of our most prized possessions. It is through our conscience that we receive inner promptings from God which, when in agreement with our actions, will point us toward a safe and eternal way.

It has been said, "A conscience is like a thermostat on an air-conditioning unit—it kicks in when things are on the verge of getting too hot."

It is possible to ignore our conscience and follow the crowd, but it is a sad waste of our lives. The conscience is the window to the soul through which we hear the voice of God, who always leads us to success and inner peace.

———⌘———

A person may sometimes have
a clear conscience simply because
his head is empty.

Reflections of Christ

Beloved, let us love one another:
for love is of God; and every one that
loveth is born of God . . . for God is love.

1 JOHN 4:7-8

A warm-from-the-oven casserole taken to the home of a sick friend . . .

A bouquet of flowers from your garden given to a neighbor . . .

A thank-you note sent to the performers who did such an excellent job during a concert or play you attended . . .

A loaf of freshly baked cinnamon bread brought to the office for coffee break . . .

A box of cookies taken to the police station on Christmas Day to encourage those who are on duty during the holiday . . .

A call to ask with genuine care and concern, "How are you doing?"

We may not think of these as acts of Christian witnessing, yet they are. Every act of loving-kindness reflects God's loving-kindness for His people. We give because Jesus Christ has so freely given His love to us. He is the example we follow.

Never dismiss an act of loving-kindness as being too small or inconsequential. God will magnify even our smallest deeds to reveal His love to others.

Each loving act says loud and clear,
"I love you. God loves you.
I care. God cares."

Who NEEDS AN ACT OF KINDNESS ON MY PART TODAY?

Sweet Trust

Whatsoever is born of God overcometh the world: and this is the victory that overcometh the world, even our faith.

1 JOHN 5:4

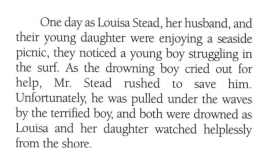

Have I
TRUSTED GOD
TO USE THE
SORROWS OF
MY LIFE FOR
HIS GLORY?

One day as Louisa Stead, her husband, and their young daughter were enjoying a seaside picnic, they noticed a young boy struggling in the surf. As the drowning boy cried out for help, Mr. Stead rushed to save him. Unfortunately, he was pulled under the waves by the terrified boy, and both were drowned as Louisa and her daughter watched helplessly from the shore.

In the sorrowful days that followed, the grief-stricken widow put pen to paper and the result was a hymn now known to millions:

> 'Tis so sweet to trust in Jesus,
> just to take Him at His word,
> just to rest upon His promise,
> just to know, "Thus saith the Lord."
> O how sweet to trust in Jesus,
> just to trust His cleansing blood,
> just in simple faith to plunge me
> 'neath the healing, cleansing flood!
> Yes, 'tis sweet to trust in Jesus,
> just from sin and self to cease,
> just from Jesus simply taking
> life and rest and joy and peace.
> I'm so glad I learned to trust
> Thee, Precious Jesus, Savior, Friend;
> and I know that Thou art with
> me, wilt be with me to the end.

Trusting Jesus, Louisa went to Africa as a missionary where she served the Lord for twenty-five years.

When we place the tragedies of our lives into God's hands and trust in Him, He can turn them around for His glory and our gain. Let God mend your broken heart today.

The highest pinnacle of the spiritual life is not joy in unbroken sunshine but absolute and undoubting trust in the love of God.

Reliability and Wisdom

*Seest thou a man that is hasty in
his words? there is more hope
of a fool than of him.*

PROVERBS 29:20

A man who had been quite successful in the manufacturing business decided to retire. He called in his son to tell him of his decision, saying, "Son, it's all yours as of the first of next month." The son, while eager to take over the firm and exert his own brand of leadership, also realized what a big responsibility he was facing. "I'd be grateful for any words of advice you have to give me," he said to his father.

The father advised, "Well, I've made a success of this business because of two principles: reliability and wisdom. First, take reliability. If you promise goods by the tenth of the month, no matter what happens, you must deliver by the tenth. Your customers won't understand any delay. They'll see a delay as failure. So even if it costs you overtime, double time, golden time, you must deliver on your promise."

The son mulled this over for a few moments and then asked, "And wisdom?" The father shot back: "Wisdom is never making such a stupid promise in the first place."

Carefully weigh your ability to deliver on your promises before you make them. A large part of your reputation is your ability to keep your word.

*One-half the trouble of this life can
be traced to saying yes too quickly,
and not saying no soon enough.*

DO PEOPLE GENERALLY THINK OF ME AS A RELIABLE PERSON?

Just You and Jesus

I am fearfully and wonderfully made.
PSALM 139:14

Regardless OF WHAT OTHERS THINK, I BELIEVE GOD HAS CALLED ME TO...

Three women on a hike came upon an unlocked cabin deep in the woods. Receiving no response to their knocks, they went inside to find one room, simply furnished. Nothing seemed unusual except that the large, potbellied, cast-iron stove was hung from the ceiling, suspended in midair by wires.

The psychologist said, "It is obvious this lonely trapper has elevated his stove so he can curl up under it and experience a return to the womb." The engineer responded, "Nonsense! This is thermodynamics! He has found a way to distribute heat more evenly in his cabin." The theologian interrupted, "I'm sure this has religious meaning. Fire 'lifted up' has been a religious symbol for millennia."

As the three debated, the owner of the cabin returned. The hikers immediately asked him why he had hung the stove by wires from the ceiling. "I had plenty of wire, but not much stove pipe." he replied.

Others may try to second-guess your motives, downplay your ideas, or insult you, but only you know why you do what you do, what you think and feel, and how you relate to God.

*Nobody can make you feel inferior
without your consent.*

The Wonder of Creation

You formed my inward parts;
You wove me in my mother's womb.

PSALM 139:13 NASB

A professor in a world-acclaimed medical school once posed the following medical situation—an ethical problem—to his students. "Here's the family history: The father has syphilis. The mother has TB. They have already had four children. The first is blind. The second had died. The third is deaf. The fourth has TB. Now the mother is pregnant again. The parents come to you for advice. They are willing to have an abortion if you decide they should. What do you say?"

The students gave various individual opinions, and then the professor asked them to break into small groups for consultation. All of the groups came back to report that they would recommend an abortion.

"Congratulations," the professor said. "You just took the life of Beethoven!"

A woman helps create the body of her child, and as her child grows, she nurtures its emotions and mind. God, however, creates the child's eternal soul. A soul must have a body on this earth. A body has a soul. Both God and mother are partners in the creation of a baby from the moment of conception.

No privilege is greater than the privilege of creating another human being. And no act requires greater faith!

❦

Every mother has the breathtaking
privilege of sharing with God in the
creation of new life. She helps bring
into existence a soul that will
endure for all eternity.

What CAN I DO TO PROMOTE THE IDEA OF THE SANCTITY OF LIFE WITHIN MY SPHERE OF INFLUENCE?

Qualified by Willingness

*A man's pride brings him low, but a
man of lowly spirit gains honor.*
PROVERBS 29:23 NIV

Despite MY
LACK OF
QUALIFICA-
TIONS, I AM
WILLING
TO . . .

Although he was raised in church, Dwight was almost totally ignorant of the Bible when he moved to Boston to make his fortune. There he began attending a Bible-preaching church. In April of 1855, a Sunday-school teacher came to the store where Dwight worked. He simply and persuasively urged him to trust in the Lord Jesus. Dwight did, and a month later he applied to the deacons of the church to become a church member. One fact was obvious to all: Dwight knew little of the Scriptures. His Sunday-school teacher later wrote, "I think the committee of the church seldom met an applicant for membership who seemed more unlikely ever to become a Christian of clear and decided views of Gospel truth, still less to fill any space of public or extended usefulness." Dwight was asked to undertake a year of study, which he did. At his second interview, his answers to the deacons were only slightly improved. He still was only barely literate and his spoken grammar was atrocious.

Few would have thought God could ever use a person like Dwight. But that wasn't God's opinion. He saw in Dwight L. Moody all the raw material necessary to create a major spokesman for His Word. Moody didn't need to be qualified in God's eyes, only willing.

Never mind your qualifications, are you willing?

---

*It is possible to be too big for God
to use you but never too small
for God to use you.*

A Real Traffic Stopper

See how very much our heavenly Father loves us, for he allows us to be called his children—think of it—and we really are!

1 JOHN 3:1 TLB

While driving along a freeway on a cold, rainy night, the adults in the front seat of the car were talking when, suddenly, they heard the horrifying sound of a car door opening, the whistle of wind, and a sickening muffled sound. They quickly turned and saw that their three-year-old child, who had been riding in the backseat, had fallen out of the car and was tumbling along the freeway. The driver screeched to a stop and then raced back toward her motionless child. To her surprise, she found that all the traffic had stopped just a few feet away from her daughter. The little girl had not been hit.

A truck driver offered his assistance and drove the girl to a nearby hospital. The doctors there rushed her into the emergency room and soon came back with the good news: Other than being unconscious, bruised, and skinned from her tumble, the girl was fine. No broken bones. No apparent internal damage.

As the mother rushed to her child, the little girl opened her eyes and said, "Mommy, you know I wasn't afraid." The mother asked, "What do you mean?" The little girl explained, "While I was lying on the road waiting for you to get back to me, I looked up and right there I saw Jesus holding back the traffic with His arms out."

God watches over our children with loving care and often uses them to remind us that He watches over us, too.

I NEED TO REMEMBER GOD'S CARE WHEN I FIND MYSELF AFRAID THAT . . .

God has given you your child, that the sight of him, from time to time, might remind you of His goodness and induce you to praise Him with filial reverence.

How Big a Person?

Set a watch, O LORD, before my
mouth; keep the door of my lips.
PSALM 141:3

I NEED TO
LISTEN AND
THINK
BEFORE I . . .

When William Gladstone was chancellor of the Exchequer, he once requested that the Treasury send him certain statistics upon which he might base his budget proposals. The statistician made a mistake. But Gladstone was so certain of this man's concern for accuracy that he didn't take the time to verify the figures. As a result, he went before the House of Commons and made a speech based upon incorrect information. His speech was no sooner published than the inaccuracies were exposed, and Gladstone became the brunt of public ridicule.

The chancellor sent for the statistician who had given him the erroneous information. When the man arrived, full of fear and shame, he was certain that he would be fired. Instead, Gladstone said, "I know how much you must be disturbed over what has happened, and I have sent for you to put you at your ease. For a long time you have been engaged in handling the intricacies of the national accounts, and this is the first mistake that you have made. I want to congratulate you and express to you my keen appreciation."

It takes a big person to extend mercy, a big person to listen rather than talk, a big person to think before jumping into action.

———

Kindness has converted more people
than zeal, science, or eloquence.

356

Good that Lays the Groundwork

Whatsoever a man soweth, that shall he also reap. And let us not be weary in well doing: for in due season we shall reap, if we faint not.

GALATIANS 6:7,9

In the late nineteenth century, a member of Parliament traveled to Scotland to make a speech. He traveled to Edinburgh by train and then took a carriage southward to his destination. The carriage, however, became mired in mud. A Scottish farm boy came to the rescue with a team of horses and pulled the carriage loose. The politician asked the boy how much he owed him. "Nothing," the lad replied. "Are you sure?" the politician pressed, but the boy declined payment. "Well, is there anything I can do for you? What do you want to be when you grow up?" The boy responded, "A doctor." The aristocratic Englishman offered to help the young Scot go to the university, and he followed through on his pledge.

More than half a century later, Winston Churchill lay dangerously ill with pneumonia—stricken while attending a wartime conference in Morocco. A new wonder drug was administered to him—a drug called penicillin that had been discovered by Sir Alexander Fleming. Fleming was the young Scottish lad once befriended. His benefactor? Randolph Churchill, Winston's father!

Sometimes the good that you do may come back in the form of the miracle you need.

A good deed is never lost; he who sows courtesy reaps friendship, and he who plants kindness gathers love.

God IS NUDGING ME TO DO SOMETHING GOOD FOR...

Wisdom of the Ages

There is a right time for
everything: . . . A time to laugh.
ECCLESIASTES 3:1,4 TLB

*D*O I HAVE A
TEACHABLE
SPIRIT—OR
WOULD
OTHERS SAY
I ACT AS
IF I KNOW
IT ALL?

————

When I was a boy of fourteen, my father was
so ignorant I could hardly stand to have
the old man around. But when I got to be
twenty-one, I was astonished at how much
the old man had learned in seven years.

One day a young woman confided to her minister, "I am afraid I sin each morning." The minister replied, "What makes you think so?" She answered, "Because every morning when I gaze into the mirror, I think how beautiful I am." The minister took a second look at the young woman before him and announced, "Never fear. That isn't a sin; it's only a mistake."

Egotism comes in many forms, but one positive thing about this brand of pride is that it often dissipates with age. Consider this progression of comments:

A child of five who has just completed a puzzle: Daddy, Daddy, I can do just about everything.

A twenty-one-year-old: Just ask me anything!

A forty-year-old: If it's in my line, I can tell you because I know my business like an open book.

A man of fifty: The field of human knowledge is so vast that even a specialist can hardly know all of it.

A man of seventy: I've lived a good many years, and I've come to realize that what I know is little and what I don't know is vast.

A man of ninety: I really don't know much, and I can't recall even more.

The younger you are when you realize how little you really know, the better off you'll be. One of the greatest character traits is a teachable spirit.

Overhearing It All

Let no corrupt communication proceed out of your
mouth, but that which is good to the use of edifying,
that it may minister grace unto the hearers.

EPHESIANS 4:29

A man once sat down to have dinner with his family. Before they began to eat, the family members joined hands around the table, and the man said a prayer, thanking God for the food, the hands that prepared it, and for the source of all life.

During the meal, however, he complained at length about the staleness of the bread, the bitterness of the coffee, and a bit of mold he found on one edge of the brick of cheese.

His young daughter asked him, "Daddy, do you think God heard you say grace before the meal?"

"Of course, honey," he answered confidently.

Then she asked, "Do you think God heard everything that was said during dinner?" The man answered, "Why, yes, I believe so. God hears everything."

She thought for a moment and then asked, "Daddy, which do you think God believed?"

Truly, the Lord hears everything we say during a day, not only those words that are addressed specifically to Him. Which words do you want Him to believe? Make everything you say today worthy of His hearing.

Which
WORDS THAT I
HAVE SPOKEN
TODAY DO I
WANT GOD
TO BELIEVE?

Once a word has been allowed
to escape, it cannot be recalled.

Give Courage

Stand firm in the faith;
be men of courage; be strong.
1 CORINTHIANS 16:13 NIV

How HAS MY
COMPASSION
COME BACK
TO BLESS ME?

When Salvation Army officer Shaw looked at the three men standing before him, he was moved to compassion. A medical missionary, Shaw had just been sent to a leper colony in India. The men before him wore manacles and fetters, the metal cutting into their diseased flesh. The captain turned to their guard and said, "Please unfasten the chains." The guard immediately replied, "It isn't safe. These men are dangerous criminals as well as lepers!"

Captain Shaw replied, "I'll be responsible. They're suffering enough." He personally took the keys, tenderly removed the bindings, and treated their bleeding, decaying ankles and wrists.

Two weeks later, Shaw had his first misgiving about what he had done when he had to make an emergency overnight trip. He dreaded leaving his family alone in the colony, but his wife insisted she was not afraid—God would protect her. Shaw left as planned. The following morning his wife was startled to find the three criminals lying on their doorstep. One of them said, "We know the doctor go. We stay here all night so no harm come to you."

Shaw's belief in the love of God gave him the courage to loose the lepers. Shaw's courage gave the lepers the love to protect his family. God's love changes hearts!

Courage is contagious.
When a brave man takes a stand,
the spines of others are stiffened.

Absolutely!

I will lift up my eyes to the mountains; from
whence shall my help come? My help comes from
the LORD, who made heaven and earth.

PSALM 121:1-2 NASB

At age thirty-three, golfer Paul Azinger was at the top of his game. He had only one problem: a nagging pain in his right shoulder, which had been operated on in 1991. After seeing the doctor, Paul received a call that changed his life. His doctor wanted him back in Los Angeles immediately for a biopsy. Paul forged a compromise. He'd undergo the procedure as soon as he had played in the PGA Championship Tournament (which he won) and the Ryder's Cup Challenge. Until then he would rely on medication and prayer. He tried to convince himself he had tendonitis, but the pain grew worse. He had cancer.

Paul began chemotherapy. One morning while praying in his bedroom, he was wondering what would happen if he didn't get better. Suddenly, the sun seemed to force its way through the blinds and a powerful feeling of peace welled up within him. He knew with absolute assurance that God was with him, and he was in His loving care—no matter what.

Two years later Paul rejoined the pro tour, his cancer gone. He says his main goal in life has shifted from winning tournaments to helping people see that "God is there for them."

God is always with you. Even when your circumstances would make you believe otherwise, if you trust in Him, He will take care of you so that you, too, can tell others of His great compassion.

How ARE MY CIRCUMSTANCES INTERFERING WITH MY FAITH IN GOD'S ABILITY?

[Rely] simply on Him who loves you, and
whom you love; just as a little helpless child.
Christ is yours, all yours: that is enough.
Lean your whole soul upon Him!

Change Your Character—Change Everything

Whatever you do, work at it with all your heart, as working for the Lord, not for men. . . . It is the Lord Christ you are serving.
COLOSSIANS 3:23-24 NIV

How DOES MY INNER CHARACTER MOTIVATE ME AT MY WORK?

After twenty years of selling cars, Bob Kamm had a new mission in life: to bring ethics into the car business. He joined the Nickelsen Group, a leading automotive consulting firm, and immediately helped to develop the Leadership Inventory and Transformation Retreat. The five-day event costs $1,595 and is considered an intellectual, physical, and spiritual program. "It's a very profound process that leads people to question who they are in this life," Kamm says, "and what they're going to do with the rest of it."

Car dealers who have come to the retreat center rarely leave the same as they came. Kamm says, "For car people it's the fourth gear at 6,000 RPMs. We're trying to get it into fifth gear at 2,300 RPMs." They are taught that a slower speed actually helps managers become more efficient and responsive, and therefore, more in control of decisions that impact all areas of their lives.

Each participant leaves the retreat with an action plan that often involves restructuring their routine, altering their management style, and apologizing to employees. Can such change occur in only five days? Kamm believes it can, because the real motivation to work is not tasks, it's a person's inner character. Change that, and you change everything.

The discipline of desire is the background of character.

Profitable Charity

*What is a man profited, if he shall gain
the whole world, and lose his own soul?*

MATTHEW 16:26

In *A Christmas Carol*, Charles Dickens' character, Scrooge, rails to his nephew about Christmas: "What's Christmas time . . . but a time for paying bills without money; a time for finding yourself a year older and not an hour richer; a time for balancing your books? . . . If I could work my will, every idiot who goes about with 'Merry Christmas,' on his lips should be boiled with his own pudding and buried with a stake of holly through his heart. He should!" Scrooge then gives his opinion about his nephew's celebration of Christmas, "Much good it has ever done you!"

At this, Scrooge's nephew replies, "There are many things from which I might have derived good, by which I have not profited, I dare say, Christmas among the rest. But I am sure I have always thought of Christmas time . . . as a good time: a kind, forgiving, charitable, pleasant time: the only time I know of, in the long calendar of the year, when men and women seem by one consent to open their shut-up hearts freely. . . . And therefore, Uncle, though it has never put a scrap of gold or silver in my pocket, I believe that it has done me good, and will do me good."

Christmas can be a joyous, giving time when people's hearts are most open to the love of God. Don't be so caught up in the buying, wrapping, and cooking that you forget the real reason for Christmas: a tiny Baby sent to save the world from sin. That will do you good!

I CAN FILL
ANOTHER'S
HEART WITH
GOD'S LOVE
BY . . .

_____

_____

_____

_____

_____

_____

_____

_____

_____

_____

_____

_____

_____

_____

_____

_____

_____

_____

*One hundred years from now it won't matter
if you got that big break . . . or finally traded
up to a Mercedes. It will greatly matter,
one hundred years from now, that you
made a commitment to Jesus Christ.*

Endangered Justice

He hath shewed thee, O man, what is good;
and what doth the LORD *require of thee,*
but to do justly, and to love mercy, and
to walk humbly with thy God?

MICAH 6:8

Whom
SHOULD I
TREAT MOST
JUSTLY
TODAY?

To crack the lily-white system of higher education in Georgia in the 1960s, black leaders decided they needed to find two "squeaky-clean students" who couldn't be challenged on moral, intellectual, or educational grounds. In a discussion about who might be chosen, Alfred Holmes immediately volunteered his son, Hamilton, the top black male senior in the city. Charlayne Hunter-Gault also stepped forward and expressed an interest in applying to the university. Georgia delayed admitting both boys on grounds it had no room in its dormitories, and the matter eventually ended up in federal court. Judge Bootle ordered the university to admit the two, who were qualified in every respect, and thus, segregation ended at the university level in that state, and soon, the nation.

Attorney General Robert Kennedy declared in a speech not long after: "We know that it is the law which enables men to live together, that creates order out of chaos. . . . And we know that if one man's rights are denied, the rights of all are endangered."

Justice may be universal, but it always begins at the individual level. Who might you treat more justly today?

———— ✦ ————

All virtue is summed up in dealing justly.

Motivated to Move

Consider it all joy, my brethren,
when you encounter various trials.

JAMES 1:2 NASB

When Eleanor Sass was a child, she was hospitalized for appendicitis. Her roommate was a young girl named Mollie, who was injured when an automobile hit the bicycle she was riding. Mollie's legs had been badly broken, and though the doctors performed several surgeries, Mollie faced the strong possibility that she would never walk again. She became depressed and uncooperative, and she cried a great deal. She only seemed to perk up when the morning mail arrived. Most of her gifts were books, games, or stuffed animals—all appropriate gifts for a bedridden child.

One day a different sort of gift came, this one from an aunt far away. When Mollie tore open the package, she found a pair of shiny, black-patent leather shoes. The nurses in the room mumbled something about "people who don't use their heads," but Mollie didn't seem to hear them. She was too busy putting her hands in the shoes and walking them up and down her blanket. From that day forward, her attitude changed. She began cooperating with the nursing staff, and soon, she was in therapy. One day Eleanor heard that her friend had left the hospital. She had walked out wearing her shiny new shoes.

Sometimes the only motivation a person needs in order to change an attitude and get moving is to know that someone else believes he or she can.

I CAN SHOW
MY CHILDREN
THAT I
BELIEVE IN
THEM BY . . .

Your children learn more of your faith
during the bad times than they do
during the good times.

Developing Potential into Reality

*The vision is yet for an appointed time
. . . it will surely come, it will not tarry.*
HABAKKUK 2:3

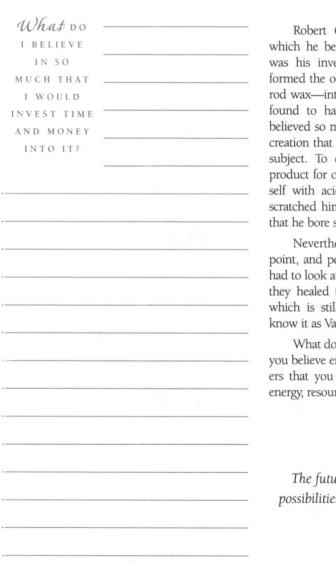

What DO
I BELIEVE
IN SO
MUCH THAT
I WOULD
INVEST TIME
AND MONEY
INTO IT?

Robert Chesebrough had a product in which he believed wholeheartedly. In fact, it was his invention. Chesebrough had transformed the ooze that forms on oil-rig shafts—rod wax—into a petroleum jelly he personally found to have great healing properties. He believed so much in the healing aspects of his creation that he became his own experimental subject. To demonstrate the benefits of his product for others, Chesebrough burned himself with acid and flame . . . and cut and scratched himself so often and so deeply . . . that he bore scars of his tests for his entire life.

Nevertheless, Chesebrough proved his point, and people were convinced. They only had to look at Chesebrough's wounds and how they healed to see the value of his product, which is still an international bestseller. We know it as Vaseline.

What do you see as a possibility today? Do you believe enough in its potential to help others that you are willing to invest your time, energy, resources, and hope into developing it?

———∞———

*The future belongs to those who see
possibilities before they become obvious.*

Powerful Positive Response

We obey his commands and
do what pleases him.

1 JOHN 3:22 NIV

When British minister W. E. Sangster first noticed an uneasiness in his throat and a dragging in his leg, he went to his physician. It was found that he had an incurable muscle disease that would result in gradual muscular atrophy until he died. Rather than retreat in dismay, Sangster threw himself into his work in British home missions. He figured he could still write and would have even more time for prayer. He prayed, "Lord, let me stay in the struggle. . . . I don't mind if I can no longer be a general." He wrote articles and books and helped organize prayer cells throughout England. When people came to him with words of pity, he insisted, "I'm only in the kindergarten of suffering."

Over time, Sangster's legs became useless. He completely lost his voice. But at that point, he could still hold a pen and write, although shakily. On Easter morning just a few weeks before he died, he wrote a letter to his daughter, saying, "It is terrible to wake up on Easter morning and have no voice to shout, 'He is risen!'—but it would be still more terrible to have a voice and not want to shout."

The person who is called is the one who hears God's call and responds with a resolute yes, regardless of his circumstances.

———— ⨳ ————

(The called man) sees himself as a steward.
. . . He's obedient rather than ambitious,
committed rather than competitive.
For him, nothing is more important than
pleasing the one who called him.

Despite ANY SUFFERING IN MY LIFE, I CAN STILL SERVE GOD BY . . .

Holy Innocents

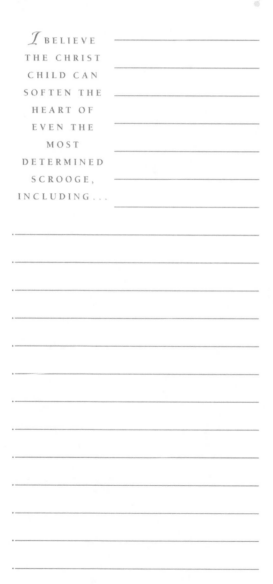

DECEMBER 25

It is appointed unto men once to die,
but after this the judgment.

HEBREWS 9:27

I BELIEVE
THE CHRIST
CHILD CAN
SOFTEN THE
HEART OF
EVEN THE
MOST
DETERMINED
SCROOGE,
INCLUDING...

Head and founder of a major contracting firm, Frank refused to celebrate the holidays, saying only, "Christmas is for children." Then one brisk December day as Frank walked to work, he saw the Child anew as he gazed at a crèche in a department store window. He started to move away, but as he did, a sign across the street caught his attention: "Holy Innocents Home." His mind raced back to a Sunday-school lesson years ago about how King Herod had feared the baby Jesus and slaughtered children in Bethlehem. He recalled the day his own son, David, had died at the age of eighteen months. He hadn't been able to speak his name since.

Frank impulsively went to the library and was surprised to learn as he researched the story that it was estimated that Herod's men killed twenty children. He left the library with a mission. Later that night he told his wife, Adele, that he had visited the orphanage, that he had given them some money, and that they were going to build a wing with it. Then he said, "They are going to name it for David." What Frank didn't tell his wife was that he had had a vision of twenty children playing in a bright new wing at Holy Innocents. As Adele hugged him, the vision came again, but this time, there were twenty-one children at play.

—❊—

Goodness is the only investment
that never fails.

The Purpose of Life

Looking unto Jesus the author
and finisher of our faith.

HEBREWS 12:2

J. C. Penney was well advanced in years before he fully committed his life to Jesus Christ. A good, honest man, in his early years, he was primarily interested in becoming a success and making money. As a clerk working for six dollars a week at Joslin's Dry Goods Store in Denver, his ambition was to one day be worth a hundred-thousand dollars. When he reached that goal he felt temporary satisfaction, but soon he set his sights on being worth a million dollars.

Both Mr. and Mrs. Penney worked hard to expand their business, but one day Mrs. Penney caught a cold and developed pneumonia which subsequently caused her death. "When she died," J. C. recalled, "my world crashed about me. To build a business, to make a success in the eyes of men, to accumulate money—what was the purpose of life? . . . I felt mocked by life, even by God Himself." Before long, Penney was ruined financially and in deep distress. It was at that point that he turned to God and experienced a true spiritual conversion. He said, "When I was brought to humility and the knowledge of dependence on God, sincerely and earnestly seeking God's aid, it was forthcoming, and a light illumined my being. I cannot otherwise describe it than to say that it changed me as a man."

Jesus gives meaning and purpose to life. He brings calm to the storm. He brings rest to the soul.

I NEED TO TRUST JESUS TO BRING CALM TO THE STORMS IN MY LIFE, ESPECIALLY . . .

Success is . . . seeking, knowing,
loving, and obeying God. If you seek,
you will know; if you know, you
will love; if you love, you will obey.

Hidden Wealth

*The ants are a people not strong, yet
they lay up their food in the summer.*
PROVERBS 30:25 AMP

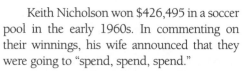

How CAN
I BE MORE
DILIGENT IN
CHOOSING
NOT TO
SPEND?

Keith Nicholson won $426,495 in a soccer pool in the early 1960s. In commenting on their winnings, his wife announced that they were going to "spend, spend, spend."

And spend they did! They purchased a luxury home for $47,600 and moved out of their low-rent city apartment, leaving behind most of their friends and family. They gave parties almost every night. In four years they managed to spend $196,000. Later Mrs. Nicholson said, "We had oodles of money but we lost our friends. The people we had known in the old days, whom we really wanted to see, never came along."

Then in 1966, Keith was killed in an automobile accident. The $5,600 car he had purchased from his winnings was totaled. After his death, $107,113 went to the government in death taxes. The remainder was invested, half in trust for the Nicholson's three children and half for Mrs. Nicholson. Her income from the trust fund—all that remained from the jackpot winnings—was $25 a week.

Having money doesn't only involve what you have available to spend, but also what you have available because you choose not to spend it. Are you saving for your future?

———— ⌘ ————

*If you would be wealthy,
think of saving as well as getting.*

Big Enough to Do "Little" Things

*The LORD seeth not as man seeth; for man
looketh on the outward appearance,
but the LORD looketh on the heart.*

1 SAMUEL 16:7

As he was returning home from the Capitol one evening, Senator John Stennis was robbed at gunpoint. Even though Stennis turned over what little he was carrying that was of value, the robbers shot him twice, hitting him in the stomach and leg. The surgeons at Walter Reed Medical Center labored for more than six hours to repair the damage and save his life.

Also on his way home that evening was Senator Mark Hatfield, who had often clashed sharply with Stennis. The two were at virtually opposite ends of the political spectrum. However, when Hatfield heard on his car radio what had happened, he immediately drove to the hospital. There, he quickly discerned that the switchboard operator was overwhelmed with the many incoming calls from fellow senators, reporters, and friends. He said to an operator, "I know how to work one of these; let me help you out." He helped answer phones until daylight when the calls finally subsided. Then without fanfare, he quietly introduced himself as he was leaving: "My name is Hatfield . . . happy to help out on behalf of a man I deeply respect."

"Bigness" means being free of pettiness, grudges, vengeance, and prejudice. It means caring unconditionally and helping unassumingly.

Have I BEEN GUILTY OF PETTINESS AND PREJUDICE LATELY?

*In taking revenge a man is but even
with his enemy; but in passing
it over, he is superior.*

Ready to Arrive

Ye are the temple of the living God;
as God hath said, I will dwell in them,
and walk in them.

2 CORINTHIANS 6:16

How CAN I
LIVE IN SUCH
A WAY THAT
OTHERS SEE
GOD IN ME?

When John Todd was only six, both his parents died. A loving aunt sent her horse and a slave, Caesar, to get John. On the way home, John asked Caesar if his aunt would be there, if he would like living with her, if she would love him, and if she would have things ready for him. Each time, Caesar replied, "Oh, yes. You fall into good hands." When they arrived, his aunt was waiting with open arms and an open heart. She became his second mother, and he loved her dearly. Years later, as his aunt was nearing death, John wrote:

> My Dear Aunt, Years ago I left a house of death not knowing where I was to go, whether anyone cared, whether it was the end of me. The ride was long but . . . there we were in the yard and you embraced me and took me by the hand into my own room that you had made up. After all these years I still can't believe it—how you did all that for me! I was expected; I felt safe in that room—so welcomed. It was my room. Now it's your turn to go, and as one who has tried it out, I'm writing to let you know that Someone is waiting up. Your room is all ready, the light is on, the door is open, and as you ride into the yard—don't worry, Auntie. You're expected! I know. I once saw God standing in your doorway—long ago!

Let God be seen in you today.

You built no great cathedrals that centuries
applaud, but with a grace exquisite
your life cathedraled God.

Matched Prayer for Prayer

Love never fails [never fades out or becomes obsolete or comes to an end].

1 CORINTHIANS 13:8 AMP

Wavie only intended to skip one day of school, but friendly strangers offered her a ride, and with each mile she traveled, the more difficult it became for her to turn around. Her parents, thinking she had been abducted, almost immediately began to search for her. Several times they thought they were close to finding her, only to have their hopes dashed. Still, they never quit praying for their daughter. They prayed that God would send their love to Wavie and that He would protect her. And they never quit believing that each ring of the phone and every mail delivery might bring word that their daughter was safe and well.

One day Wavie did return. She told of writing hundreds of letters to her parents—never mailed. Still, she did bring one of her tear-stained messages home with her. She had written, in part: "I love and miss you more than I could ever explain. I'm ashamed of what I've done. I pray every night that God will send you my love and take care of you so that one day I'll see all of you again."

Throughout the time she was away, Wavie's prayer for her parents had been nearly identical to that of her parents for her!

Never quit praying. Never quit believing. God will answer your prayers and the prayers of someone who is praying for you.

⸻

There is no greater love than the love
that holds on where there seems
nothing left to hold on to.

Today I COMMIT TO PRAYING REGULARLY FOR...

Balancing the Books of Life

*The heart of her husband doth
safely trust in her, so that he
shall have no need of spoil.*

PROVERBS 31:11

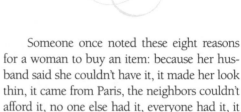

I CAN FIND
A BALANCE
BETWEEN
BEING
MISERLY AND
BEING
WASTEFUL
WITH MY
MONEY BY...

Someone once noted these eight reasons for a woman to buy an item: because her husband said she couldn't have it, it made her look thin, it came from Paris, the neighbors couldn't afford it, no one else had it, everyone had it, it was different, and "just because."

Consider the example, however, of Bill Hughes, a shipyard worker. London tax officials thought they could prove Hughes was involved in illegal activity when they found he had a savings account of $16,800, yet earned only $56 a week. Instead, Hughes told them his secrets: He never ate candy, smoked, drank, or went out with women. He shaved with his brother's razor blades, charged his grandmother 12 percent interest on money she borrowed from him, worked a night shift, and wore his father's shoes to save on shoe leather. He also went thirteen years without buying a new suit, never bought a single flower, only saw one movie in his entire life, ate everything served to him at mealtimes even if he didn't want it, and patched everything he owned until the patches wouldn't hold (including his underwear). Finally, Bill never took a holiday trip that cost more than 56 cents in fares and fees.

There is a balance to be found between spending too much and spending too little! Don't be a miser—be wiser. Enjoy life!

---

*My wife is very punctual. In fact,
she buys everything on time.*

Reflections

Reflections

Reflections

Acknowledgments

Charles Meigs (12), William James (15), Mother Teresa (18,356), Jean Hodges (19), Tagore (23), Robert Schuller (24), Henry Ward Beecher (25,38,156,283), Henry W. Longfellow (26,111,256), Vince Lombardi (27), Dwight L. Moody (31,52,232,245,342), Sir John Buchan (Lord Tweedsmuir) (32), Mike Murdock (33), Gary Smalley and John Trent (35,157), Freeman (36), Harry Emerson Fosdick (37,181), Dr. Eugene Swearingen (40), James Dobson (43,248,294,303), Elbert Hubbard (45), Solon (47), Duncan Stuart (49), George Dana Boardman (50), Thomas Jefferson (54,70), Syrus (59,219), George J. Haye (62), Orlando A. Battista (64), Martin Luther (65), Oliver Wendell Holmes (66,83,112), Josh Billings (67), Seneca (77), Dennis Rainey (78), William H. Danforth (79), Charles H. Spurgeon (85,235,243,263), Jim Patrick (88), Ruth Bell Graham (89,194), David Dunn (93), Edward John Phelps (94), Mark Twain (95,119,230,277,294,358), Bern Williams (96), Pauline H. Peters (98), George Sala (99), Miguel de Unamuno (102), Pope Paul VI (104), Dr. Anthony P. Whitham (109), Frank Crane (114), Alvin Vander Griend (116), H.E. Jansen (118), Jewish Proverb (122), Wilson Mizner (126), Abraham Lincoln (129,187), Sebastian-Roche (130), Jeremy Taylor (133), George M. Adams (134), Robert South (135), Norman Vincent Peale (138), Larry Christensen (141), Caroline Fry (142), Hannah More (143), Elton Trueblood (146), Henry Ford (147), William Feather (149), Maurcel Pagnol (150), Thomas Carlyle (153), James Huxley (155), Joseph Addison (159), Dr. John Olson (160), Merceline Cox (161), Peter Marshall (162), Cyrus (164), Margaret E. Sanger (166), Ronald Reagan (167), G.W.C. Thomas (169,373), Friedrich Wilhelm Nietzsche (173), Paul Lewis (174), Ralph Waldo Emerson (175), William Carey (176), Winifred Newman (179), John Wesley (182,252,361), Billy Sunday (185), Lorrie Morgan (190), Matthew Prior (192), R. Kent Hughes (195), Terence (200), Doug Larsen (201), Mary Gardner Brainard (202), Moliére (204), Cervantes (205), Charles C. Noble (209), Victor Hugo (210), Thomas Fuller (214,371), Calvin Coolidge (215), Denis Diderot (216), Billy Graham (221,360), Francis Bacon (222), Ed Cole (223), Oswald Chambers (225), John D. Rockefeller Jr. (233), Thomas Paine (239), Robert Browning (240), Paul Tillich (241), Theodore Roosevelt (242), Jim Elliot (244), Hawthorne (251), Thomas à Kempis (254), Zig Ziglar (255), Albert Schweitzer (257), Benjamin Franklin (259,351,370), Washington Irving (260), Euripides (261), Woodrow Wilson (262), Bob Bales (264), Roy L. Smith (265), H.L. Menken (267), Anne Bradstreet (270), Samuel Butler (271), M. Scott Peck (273), Bill Cosby (275), Betty Mills (276), James Whitcomb Riley (280), Hugh Prather (281), Josh McDowell (286), Builder (289), Hazel Scot (290), Anthony Evans (295), Arnold H. Glasgow (296), Sydney J. Harris (298), Aristotle (299), A.W. Tozer (301), T.L. Cuyler (305), Marcus Aurelius (307), Confucius (309), Earline Steelburg (310), William Lyon Phelps (312), Descartes (315), Oprah Winfrey (316), Margaret Fuller (317), H.P. Liddon (318), André Maurois (326), Bill Copeland (327), Robert W. Burns (329), Andrew Carnegie (334), Lillian Dickson (336), Henry Home (346), Martin Luther King Jr. (347), Ralph W. Sockman (348), Joyce Heinrich and Annette La Placa (349), A.W. Thorold (350), Eleanor Roosevelt (352), James Keller (353), Christian Scriver (355), St. Basil (357), Horace (359), John Locke (362), David Shibley (363), Beverly LaHaye (365), John Sculley (366), Richard Exley (367), Charles Malik (369), Thomas Fessenden (372).

References

Unless otherwise indicated, all Scripture quotations are taken from the *King James Version* of the Bible.

Scripture quotations marked NIV are taken from the *Holy Bible, New International Version®*. NIV®. Copyright © 1973, 1978, 1984 by International Bible Society. Used by permission of Zondervan Publishing House. All rights reserved.

Scripture quotations marked NASB are taken from the *New American Standard Bible*. Copyright © The Lockman Foundation 1960, 1962, 1963, 1968, 1971, 1972, 1973, 1975, 1977, 1995. Used by permission.

Verses marked TLB are taken from *The Living Bible* © 1971. Used by permission of Tyndale House Publishers, Inc., Wheaton, Illinois 60189. All rights reserved.

Scripture quotations marked AMP are taken from *The Amplified Bible. Old Testament* copyright © 1965, 1987 by Zondervan Corporation, Grand Rapids, Michigan. *New Testament* copyright © 1958, 1987 by The Lockman Foundation, La Habra, California. Used by permission.

Scripture quotations marked NKJV are taken from *The New King James Version*. Copyright © 1979, 1980, 1982, 1994, Thomas Nelson, Inc.

Scripture quotations marked RSV are taken from *The Revised Standard Version Bible*, New Testament Section copyright © 1946, Old Testament section copyright © 1952 by the Division of Christian Education of the Churches of Christ in the United States of America and is used by permission.

If you have enjoyed this book, or if it has
impacted your life, we would like to hear from you.
Please contact us at:

Honor Books
Department E
P.O. Box 55388
Tulsa, Oklahoma 74155
Or by e-mail at info@honorbooks.com

Additional copies of this book and other titles
in our Devotional Series are available
from your local bookstore.

God's Little Devotional Book
God's Little Devotional Book, II
God's Little Devotional Book for Moms
God's Little Devotional Book for Dads
God's Little Devotional Book for Students
God's Little Devotional Book on Prayer
God's Little Devotional Book on Success

Honor Books
Tulsa, Oklahoma